ENTERPRISING WOMEN

Published in association with

THE SCHLESINGER LIBRARY
RADCLIFFE INSTITUTE OF ADVANCED STUDY
HARVARD UNIVERSITY

by

THE UNIVERSITY OF NORTH CAROLINA PRESS

Chapel Hill and London

ENTERPRISING
Women

250 YEARS OF AMERICAN BUSINESS

Virginia G. Drachman

Published in association with the Schlesinger Library, Radcliffe Institute of Advanced Study, Harvard University, by the University of North Carolina Press, Chapel Hill and London

Enterprising Women: 250 Years of American Business, by Virginia G. Drachman, is published in conjunction with the exhibition of the same title organized under the auspices of the Schlesinger Library, Radcliffe Institute of Advanced Study, Harvard University, Cambridge, Massachusetts, and the National Heritage Museum, Lexington, Massachusetts. The exhibition was curated by guest curator Edith P. Mayo and designed by Staples & Charles Ltd.; website and audio-visual materials designed by Picture-Projects.com.

This exhibition and its national tour are made possible by the generous support of Ford Motor Company and AT&T.

Ford Motor Company   ◉ **AT&T**

Additional support is provided by the Cabot Family Charitable Trust and in-kind support from the U.S. Small Business Administration.

EXHIBITION DATES:

National Heritage Museum, Lexington, Massachusetts   October 2002–February 2003

New-York Historical Society, New York, New York   March–May 2003

Atlanta History Center, Atlanta, Georgia   June–September 2003

National Museum of Women in the Arts, in collaboration with
   the National Museum of American History, Smithsonian Institution, Washington, D.C.
   October 2003–January 2004

The Women's Museum–An Institute for the Future, Dallas, Texas   February–May 2004

Los Angeles Public Library, Los Angeles, California   June–September 2004

Detroit Historical Museums, Detroit, Michigan   October 2004–January 2005

Pictures on pages ii–iii (from left to right): Martha Coston, Polly Bemis, Carrie Marcus Neiman, Maggie Lena Walker, Elizabeth Keckley, Hattie Carnegie, Ruth Handler, Katharine Graham (for full description and picture credits, see Picture Credits, pages 176–77).

Edited, designed, and produced by Vernon Press, Inc., Boston, Massachusetts

Designer: Jean Hammond

Library of Congress Cataloging–in–Publication Data

Drachman, Virginia G., 1948–
   Enterprising women : 250 years of American business / Virginia G. Drachman.
      p. cm.
 Includes bibliographical references and index.
   ISBN 0-8078-2762-2 (cloth : alk. paper) –– ISBN 0-8078-5429-8 (pbk. : alk. paper)
   1. Businesswomen––United States––Biography. 2. Businesswomen––United States––History.
 3. Businesswomen––United States––Exhibitions. I. Title.
   HC102.5 .D73 2002
   338.7′092′273––dc21

                              2002006428

casebound 06 05 04 03 02 5 4 3 2 1
paperbound 06 05 04 03 02 5 4 3 2 1

Printed in Italy

CONTENTS

COLORPLATES (FOLLOWING PAGE 104)

INTRODUCING ENTERPRISING WOMEN   1

"To live & act as I please"
SEEKING INDEPENDENCE, 1750–1830   6

"To guide and encourage other women in business"
PROFIT IN THE SERVICE OF WOMEN, 1830–1890   28

"A field that is their own province"
FASHIONING THE BUSINESS OF BEAUTY, 1890–1960   74

"The cleverest women…have entered most of the business fields"
BREAKING NEW GROUND, 1890–1960   108

"Go ahead, go ahead, go ahead. Let's go."
WOMEN TAKE CHARGE, 1960–2000   148

NOTES   162
FURTHER READING   174
PICTURE CREDITS   175
INDEX   177
ACKNOWLEDGMENTS   181

FORD MOTOR COMPANY

✑ "Enterprising Women" expands the history of American business to include the little-known stories of bold and ingenious women and celebrates the many faces of the American entrepreneur. At Ford Motor Company, we are proud to support a project that recognizes the unsung visionaries who have contributed to American society throughout our country's history.

The biography of Ford Motor Company founder and twentieth-century entrepreneur, Henry Ford, is well known. His innovations in business and technology as well as his commitment to supporting American cultural and community life established him as the quintessential American entrepreneur. Throughout the earliest years of Ford Motor Company, he embraced the arts by supporting institutions and cultural programs nationwide.

We are proud to continue this commitment today by supporting "Enterprising Women." Through this project, thousands of people nationwide will have a special opportunity to explore the histories of these innovative and talented women. We salute the Arthur and Elizabeth Schlesinger Library on the History of Women in America and the National Heritage Museum for organizing this extraordinary project.

John M. Rintamaki
Chief of Staff, Ford Motor Company

AT&T

    At AT&T, we have long held that communication is the beginning of understanding. For more than a century, the people of AT&T have concentrated on building the world's most comprehensive telecommunications network, serving and delighting our customers, and encouraging the diversity and creativity of our associates.

Since the 1940s, we have supported creative expression as one of the most profound forms of communication, and we have been proud to help bring a diverse array of cultural ideas to a wider public.

With our support of "Enterprising Women: 250 Years of American Business," we continue that long-term commitment by recognizing past and present enterprising women. By telling the story of women in American businesses, from the colonial era to the millennium, "Enterprising Women" will help to illustrate the role that women have played in business throughout our history.

The people of AT&T congratulate the people of the Arthur and Elizabeth Schlesinger Library on the History of Women in America and the National Heritage Museum for bringing these important stories to millions of Americans.

Betsy Bernard
President and CEO, AT&T Consumer

To the Memory of

Charles Brand

and

Helen G. Rudolph

INTRODUCING ENTERPRISING WOMEN

Meet Katherine Goddard, publisher of the first signed copy of the Declaration of Independence and owner of a print shop, and Katharine Graham, publisher of the Pentagon Papers and owner of the Washington Post Company; meet Madam C. J. Walker, whose hair-care products brought her from her slave parents' dilapidated cabin to her own Hudson River estate down the road from the Rockefellers and the Vanderbilts; meet Lane Bryant, whose maternity fashions freed expectant mothers from the restrictions of confinement while liberating Bryant from the oppression of the New York City sweatshops; and meet Hazel Bishop, whose "kissable" lipstick left an indelible mark on the cosmetics industry while her place in her company disappeared.

These are but a few of the women whose lives unfold in this history of enterprising women in America. Their stories span two hundred and fifty years of American history, from the birth of a new nation to the dawn of the twenty-first century. They are from different racial, ethnic, and socio-economic groups; they come from every region of the country; their businesses range from iron production to dress patterns, from pyrotechnics to cosmetics. They are indeed a diverse group, and they mirror the evolution of that diversity in America. Both African American women and Jewish immigrant women were minorities among women entrepreneurs at the end of the nineteenth century and made significant headway in the early decades of the twentieth. Yet, while Jewish women entrepreneurs were part of the mainstream by the middle of the twentieth century, African American women entrepreneurs remained a minority, having lost significant ground due to the Jim Crow laws that redefined race relations for the first half of the twentieth century. Latinas and Asian Americans emerged as new minorities among women business owners in the latter part of the twentieth century.

While the women entrepreneurs featured here are different in many ways, they share several important features. They all believed in the possibilities and opportunities of American capitalism and set out to reap its rewards for themselves. They all owned their business ventures, whether inherited or built from scratch. And they were all successful, at least for a while. They are part of an impressive roster of women entrepreneurs whose ventures have left their mark on two hundred and fifty years of American business and life. But behind them are hundreds of thousands, indeed millions, of lesser-known women business owners who have achieved different degrees of success. Measured against the entire community of women business owners, most of the women included here are exceptional. They earned sizable fortunes and widespread public recognition for their day. They take their place among the notable women in American history who made it in the public sphere when measured by men's standards of success.

Yet, a focus on these women reveals much more than the fact of their achievements. It reveals the hard truth that even the most successful women entrepreneurs faced severe restrictions and limitations. Simply put, the stories of these successful women entrepreneurs reveal at once the opportunities and the limits of success for enterprising women. As exceptional as they were, these enterprising women shared much in common with the millions of less successful women business owners in American history. They enjoyed the independence of ownership and understood the simple truth that entrepreneurship, not just a job in the workplace, was the route to economic freedom and independence for women. At the same time, they faced the same challenges–legal and institutional discrimination, cultural restrictions, and the burdens of work and family–that confronted all women entrepreneurs, indeed all women who have strived for a meaningful career beyond the home. From this perspective, the stories of these enterprising women are the stories of America's women.

This history spans the transformation of the nation from an agricultural economy that linked work and family in the eighteenth century; to an industrial economy in the nineteenth century that separated work from family and defined the home as woman's proper place; to the rise of great corporations, modern business institutions, and the modern woman in the early twentieth century; to the rapid expansion of high technology and new opportunities for women at the end of the twentieth century. Women entrepreneurs were present at every stage of this growth and change. They linked the struggle for political independence to the country's economic independence in the eighteenth century; they fused their own quest for political and economic independence, helped the Union war effort, and spearheaded social reform, especially for women and children, in the nineteenth century; drawn by the promise of opportunity, they immigrated to the nation's cities with dreams of economic and social mobility in the early twentieth century; they participated in the creation of a consumer culture, building unique businesses for women, children, and families throughout the twentieth century; and they incorporated the values of gender equality, meritocracy, and cultural diversity into their businesses in the late twentieth century.

This consideration of enterprising women reveals a powerful story. It is intended to be neither general history nor one that compares female and male business owners. Instead, it presents women entrepreneurs on their own terms. Of course, enterprising women shared certain fundamental experiences with their male counterparts. What is of interest here, however, is the story of women who understood the value of a good idea, found the capital to finance it, assembled the team to implement it, launched the advertising campaign to market it, and ultimately built a profitable enterprise. It is a story of women who negotiated with suppliers, sellers, and employees, who targeted and cultivated their clientele, who kept up with the latest trends, and who were firmly planted in the world of business and finance. It is a story of women who believed in the power of individualism, ingenuity, and hard work; who were motivated by the promise of economic opportunity and upward mobility; who were willing to take a risk; and who believed that success is possible for anyone with creativity, ambition, courage, and commitment. It is a story of the possibilities and the limits of the American dream. It is America's story.

Still, enterprising women shared experiences that distinguished them from their male counterparts. For one, sexual discrimination was a persistent theme in their history. Even as they embraced the belief in equality of opportunity, they encountered obstacles that restricted their chances for success. Eighteenth-century women had no legal right to own property; nineteenth-century women could not vote; early-twentieth-century women were excluded from the elite business schools and large corporations that redefined modern business; women in the last quarter of the century were unwelcome at bars or on golf courses, the venues where businessmen socialized, networked, and often arranged the big deals; and women today receive little venture capital and continue to collide with the glass ceiling.

Second, a history of enterprising women is a story of family ties, marriage, and motherhood. For women entrepreneurs, public and private life have always been inextricably linked; business ventures occurred in relationship to, not independent of, roles as daughters, wives, widows, and mothers. Sometimes daughters got their start from supportive parents. Sometimes daughters left the shelter of the family and found new opportunities in marriage. Marriage shaped the lives of most. It made business easier for some, like Myra Bradwell and Ida Rosenthal, who started ventures with their husbands; it intruded on others, like Madam C. J. Walker and Elizabeth Arden, who divorced their husbands and continued their businesses. And it shielded others, like Rebecca Lukens and Katharine Graham, within the circle of domesticity until widowhood thrust them into ownership of their husbands' businesses. Likewise, motherhood presented challenges to all married women entrepreneurs. And for the few who remained single, like Katherine Goddard, business was still tightly tied to their position in the family as daughter and sister.

Third, the persistence of traditional ideas about femininity and woman's proper place forces the woman entrepreneur to straddle two worlds. As a woman, her "place" was at home, as the caretaker of the family. But as an entrepreneur, she belonged outside the home, the builder of a business. As a woman, she was dependent on her husband for her financial security; as an entrepreneur she stood on her own. As a woman, she had to protect her family's emotional needs; as an entrepreneur she had to be rational and ready to take risks. As a woman, she had to be nurturing and self-sacrificing, placing the needs of others before her own; as an entrepreneur, she had to be independent and acquisitive, seeking profit for herself.

These conflicting roles created a unique and enduring dilemma: how to be at once a woman and an entrepreneur. Sometimes women entrepreneurs took a unique interest in the welfare of their employees. But not always. Bradwell rejected the collective demands of her printers, as did Graham a century later. This did not mean that they were insensitive, dispassionate women, but it did make them successful businesspeople. Ultimately, the same gender roles that supposedly made a woman unfit for a life of competition and capital actually prepared her for a life in business. Over the generations, women long understood that their duties in the home—that is, keeping detailed account books, balancing the family budget, negotiating conflict, and managing myriad household tasks—provided them with excellent training for business. Paradoxically, femininity and domesticity have simultaneously excluded and prepared women for entrepreneurship.

Despite the challenges they faced, women entrepreneurs often made it in the competitive world of business. Some succeeded in typically male arenas of enterprise. In doing so, they contributed to major historic developments of their day. Rebecca Lukens's iron mill produced steel for ships and trains during the transportation revolution in the early nineteenth century; Martha Coston's pyrotechnics firm produced maritime technology that was indispensable to the Union navy during the Civil War; Olive Beech's aircraft company built military airplanes for World War II and the Korean War. What connects these women of different eras and diverse industries is an accident of their private lives: widowhood transformed them from wives to entrepreneurs. They were not alone. Rose Knox artfully managed her husband's gelatin business after he died, while Marjorie Merriweather Post inherited her father's Postum Cereal Company and expanded it into the General Foods Corporation. Their access to business uncovers a pattern: women who owned traditionally male businesses often inherited rather than initiated their enterprises, at least until the turn of the twenty-first century.

Throughout American history, women entrepreneurs were excluded from the nation's largest and most powerful industries, such as oil, steel, railroads, and automobiles. When women launched enterprises, on their own or with a husband, they typically created businesses geared specifically to women. It was a successful and familiar strategy for women who sought to enter male-dominated careers. Women doctors carved out professional space by claiming the health of women and children as their "womanly responsibility"; women lawyers rejected the acrimony and publicity of the courtroom but claimed office work, with its reliance on the housewifery skills of organization, detail, and compromise, as their province. Similarly, women entrepreneurs capitalized on their understanding of women's needs and desires and carved out a niche that reached the hearts and pocketbooks of the female consumer. In the middle of the nineteenth century, Ellen Demorest sold paper dress patterns just as the sewing machine became an indispensable item in middle-class homes, while Lydia Pinkham sold herbal medicines that promised women the relief from gynecological ailments that contemporary doctors could not provide.

In the twentieth century, this female niche exploded into a separate and thriving arena of women's business as fashion and beauty became important consumer industries. Ida Rosenthal sold bras that promised women comfort and health, and Hattie Carnegie sold elegant suits and dresses to fashionable women willing to pay a high price for high fashion. Elizabeth Arden and Helena Rubinstein created cosmetic companies that turned women's beauty into big business. Meanwhile, African American entrepreneurs like Madam C. J. Walker, Sara Spencer Washington, and Annie Turnbo Malone carved out a corner of women's business, selling specially concocted hair and beauty products to the women of their race. Other women entrepreneurs, including Isabella Greenway and Jennie Grossinger, established resorts that sold leisure to couples and families. Together, these enterprising women reveal that women were not simply consumers in the new consumer and leisure economy of the twentieth century; rather, they took their place alongside men and played an important role in the creation of that economy.

Enterprising women cultivated and expanded the separate sphere of women's consumer business throughout the twentieth century. Some took women's passion for beauty in new business directions: Patricia Stevens started modeling agencies and schools; Jean Nidetch succeeded with Weight Watchers. Others found inspiration in their kitchens and created popular food companies, like Joyce Chen's Chinese restaurants and foods and Margaret Rudkin's Pepperidge Farms bakeries. Lillian Vernon sat at her kitchen table and began a mail-order catalogue business that catered to women's desire to shop at home. Martha Stewart moved well beyond the confines of the kitchen to claim every corner of the home as her domain and made a fortune transforming domesticity into a thriving and lucrative lifestyle industry. Similarly, Oprah Winfrey took women entrepreneurs' long-held commitment to social reform and self-improvement to new heights, marketing her television show, magazine, and book club to an audience in search of a better world and a better self. Perched at the absolute pinnacle of entrepreneurial success, and known to all simply as Martha and Oprah, they are beacons for women's businesses, proof that enterprising women are here to stay.

Back in the 1920s when President Calvin Coolidge declared that "the chief business of the American people is business," he was not thinking about women. But women's business has always been part of America's business. Whether they inherited or initiated their businesses, whether they marketed to women or to the general public, enterprising women have contributed to the vitality of the nation from its inception to the present day. This is their story.

1776 Thomas Paine publishes *Common Sense*
• Declaration of Independence
• "Remember the Ladies" letter from Abigail Adams to John Adams

1783 Treaty of Paris ends American Revolutionary War
• Noah Webster publishes *American Spelling Book*

1790 Samuel Slater's spinning mill established, Pawtucket, R.I.

1793 Eli Whitney designs cotton gin

CHAPTER ONE

"To live & act as I please"

ELIZABETH MURRAY

1750–1830

SEEKING INDEPENDENCE

One customarily thinks of enterprising women as the contemporary businesswomen of the twentieth century, busily leading their corporations into the frontiers of economic competition and success. While that picture is partially true, the story of the enterprising women of America begins well over two hundred years ago, when America was but thirteen colonies under the relatively inefficient control of England. In 1750 the colonial American economy looked quite different than the United States' economy of one hundred or two hundred years later. America was a rural, undeveloped land with farming communities dotting its Atlantic seaboard. Seaports served as com– mercial centers for colonial American traders, women and men alike, and were centers for economic activities that relied on the produce of agricultural hinterlands. Most colonial Americans earned their

1801 Thomas Jefferson becomes President of the United States

1804 Lewis and Clark begin exploration of Louisiana Territory

1816 Second Bank of the United States chartered

1825 Frances Wright publishes *A Plan for the Gradual Abolition of Slavery*
• Erie Canal completed
• New York Stock Exchange opens

livings from the land by both subsistence and cash farming. The economy of the northern colonies depended primarily on subsistence farmers who gradually developed commercial trading, dominated by such major seaports as Boston, New York City, Philadelphia, and Baltimore. In the southern colonies, subsistence farmers shared the land with larger plantation owners, who developed the institution of slavery. While the economies of the northern and southern colonies gradually grew more distinct because of the presence of slavery in the South, the underlying features of each were both the agricultural rhythms of life and the expansion of an Atlantic economy. The emergence of both export and import markets at home and abroad laid the foundation for the place enterprising women would take in early American society.[1]

Typically, husbands, wives, and children in colonial America worked together in the "family economy," plowing fields, harvesting crops, preserving food for the winter months, sewing and making clothes, and bartering and trading crops for goods not produced on the farm. Similarly, in the seaports, families lived and worked together, with each family member augmenting the household income. Laborers migrated from farm to seaport and back again, depending on the agricultural cycle. Whether in the farming village or the commercial seaport, women's lives were tied to and dependent on their husbands' economic ventures. A bad crop or a maritime disaster could mean poverty and dependence on the local welfare rolls or on the charity of churches and neighbors. In the seaports, women equally relied on their husbands' place in the economic structure, riding through good times and bad with little ability to work independently. It was not unusual for the wives whose husbands were absent from the farm or the seaport due to their work, or military or political service, to participate in the maintenance of the family economy. These "goodwives" or "helpmeets," as they were known, ran family farms, kept accounts, and did what was needed to feed and clothe their families.[2]

Still, all colonial women were burdened by their legal status as *feme covert*: married women were defined legally by the status of their husbands and could not own property or make contracts in their own names. Single women, in contrast, had all of these rights but lost them upon marriage. No woman, single or married, could vote.[3]

Remarkably, despite the severe limitations on women in colonial American society in 1750, the idea of the entrepreneurial woman began to take shape. While the term *entrepreneurial* has come to be considered a modern economic category, the beginnings of the risk-taking, active, independent woman in a business can be found in eighteenth-century America. The entrepreneurial women of the colonial and Revolutionary era were energetic, ambitious, and self-reliant; they displayed a striking sense of independence when compared with other women of their day.

In contrast to the goodwives of the era, women like Eliza Lucas Pinckney, Mary Katherine Goddard, and Elizabeth Murray were precursors of the American entrepreneurial tradition, engaging in economic pursuits well beyond the maintenance of the household. Pinckney's agricultural experiments in colonial South Carolina turned indigo into the major commercial crop of the region, and led the way for other plantation

(page 6)
The Declaration of Independence—the first with signatures attached—was printed by order of Congress, January 18, 1777, by Mary Katherine Goddard.

owners to grow an alternative to rice for export to England. Goddard–who emerged from a family of newspaper publishers and developed into one of Baltimore's leading publishers as sentiment grew for a war for independence–became so prominent that she was commissioned to print the first signed version of the Declaration of Independence. Murray, tied to the export business of the seaport of Boston, opened her own dry goods store, where she sold the latest accouterments of fashion and social class, which helped middle- and upper-class women define a new urban lifestyle in revolutionary and postrevolutionary Boston.

Between 1750 and 1830, as colonial America became the new nation, political and economic freedom became inextricably linked. The principles of democracy–each individual's right to life, liberty, and the pursuit of happiness–mirrored the rise of capitalistic culture, which encouraged individual competition in the market economy. Entrepreneurial women like Pinckney, Goddard, and Murray believed themselves to be part of this emerging society that fused democracy with entrepreneurship. Rather than acting on behalf of husbands, fathers, or brothers, they exerted initiative, acted independently, and developed a consciousness of themselves as the owners of businesses. In doing so, they redefined their roles in the economic and social order of the new republic, leaving little doubt that women were part of the emerging American entrepreneurial tradition.[4]

When Eliza Pinckney (1722–93) was sixteen, her father, an officer in the British army, was obligated to leave his family for military service.[5] His wife ailing and unable to take over, Colonel George Lucas entrusted his household and plantations to Eliza, the eldest of his four children. This personal decision would have significant public ramifications: left to manage the family business, this dutiful daughter became an independent and enterprising woman.

Although Colonel Lucas had the means to hire a man to manage his three plantations, he chose to have Eliza run the properties. He had prepared his daughter well, doing everything he could to encourage her education. Schooled in England, she devoured the books from her father's private library and was well versed in the works of Milton, Locke, and Plutarch. "My father has left me most of his books," she wrote with delight.[6] Lucas's faith in his daughter was not misplaced. While he was serving his military duty in Antigua, his daughter not only ran the household and cared for her ailing mother, she turned the family's plantations into a thriving business that ultimately changed the economy of the South Carolina colony.

Pinckney's dual responsibility for home and plantation placed her squarely in two arenas: the domestic world of eighteenth-century women and the business world of men. For American women of the time, daily life revolved around household tasks and agricultural labor. Women were responsible for feeding and clothing their families, keeping clean homes, and caring for children. Their duties also extended beyond the walls of the home since they tended family gardens, raised chickens, and sometimes went out to work in the fields. Of course, while all women were responsible for these domestic tasks, how they met those responsibilities–that is, how they lived their lives day in and day out–varied depending on each woman's social position. Wives of subsistence farmers did most of the work themselves, relying on the assistance of their daughters and perhaps a female servant if they could afford one. In the South the institution of slavery freed the wives of planters from heavy physical labor. They managed the household while their daughters spent their time learning the finer arts of music, needlework, and French.

As a young single woman of the planter elite, Pinckney was part of this privileged female world of the colonial South. Besides being schooled in the gentle arts, twice a week she visited her friends or entertained them in her home. But her time was not filled totally with these leisurely pursuits. From her father she had absorbed the importance of learning. Each morning for at least an hour she read or studied and then taught reading to her younger sister as well as to two slave girls. While other southerners of her day believed in the mental inferiority of their slaves, Pinckney believed in educating all the slave children on her father's plantation; her goal was to open a school on her family's land with these two slave girls as the teachers. Still, she was a product of the privileges she derived from her race and class. She never questioned the institution of slavery, and though she treated her slaves with kindness, they freed her from all physical work, and she made her profits from their labor.

From the time she was sixteen years old, Pinckney's experiences expanded well beyond the boundaries of traditional femininity. "I have the business of 3 plantations to transact," she wrote to a close friend, trying to explain the demands of the job. It "requires much writing and more business and fatigue of other sorts than you can imagine." She was up every morning at five o'clock and walking the plantations by seven o'clock. She devoted Thursdays to "the business of the plantations." While her friends thought she was working too hard, Pinckney reassured them that she thrived on the activity and responsibility. "Least you should imagine it too burthensom to a girl at my early time of life, give me leave to answer you: I assure you I think myself happy that I can be useful to so good a father, and by rising very early I find I can go through much business."[7]

In fact, Pinckney was delighted with the job her father had entrusted to her. "I love the vegitable [sic] world extremely," she confessed, and she brought this passion for the land–along with her intelligence, self-confidence, love of hard work, willingness to take risks, and drive for success–to the endeavor of running her father's business.[8] It was a winning combination.

Rice was the only exportable crop in South Carolina when Pinckney took over her father's plantations. This made the colony economically vulnerable since it traded heavily with Europe for manufactured goods. Determined to make a profit off her father's land, Pinckney began her search for other crops that would thrive in the South Carolina soil. She experimented with indigo, ginger, and cotton. She planted an orchard of fig trees and calculated the profits she would make from exporting the figs. With the independence and initiative of a budding entrepreneur, she created a "large plantation of oaks which I look upon as my own property, whether my father gives me the land or not."[9] Her primary interest was the indigo plant; its deep blue dye, used to color cotton and wool, would make it a desirable commodity for cloth manufacturers in England and a lucrative crop for her family. Confident in her business acumen and in her ability to profit from indigo, she wrote her father: "I make no doubt Indigo will prove a very valuable Commodity in time."[10]

Pinckney's prediction was, indeed, correct, but cultivating indigo was no simple task (colorplate 2). After her first attempts were destroyed by frost, she urged her father to send her indigo seed from the East Indies earlier in the spring so she could harvest the crop before the frost. But timely planting was only part of the problem. Extracting the blue dye from the indigo plant was a complicated and delicate process. To get the highest-quality dye required a number of carefully executed steps: timely cutting and soaking of the leaves, monitoring of the colored liquid extracted from the leaves, and, finally, forming and drying the cakes of indigo sediment. Aware of the delicate nature of cultivating indigo, Colonel Lucas hired an expert from the French island of Montserrat to oversee production. But the overseer only made Pinckney's job more difficult. In fact, afraid that the successful cultivation of indigo in South Carolina would threaten his own country's indigo trade with England, he destroyed the dye by diluting it with limewater. This man must have believed it would be easy to deceive his young female employer, but she discovered the sabotage and fired him.

While Colonel Lucas supported his daughter's agricultural successes, he began to worry about the impact of her independent spirit on her personal life. Quite simply, he wanted her to marry, and he began to present her with the names of suitable mates. But Pinckney was too independent to marry just anyone. She resisted marriage and rebuffed her father's choices, claiming that even "the riches of Peru and Chili [sic]" would not change her mind. Instead, the eighteen-year-old young woman explained to her father that she would marry only when she was ready. "Give me leave to assure you, my dear Sir, that a single life is my only Choice and if it were not as I am yet but Eighteen, hope you will [put] aside the thoughts of my marrying yet these 2 or 3 years at least."[11] Her refusal to follow her father's advice reveals that she felt no need to marry simply to satisfy him. Her knowledge about her family's finances and her management of their property gave Eliza autonomy and economic power that she was not anxious to give up.

Ultimately, in 1744, at the age of twenty-two, Eliza Lucas did marry, but on her own terms. The man she chose was Charles Pinckney, a prominent South Carolina planter and lawyer, and a widower twenty years older than she. This was far from an impulsive marital choice for her. She had been good friends with Charles Pinckney and his first wife, and she had relied on Pinckney for educational guidance when her father left home for military service. She knew very well what she was doing, and the marriage was a good one, based on mutual friendship and respect.

Newly married, with a wedding gift from her father of the entire indigo crop from one of his plantations, Pinckney turned her attention to the traditional responsibilities of a wife. Her goal was "to make a good wife to my dear Husband . . . to make all my actions Corrispond with that sincere love and Duty I bear him. . . . To do him all the good in my power; and next to my God . . . to make it my Study to please him." Mother-hood soon followed. In the first six years of her marriage, Pinckney had four children, three of whom survived, and she devoted herself to their care. "I am resolved to be a good Mother to my children; to spair no paines or trouble to do them good; to correct their Errors whatever uneasiness it may give myself; and never omit to encourage every virtue I may see dawning in them."[12]

Over the years, Pinckney tended closely to the emotional and intellectual develop-ment of her children, sending them to schools in England, urging them to read the books she recommended, and advising them on virtue and behavior. In an era when women contributed to society by raising their sons and daughters for the future, Pinck-ney was a model of republican motherhood. She instilled a fierce patriotism in her sons, who grew up to become important politicians in South Carolina and leaders among the first generation of post–Revolution Americans. Her eldest, Charles, was a signer of the United States Constitution, while Thomas served as governor of South Carolina and arranged the famous Pinckney Treaty of 1795, which settled land disputes between the United States and Spain in Florida and along the mouth of the Mississippi River.

As wife and mother of a plantation household, Pinckney fit perfectly the ideal pre-scription for women of her social class in the southern colonies. Still, she remained an enterprising woman. In 1744, the year of her marriage, she took a major financial risk by devoting her entire crop to the cultivation of indigo seed. The strategy paid off, assuring Pinckney her place as a successful planter for the rest of her life. This proved particularly important to her in 1758, when her husband died from malaria, just fourteen years after they married. Emotionally bereft by the loss, she immersed herself in the business of managing the plantations; the work saved her. "Had there not been a necessity for it, I might have sunk to the grave by this time . . . but a variety of imployment gives my thoughts a relief from melloncholy subjects."[13] Unlike other widows of the day, who were unprepared for the task, Pinckney was simply returning to the work of her younger years.

More immediately, Pinckney's 1744 decision to cultivate only indigo freed her from buying seed from the East Indies and launched her as a successful indigo grower. Hop-ing to spread the cultivation of indigo throughout the region, Pinckney gave much of her own seed away to neighboring planters, who also began to grow the plant. Her goal was to make the colony of South Carolina the major supplier of indigo to England. "We please ourselves with the prospect of exporting in a few years a good quantity from hence and supplying our Mother Country with a manifacture for which she has so great a demand, and which she is now supplyd with from the French Collonys."[14]

Silk for this gown, which belonged to Eliza Lucas Pinckney, was produced on her plantation and sent to England to be woven and dyed.

In a few short years Pinckney had achieved her goal. In 1747, South Carolina exported one hundred thousand pounds of indigo to England. Only too happy to trade with its own colony, England offered Pinckney and the other indigo planters of South Carolina a bounty for their indigo that enabled them to double their capital in three or four years. With England eagerly buying indigo from South Carolina, it quickly became the chief cash crop of the highland region of the colony. Just before the Revolution, South Carolina was annually exporting over one million pounds of indigo to England. This was over one-third of the colony's total exports. After the Revolution, indigo once again was cultivated, but it never regained this prominence. Indigo from the East Indies, the end of bounties from England, and greater interest in cotton arising from the development of Eli Whitney's cotton gin in 1793 all contributed to its demise in South Carolina. Nevertheless, indigo was the driving force of the colony's economy in the decades leading up to the Revolution.

When Colonel Lucas left sixteen-year-old Eliza in charge of his plantations, he had confidence that she could manage his estate. And indeed she did; but she accomplished much more. What seemed unthinkable at the time, yet ultimately proved incontrovertibly true, was that a young southern girl, privileged yet unafraid of risks, leisured yet willing to work hard, domestic yet driven to succeed on the plantation, would not only bring remarkable profit to her own family but also leave a permanent mark on the economic history of colonial South Carolina.

⟨⟩ Just as Eliza Lucas Pinckney's successful indigo enterprise helped strengthen colonial South Carolina, Mary Katherine Goddard's publishing ventures contributed to the birth of the new nation a generation later. Along with her mother, Sarah Updike Goddard, and her brother, William Goddard, Mary Katherine Goddard (1738–1816) was among the first publishers in the American colonies. Her careful, steady, day-to-day work on the family newspaper made her an important figure in this precarious era when America was emerging as a new republic. On a more private level, Goddard's story reveals the significance of family ties and gender roles in the late eighteenth century. It is a story in which one-time sibling loyalty and support gradually deteriorated into sibling conflict and competition.

Born in 1738, the eldest of four children of Giles and Sarah Goddard, Katherine grew up in New London, Connecticut, where her father was a doctor and the postmaster.[15] Her mother managed the household and educated Katherine and her younger brother, William. In 1757, when his daughter was nineteen, Giles Goddard died, marking the end of traditional patriarchy in the Goddard household. Sarah Goddard bypassed her first-born and turned to William, then seventeen, to support the family. Her choice reflected prevailing ideas about men's and women's roles in mid-eighteenth-century America. Though younger than his sister, William was deemed best suited to venture beyond the boundaries of the family to engage in entrepreneurial activity. Having inherited the substantial sum of £780 from her husband, Sarah Goddard gave William £300, which he used to open a printing shop and found the *Providence Gazette*, the first newspaper in Providence, Rhode Island. But mother did not bypass daughter entirely. Having helped her son to establish his business, she moved with Katherine to Providence in 1762 to participate in the new family enterprise.

This began a pattern of family migration and work: William started newspapers and Katherine and their mother took over the work of running them when he moved on to new projects. Just three years after Katherine and Sarah Goddard had settled down in Providence, William left town. With few subscribers to the *Gazette*, he hoped to find better publishing opportunities in New York and Philadelphia. Goddard and her mother stayed behind, and for the next three years they continued to publish the *Gazette* while they also ran a bookshop and bindery, all on their own. In 1768, however, they sold these businesses and followed William to Philadelphia, where he had opened a new printing office, one of the largest in the colonies, and in 1767 had founded the *Pennsylvania Chronicle*. Again Katherine and her mother set to work, this time helping William run his new printing office as well as publish his newspaper. But two years later, Sarah died.

Katherine continued to run the *Chronicle* and manage William's printing business, as she had done with her mother. William, meanwhile, left his sister in Philadelphia and moved once again. This time he went to Baltimore, where he started the city's first newspaper, the *Maryland Journal*, in 1773.

The following year, Goddard once again followed her brother, but this would be the last time. When she arrived in Baltimore in 1774, William had already shifted his attention to the task of establishing a national postal system and he needed his sister to run the *Journal*. Katherine took over the paper, but she was no longer willing to do it behind the scenes. Perhaps it was the self-confidence she had developed from her years of running William's newspapers and printing offices with her mother. Perhaps it was the new-found independence she discovered after the death of her mother. Perhaps it was simply that she was now highly experienced in the business of newspaper publishing. In any event she wasted little time before claiming credit for her role. The following spring, in the May 10, 1775, issue, Goddard publicly announced that she was running the newspaper. The new masthead read simply: "Published by M. K. Goddard." It left no ambiguity about the fact that she, and not William, was officially in charge of the *Maryland Journal*.

When Katherine Goddard took over the *Journal*, she was not the first woman to publish a newspaper in the colonies. Women had been running them since the early eighteenth century and between 1739 and 1820 Goddard was one of thirty-two women newspapers publishers.[16] But most of them were widows who took over their husbands' papers to support themselves and their families. Goddard was different. She was an independent, single woman who deliberately took the newspaper away from her brother.

Goddard took over the *Maryland Journal* in a period of significant growth in newspaper circulation. The number of newspapers in the colonies more than doubled from seventeen in 1760 to forty in 1775.[17] This expansion reflected the growing reliance on the press during an era of heightened political agitation. Colonists increasingly turned to newspapers for discussion of political ideas and for information; newspapers such as the *Journal* helped create a climate of revolution. As publisher of the *Journal*, Goddard assumed an important public position. She took over the newspaper at a time when citizens were becoming increasingly aware of the power of the press to give voice to the idea of freedom. She was a woman at the very heart of the politics of revolution, playing a vital role in the creation of a national consciousness.

Running the *Maryland Journal* as a steady, profitable business in the era of the Revolution was no small feat. Most colonial publishers of the day found it difficult to print a newspaper on a regular schedule. A major obstacle was the paper shortage. Paper had been at a premium for several years. In 1773, the American Philosophical Society appealed to colonists to donate rags to the paper mills, offering prizes as incentives. And during the Revolution, paper makers could often get military exemptions because of the urgent need for their product. The *Maryland Gazette*, which had been published weekly in Annapolis since 1738, closed because of the scarcity of paper. For a while,

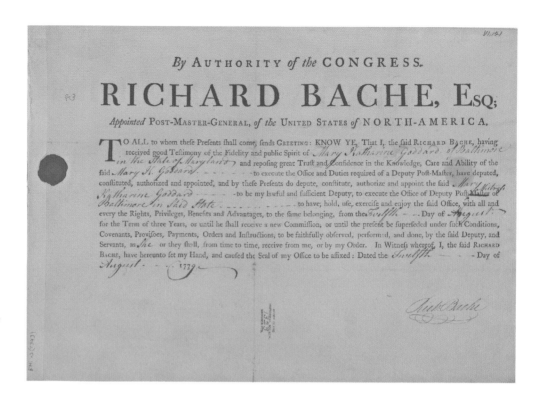

By AUTHORITY of the CONGRESS.

RICHARD BACHE, Esq;

Appointed POST-MASTER-GENERAL, of the UNITED STATES of NORTH-AMERICA.

TO ALL to whom thefe Prefents fhall come, fends GREETING: KNOW YE, That I, the faid RICHARD BACHE, having received good Teftimony of the Fidelity and public Spirit of *Mary Katharine Goddard, of Baltimore in the State of Maryland* and repofing great Truft and Confidence in the Knowledge, Care and Ability of the faid *Mary K. Goddard* - - - - -to execute the Office and Duties required of a Deputy Poft-Mafter, have deputed, conftituted, authorized and appointed, and by thefe Prefents do depute, conftitute, authorize and appoint the faid *Mary Katharine Goddard* - - - - -to be my lawful and fufficient Deputy, to execute the Office of Deputy Poft-Mafter of *Baltimore in faid State* - - - - - - - - -to have, hold, ufe, exercife and enjoy the faid Office, with all and every the Rights, Privileges, Benefits and Advantages, to the fame belonging, from the *Twelfth* - - -Day of *August* for the Term of three Years, or until he fhall receive a new Commiffion, or until the prefent be fuperfeded under fuch Conditions, Covenants, Provifoes, Payments, Orders and Inftructions, to be faithfully obferved, performed, and done, by the faid Deputy, and Servants, as *fhe* or they fhall, from time to time, receive from me, or by my Order. In Witnefs whereof, I, the faid RICHARD BACHE, have hereunto fet my Hand, and caufed the Seal of my Office to be affixed: Dated the *Twelfth* - - - -Day of *August* - - - *1779*

Goddard's appointment to the position of Post-Master of Baltimore, August 2, 1779, by Richard Bache, Post-Master-General

Goddard also had trouble getting paper and used the *Journal* to advertise for linen rags. Nevertheless, she managed to turn out the newspaper on a regular basis during those difficult years, until 1777, when her brother's part-ownership in a paper mill gave her ready access to paper.

Inflation also threatened the newspaper business in the Revolutionary era. Goddard continually faced the need to raise prices simply to survive. When William first published the *Journal* in 1773, subscribers paid ten shillings per year. By 1777, however, she had been forced to double the annual subscription rate. A year later, she raised the annual rate to fifty-two shillings, doubling it once again in the spring of 1779. By October 1779, subscribers were paying ten pounds per year to read the *Journal*.[18] This was no small sum. To hold on to her readers, Goddard turned to the common practice of barter, willingly accepting a range of commodities including beef, grains, vegetables, feathers, and linen rags in place of cash.

As busy as she was with the newspaper, Goddard found time for other work as well. In 1775 she was put in charge of the Baltimore post office, part of the colonial postal system her brother had helped create. This appointment made her the first woman postmaster in the colonies. In addition to administering the daily business of the Baltimore post office and turning out the *Maryland Journal* on a weekly basis, Goddard began a number of related ventures. She ran her own book-binding and selling businesses. Using the *Journal*, she advertised both her "complete and elegant Bookbinding room" and her books, which she sold "cheap, for cash."[19] In addition, Goddard published a popular almanac, which was an important source of income.

Together, these ventures established Goddard as one of the remarkably successful entrepreneurs of her day–male or female. That she was a woman makes her accomplishments all the more noteworthy. To be sure, she benefited from the Goddard family name as well as from her brother's reputation. But William did not assist her in any of the day-to-day responsibilities, and she had no husband or father to help. On her own, as a single, independent woman, Goddard ran the *Maryland Journal*, administered the Baltimore post office, managed her bookshop and bindery, and published an almanac.

And yet, as important as all of her accomplishments were, Goddard's most noteworthy achievement occurred in 1777: she was chosen by the Continental Congress to print the first copy of the Declaration of Independence with the names of the signers included. This was no small attainment. At a time when women were deemed inferior to men, legally, socially, and politically, when the Declaration of Independence itself did not mention the rights of women, Goddard's reputation as a respected publisher and entrepreneur earned her a special place in the history of the new nation. She became a symbol of the unique relationship between political freedom and economic progress that blossomed after the Revolution and ultimately became a part of the national character. But because Goddard was a woman, her contribution carried added significance. Entrepreneurship, patriotism, and gender were inextricably and forever united in 1777 with five simple words at the bottom of the first official copy of the Declaration of Independence: "Printed by Mary Katherine Goddard."[20]

Baltimore's first post office, where Goddard is believed to have worked as postmaster

While Katherine's businesses and reputation thrived, William was less successful in his own pursuits. Describing his sister as "an expert & correct Compositor of Types," he well understood that he could entrust the business of the *Journal* to her while he devoted his time to other endeavors.[21] But his work in the postal system did not turn out as he had hoped. William had his eye on the position of comptroller, but Benjamin Franklin, who was in charge of its administration, appointed his son-in-law instead. William ended up in the low-paying position of surveyor of the system. Unhappy and insulted by this appointment, William first sought a commission to the army, but General Washington turned him down. His performance as surveyor was disappointing, earning him a reputation for working "in a very careless, slovenly manner."[22] William returned to Baltimore in 1777, where he focused on his paper mill and assisted his sister with the *Journal*.

William quickly grew restless in his background role, and the relationship between brother and sister began to deteriorate. First William made plans to establish a press that would compete with Katherine's. Perhaps he expected his sister to support him as she had always done, but those days were over. Instead, she headed off her brother's plan by announcing in the *Journal* her discovery of a scheme "to diminish her Business, and compel her to quit the same."[23] William backed off, and for a few years he continued to help Katherine.

But in 1784 he took control of the *Maryland Journal* away from his sister. That same year, he published a competing almanac and publicly derided Katherine as "a certain *hypocritical Character*" who published her almanac "for the dirty and mean Purpose of Fraud and Deception."[24] In his attempt to reestablish his publishing career, William destroyed their relationship. For almost a decade, she had overseen the daily routine of running the newspaper, nursing it through the difficult times of shortages and inflation, and celebrating its success. Because she was a single woman with no family, in important ways the *Journal* was her child, and the bookshop and post office were the rest of her family. William wrested the *Journal* back because he did not get the postal position he believed he deserved, and Katherine never forgave him.

Although the *Journal* was no longer her own, Goddard still had her other ventures, and she continued to run them for the next few years. Even though she ran the Baltimore post office more efficiently than most postmasters of her day operated theirs, ultimately her competence was unable to transform contemporary patriarchal attitudes. In 1789 she learned that a man would replace her. The new postmaster would be required to travel frequently by horseback beyond the city limits. He would need the physical strength, which a woman supposedly did not have, as well as the freedom to travel alone, an undertaking which was deemed unsafe and inappropriate for any proper woman of the day. But Goddard had earned such a strong reputation for outstanding work that over two hundred of the leading businessmen of Baltimore signed a petition requesting that she be allowed to keep her position. Neither President Washington nor the United States Senate came to her support. Goddard fell victim to the gendered constraints of post-revolutionary America.

Goddard continued to run her bookshop. She never reconciled with her brother; in her will she freed her personal slave and, bypassing William completely, left her all of her property. Though Goddard died without family ties, for many years she was one of the most important participants in the life of colonial Baltimore. Her entrepreneurial ventures in publishing and printing contributed to the transition of America from thirteen British colonies to an independent country, and Goddard took her place at the center of an emerging national culture linking free enterprise and an independent press to political freedom. Moreover, while most women publishers a generation later would make their fortunes speaking specifically to a female audience, Katherine Goddard succeeded by speaking to the citizenry, male and female. Her printing of the Declaration of Independence was testimony to her important role as a publisher, independent of gender, and made her a major participant in the most important political issues of the day.

⟳ Elizabeth Murray (1726–85) did not shake the world (colorplate 1). Unlike Eliza Pinckney, whose indigo investments revitalized the economy of colonial South Carolina, and Katherine Goddard, whose printing business helped propel the American Revolution, Murray followed the path of many women of her day: she ran a simple dry goods shop. In fact, she was but one among hundreds of "she-merchants" who ran such shops in the major northern colonial seaports of New York, Boston, and Philadelphia from 1740 to 1775.[25]

Shopkeeping was certainly a reasonable public venture for a colonial woman: it required little formal training beyond arithmetic and an ability to read and write, and it enabled a woman to earn an income without straying from acceptable gender roles. To be sure, most independent female shopkeepers were widows who took over their late husbands' shops. Single women owned shops, as well, without risking community acceptance of their behavior. They could hardly be defined as overstepping their bounds. Indeed, a woman shopkeeper typically sold dry goods and luxury items to other women. Her shelves were stocked with such fashion-related items as cloth and trimmings and such household wares as teapots and china. She was not in the business of selling hardware, guns, locks, or tools. Nor was she a merchant engaged in wholesale transactions between Britain and the colonies. Those were men's activities at the time.

Murray was one of the most successful women shopkeepers of her day, but her significance lies as much in the ways that her story reveals the patterns of work and life for she-merchants of her time. Female shopkeepers were a highly visible and integral part of the business world of colonial America. Though largely uncelebrated today, they were part of the economic, political, and social backbone of colonial America. In an age of increased importation and consumption of British luxury goods, she-merchants were crucial to the transatlantic commercial trade between England and the colonies.[26] As the century progressed, they found themselves thrust increasingly into the middle of the burning political issues of the Revolution. Well after the revolutionary era, she-merchants like Murray left their marks, sowing the seeds of a consumer economy that would blossom a century later.

Murray must always have had an independent streak. Born in Unthank (Roxburghshire), Scotland, in 1726, she journeyed to colonial North Carolina in the late 1730s

Elizabeth Murray, 1769 (detail of the Copley portrait, colorplate 1)

with her eldest brother, James, to be his housekeeper.[27] Ironically, this traditional domestic role helped prepare Murray for a life of business; as her brother's housekeeper, she observed James's business ventures and wrote much of his business correspondence. A few years after settling in North Carolina, Murray and her brother returned to Scotland, where James married. Several years later, they set sail for North Carolina yet again, this time accompanied by James's wife and daughter—and a stock of dry goods brought by Elizabeth. James, disappointed in his trading ventures during his first trip to North Carolina, planned to concentrate on running his plantation and took comfort in knowing that Elizabeth would be housekeeper to his expanding family.

But his sister had different plans. When their boat docked briefly in Boston, twenty-three-year-old Murray decided to stay there on her own and open a dry goods shop. It was a brave step: Murray was alone in an unfamiliar city, thousands of miles and an ocean away from home. Since James continued to North Carolina as originally planned, she had no family or friends to whom to turn. But she had her brother's support, both emotional and economic.

What Murray needed to succeed in her business venture were the requisites of any successful business: capital, credit, a stock of desirable merchandise, and a solid reputation. She turned to James, who supplied the credit, reputation, and merchandise that enabled his sister to get started. Murray had some capital of her own, namely three slaves, which James sold for £145 on her behalf. He also promised £100 of his own credit and persuaded their brother John to do the same. Siblings and slavery brought Murray the capital she needed to become an entrepreneur.

Backed by sufficient funding, the other elements of the start-up plan fell into place. James brought together a team in London—a well-known mercantile company, a respected seamstress, and a fashion-conscious buyer—to insure that his sister received the best merchandise at the best price and in a timely way. The combination of the male-run mercantile company with the needlewoman and female buyer mirrored the sexual division of labor of the era and provided the ideal balance of aesthetics and economics to help Murray survive the tough competition among Boston's shopkeepers.

With everything in place, Murray launched her career as a colonial she-merchant. The growth of her business reflects her evolution as an entrepreneur. In a few short years she gave up her financial and emotional dependence on her brother and gradually matured into a successful businesswoman, free to assert her autonomy within her family.

Murray began with a simple plan: keep a well-stocked shop of fashionable merchandise, avoid debt, pay creditors on time, and get the word out. While most female shopkeepers relied on word of mouth, Murray took a more public approach, distributing flyers and buying advertising space in newspapers on a regular basis. In her advertisements, she made sure everyone knew where to find her—across the street from the well-known Brazen Head, where another female shopkeeper sold baking tins, cutlery, and other domestic metal products. Her advertisements also defined her as a woman of

Trade bill, ca. 1749, describing the broad range of goods Elizabeth Murray offered at her Boston shop

fashion and cosmopolitan sophistication. Anyone who read these notices knew that her shop was filled with the latest English luxury items including satin gloves, lace, silks, velvets, feathers, and ribbon. Appealing to a clientele of women with both fashion and cost in mind, Murray made it clear that she was an arbiter of style and that her shop was the place to go for the latest goods imported from London at a reasonable price.[28]

Murray encountered a number of unanticipated obstacles in the early years of her business. First, the woman in London responsible for selecting much of the merchandise for her shop failed to get them at a reasonable price. Murray was forced to risk her reputation and goodwill as she tried to sell the overpriced merchandise to angry and uninterested customers. She turned once again to James: he dismissed the woman and, with his own money as backing, set his sister up with a London wholesaler who insured that the overpricing fiasco would not happen again. Then, in 1753, Murray ran out of stock. The image of luxury and abundance so important to the success of her business quickly dissolved when customers entered a shop with empty shelves and barren walls. Murray's reputation as an arbiter of fashion gave way to "the broken shop keeper" who could not even keep her store fully stocked.[29] Understanding that success lay as much in image as in reality, she sought to create the appearance of constant inventory. She purchased twelve dozen boxes, which she kept labeled, yet empty, on her shelves. Then in the fall of that year, Murray received a shipment of summer merchandise. This was the last straw.

Without consulting James this time, Murray took an inventory of her merchandise, found a widow to run her shop, and set sail for London. This was no small step for a single woman of her day, but Murray had changed in significant ways since her arrival in Boston just four years before. She was financially independent, managed her own shop, and had business experience. Journeying to London with a purpose–to improve the circumstances of her business–she declined invitations to visit family members in Scotland. Murray stayed in London, learning new bookkeeping methods and selecting a fresh assortment of merchandise. She returned to Boston in the spring of 1754 with a heightened sense of confidence and resolve. She had made the round-trip journey to London on her own, learned important financial lessons, solidified her business contacts, and purchased a new stock of goods, the latest fashions for the coming season.

Around this time, just as she put her public life in order, Murray finally did what a twenty-nine-year-old woman in her era typically would have done years earlier: she married. In 1755 she married Thomas Campbell, a sailor and trader who shared her Scottish heritage and interest in commerce. Moreover, Campbell had known James in North Carolina, and he had carried letters between brother and sister on his sailing voyages. As the eldest male of the family, James heartily approved of the match, certain that his sister had "not much time to wait for further Choice."[30] In these matters, his sister would surprise him, for she married a total of three times.

While Thomas brought business experience to the marriage, Elizabeth's decision to marry him affected her economic autonomy. The English common law of feme covert defined a married woman as legally dead. She had no right to own property, to make a contract, or to buy or sell property in her own name. Elizabeth's business immediately became the legal property of her husband; fortunately for her, Thomas had no inclination to take it from her. They made a good team, and the business thrived under their

THE
LADY's LAW:
OR, A
TREATISE
OF
Feme Coverts:
CONTAINING

All the **Laws** and **Statutes** relating
to WOMEN, under several HEADS:

VIZ.

I. Of Discents of Lands to Females, Coparceners, &c.

II. Of Consummation of Marriage, stealing of Women, Rapes, Polygamy.

III. Of the Laws of Procreation of Children; and of Bastards or spurious Issue.

IV. Of the Privileges of *Feme Coverts*, and their Power with respect to their Husband, and all others.

V. Of Husband and Wife, in what Actions they are to join.

VI. Of Estates Tail, Jointures and Settlements, real and personal in Women.

VII. Of what the Wife is entitled to of the Husband's, and Things belonging to the Wife, the Husband gains Possession of by Marriage.

VIII. Of Private Contracts by the Wife, Alimony, separate Maintenance, Divorces, Elopement, &c.

The SECOND EDITION.

To which is added,
Judge HIDE's very remarkable Argument in the *Exchequer-Chamber, Term. Trin.* 15 *Car.* 2. In the Case of *Manby* and *Scot*, whether, and in what Cases, the Husband is bound by the Contract of his Wife:

And Select *Precedents* of *Conveyances* in all CASES concerning Feme Coverts.

In the SAVOY:

Printed by E. and R. NUTT, and R. GOSLING, (Assigns of *E. Sayer*, Esq;) for *H. L.* and Sold by C. CORBETT, at *Addison's* Head, and E. LITTLETON, at the *Mitre*, both against St. *Dunstan's* Church in *Fleetstreet.* 1737.

Treatise of Feme Coverts (1737) that defined and described the legal disabilities of women in eighteenth-century America

division of labor: he took care of the business correspondence; she ran the shop. Meanwhile Elizabeth became pregnant, but she either miscarried or bore a child who died shortly after birth. She never became pregnant again. This was not the only loss she suffered in this period of her life, for Thomas died during her pregnancy, the victim of a measles outbreak in Boston in the winter of 1759.

With her private life shattered, Murray faced economic uncertainty, made even worse by the suspicions of her husband's relatives, who did not trust her to settle Thomas's estate. Overwhelmed by the legal and financial complications of widowhood, she once again turned to James, who helped her settle the immediate matters. She moved her shop and resumed her business, but it was her second marriage that enabled her to recapture and hold on to her economic independence.

In 1760, barely a year after Thomas died, Elizabeth Murray Campbell married seventy-year-old James Smith, a man twice her age, and one of the wealthiest men in Boston. Elizabeth had learned a crucial lesson from her first marriage: never to relinquish her financial independence again. This time she insisted on a prenuptial agreement allowing her to keep control of her own property and to dispose of it as she chose at her death. In addition, it guaranteed her the sum of £10,000 from her husband's estate.[31] The terms of Murray's second marriage promised her a future of economic independence.

The marriage lasted nine years, during which Elizabeth devoted most of her time to caring for her elderly husband. His death in 1769 brought her relief from care-giving obligations and left her financially independent. Writing to her friend Christian Barnes, Elizabeth explained that she was now able "to live & act as I please."[32] Relieved and exhausted, Elizabeth visited Great Britain, taking the long transatlantic voyage once again. She rested, reunited with family for two years, and returned reinvigorated to Boston in 1771. But in her absence circumstances had changed dramatically, both in her personal life as well as in the community.

Murray discovered that in the absence of her vigilant watch, her inheritance had dwindled and her financial matters had fallen into disarray. The situation motivated her once again to marry, this time Ralph Inman, a long-time friend, whom she believed would help bring order back to her financial situation. Despite her trust in her new husband, she again insisted upon a prenuptial agreement. The contract not only preserved all of Murray's property in her name, but also guaranteed her the right to make a will as she chose, so that she could pass on her property to whomever she wished, even if she predeceased her husband. The latter provision was especially important to Murray, and to her brothers, who by this time were less financially secure than she.

Murray's visit to Great Britain had coincided with a number of developments in Boston that made it increasingly difficult for her, or anyone else with Loyalist sympathies, to be there. In 1770, British soldiers killed several Boston citizens in what would become known as the Boston Massacre. No one in Boston could ignore the incident. Indeed, since Murray's departure in 1769, the colonists maintained a boycott of British luxury goods in order to force Parliament to repeal taxes on imported items, especially tea. Many merchants supported the boycott, known as the nonimportation agreement, and refused to carry British products; similarly, many customers refused to purchase them.

Some colonists, however, resisted the boycott, but not without consequences. Sisters Anne and Elizabeth Cuming faced constant threats and ridicule as they continued to import British goods for their dry goods shop. Despite pressure and threats from the press and from merchants who supported the boycott, they refused to succumb, insisting that they were simply two hardworking single women trying to survive. In reality, their actions were highly political. Their vilification in the press and their ostracism by many who had previously frequented their shop galvanized Loyalist supporters to buy from the Cuming sisters. Thus, Loyalist women, shopkeepers and consumers alike, deliberately ignored the boycott, thereby demonstrating the tight connection between their pocketbooks and their politics. Not all Loyalist she-merchants fared as well as the Cuming sisters. Murray's friend Jane Eustis, who had successfully run a shop for two decades, faced financial ruin when the *Boston Chronicle* included her name on a list of shopkeepers unsympathetic to the policy of nonimportation.[33]

The anti-British sentiment Murray encountered when she returned to Boston in 1771 increased over the next few years. In 1773 a group of colonists dumped a shipload of imported tea into Boston harbor. The British government responded harshly to this act of colonial aggression, closing the port of Boston, sending more British soldiers to the city, and placing the city under the military rule of General Gage. These "Intolerable Acts" of 1774 helped make Boston the hotbed of revolutionary furor.

It was a dangerous time for Loyalists like the Inmans. In 1775, as British troops made their way from Boston to Concord, Ralph was in Boston visiting friends, while Elizabeth was alone at their Cambridge farm. Afraid of an impending war, Ralph's initial response was to flee Boston for London, leaving his wife to fend for herself. Determined to protect her large hay crop, she stayed alone at the farm, even as American troops took it over to house soldiers, reassuring her friends that she had "no personal fear" and that she could easily survive alone on "water-gruel, and salt . . . with a bit of meat, [and] a few greens or roots."[34] Ultimately Ralph did not leave Boston, but Elizabeth never forgave him. Exercising the right she had demanded in her prenuptial agreement to make her own will, she carried her disappointment to her grave, leaving Ralph very little of her substantial property.

Instead, Murray left most of her property to her nieces and to other women whose lives she had touched. This was but her final act in a lifetime committed to helping women become self-supporting. While Murray never had any children of her own, she became a surrogate mother to several of her nieces. As an experienced she-merchant who had learned the pitfalls and opportunities of marriage, she well understood the link

*The Inman House,
Cambridge, Massachusetts,
the estate where Elizabeth
Murray lived with her third
husband, Ralph Inman*

between business and independence. Her mothering took the form of nourishing her nieces' independence through education and useful work. "I prefer an usefull member of society to all the fine delicate creatures of the age," she once wrote to a friend. She began with James's eldest daughter, Dottie, who left North Carolina to live and study with Murray in Boston. Murray made accounting a crucial part of her niece's education "[so that] your papa will let you keep his Books. . . . [H]ow many familys are ruined by the women not understanding accounts," she explained.[35] Elizabeth took responsibility for the education of her four other nieces as well, providing two of them with the financial backing for a millinery shop. Beyond her family circle, she helped women start a sewing school for the daughters of Boston's elite and set up the orphaned Cuming sisters in their own shop.

For Elizabeth Murray, the link between business and independence was the defining connection in her life. Two years before she died, looking back on her life, she reflected on the "spirit of Independence" that had propelled her to work quietly yet persistently, unobtrusively yet with enormous deliberation, to become a financially independent woman.[36] Indeed, it was this very "spirit of Independence" combined with self-discipline and a passion for hard work that Murray shared with Eliza Pinckney and Katherine Goddard. All three women embraced the belief in individualism, progress, and prosperity that was emerging as the foundation of the American entrepreneurial spirit.

Pinckney, Goddard, and Murray shared another bond, however—namely, the powerful influences of their private circumstances on their public lives. Family ties profoundly affected their economic independence; they all relied on the men in their nuclear family to set them on their enterprising paths; and, ironically, to varying degrees they also depended on the institution of slavery. Moreover, in an age of feme covert, all three women escaped the misfortunes that marriage could bring upon a woman. Ultimately, none of them could separate their entrepreneurial ventures from the circumstances of their private lives, which continued to be an enduring theme for women entrepreneurs. Finally, Pinckney, Goddard, and Murray share a common legacy: they are role models for women of generation to come. Each was a fiercely independent-minded and success-ful entrepreneur, who linked business with politics, thus symbolizing the contributions and potential of enterprising women in the new republic.

THE EVER-BLOOMING.

A NEW INDUSTRIAL SPECIES, AND A REPRESENTATIVE DEVELOPMENT OF THE NINETEENTH CENTURY,

1837 Panic of 1837
• Oberlin College becomes first coeducational college
• Mount Holyoke Female Seminary opens; first U.S. college for women
• New Mexico's Californios rise against Mexican government

1848 First woman's rights convention, Seneca Falls, New York
• New York passes Married Women's Property Rights Act
• Gold discovered, California
• Elizabeth Blackwell trains at Philadelphia Hospital

1851 Harriet Beecher Stowe publishes *Uncle Tom's Cabin*
• Amelia Bloomer urges reform of women's clothing
• Isaac Singer improves sewing machine

1861 Abraham Lincoln becomes President
• Fort Sumter attack marks the beginning of Civil War

CHAPTER TWO

"To guide and encourage other women in business"

ELLEN DEMOREST

1830–1890

PROFIT IN THE SERVICE OF WOMEN

Rebecca Lukens was raised for a life of domesticity. Married at the age of nineteen, she settled comfortably into matrimony and motherhood. But her life changed dramatically in 1825 when her husband suddenly died, and she inherited the family iron business, the Brandywine Iron Works and Nail Factory Company. For the next two decades Lukens was not simply a widow with six children; she was an iron manufacturer, supplying boilerplate for steamships and locomotives in the new industrial age.

Like Rebecca Lukens, Lydia Pinkham planned to devote her life to her husband and children, but a family crisis led her into the world of business. A half–century after widowhood made Lukens the owner of her family's iron works, Pinkham, who was married with five children, helped reverse her

1865 Robert E. Lee surrenders at Appomattox
• President Lincoln assassinated
• Freedmen's Bureau established
• Thirteenth Amendment abolishes slavery
• Vassar College opens

1869 National Woman Suffrage Association formed
• Transcontinental railroad completed
• Wyoming Territory enacts women's suffrage
• Founding of Knights of Labor

1876 Alexander Graham Bell invents telephone
• Battle of the Little Big Horn
• Centennial Exposition in Philadelphia

1886 Haymarket Massacre, Chicago
• Organization of the American Federation of Labor

husband's economic ruin by turning a private herbal recipe for "female complaints" into a thriving family enterprise. Within a few short years, thousands of women across the country eagerly purchased Pinkham's vegetable compound, and the Lydia E. Pinkham Medicine Company became one of the most successful patent medicine companies of its day.

The stories of nineteenth-century women entrepreneurs like Lukens and Pinkham reveal both the change and the continuity in the lives of enterprising women since the era of Eliza Pinckney, Katherine Goddard, and Elizabeth Murray in the eighteenth century. In some ways, life for women in 1830 was very much like it had been in the previous century. America continued to be primarily a rural society and most women lived and worked on the family farm, keeping them tied to the family economy. Women entrepreneurs in the 1830s continued to engage in business in the context of their family position as wives, widows, or daughters. Like their male counterparts, they ran small businesses. In 1832 the overwhelming majority of American businesses had assets of only a few thousand dollars and no more than a dozen employees. They were personal, family-run affairs; most entrepreneurs, male or female, lived near or above their shops.[1] A small number of women could be found taking part in one or more of the many enterprises dominated by men, such as publishing and manufacturing. Among this smaller group of women, most did not establish a new business; rather, like Lukens, they took over a family enterprise. In contrast, most women entrepreneurs of this period, like Pinkham, followed the path of the hundreds of she-merchants of the eighteenth century, and continued to cluster more narrowly in such ventures as millinery, dressmaking, and retail shopkeeping that catered specifically to the female consumer.

While the United States was still primarily an agricultural society in 1830, the rapid growth of industrialization in the decades before the Civil War gradually transformed American business; large corporations began to overshadow small, family-run ventures. Iron production, made possible by the mining of anthracite coal in Pennsylvania, increased, leading to expanded production of such tools as axes, hoes, and plows, and stimulated the production of interchangeable parts in items from clocks to sewing machines. The availability of coal, iron, and machinery led to the growth of factories. The first factories—textile mills in northern New England—drew young men and women away from the family farm to the new mill towns, which led to a gradual decline of the rural family economy. Meanwhile, immigrants, particularly from Ireland, provided an inexpensive industrial labor force. Other industries moved from home to factory, threatening the artisan and small, independent business owner. While most businesses were small in this era of change, as early as 1832 there were already more than a hundred manufacturing firms with capital assets of over $100,000 and another 143 businesses with at least $50,000 in assets.[2] Though few in number, these larger firms signaled the future—the emergence of the modern business corporation in the last quarter of the nineteenth century.

(page 28)

Advertisement from Demorest's Monthly Magazine, 1875, used a tree as a symbol to illustrate the nationwide extent of Demorest's dressmaking-pattern business

Out of Bondage
Polly Bemis

Polly Bemis (1853–1933) overcame the cruel circumstances of her youth to become one of the founding settlers and landowners in the Pacific Northwest. Born Lalu Nathoy, to peasants in China, she labored in the fields with her parents. She was either sold or captured and shipped across the Pacific Ocean to California, like thousands of

Chinese immigrant women of her time. Bought by a saloon owner, who renamed her Polly, she entertained his customers– men who worked in Warrens, a mining town near Portland, Oregon.

Though she was but four feet tall, Polly overcame the obstacles of her bondage and became a successful businesswoman. She was befriended by Charles Bemis, a saloon patron, who helped her open a boarding house. Polly plunged into the endless work of cooking, sewing, and washing for her boarders. At the same time, she earned a reputation as a woman of warmth and generosity.

In 1894, when she married Bemis (in the picture at right she wears her wedding dress), she gained the legal rights to American citizenship and to independent property ownership in her own name. Meanwhile, her successful boarding house business enabled her to buy land along the Salmon River in Idaho. Through her tireless work, she created Polly Place, a self-sufficient ranch, where she harvested fruit, grew wheat, ground flour, and raised livestock. Tenacity, hard work, and a relentless drive for independence, combined with the help she received from Charles Bemis, enabled Polly Bemis to become a successful entrepreneur on the Western frontier. ✎

At the same time, transportation, first by canals and later by rail, opened up new markets, making it possible to move greater quantities of goods more quickly and reliably around the country and enabling migration from New England farms to urban areas and westward to unsettled territories. The railroad boom in the 1840s and 1850s literally transformed the nation's landscape and provided the fast, regular transportation needed to distribute a high volume of goods beyond local markets. The railroads that were first built in the 1830s and 1840s supplemented water-borne transportation and linked existing commercial centers, such as Boston with Lowell and Baltimore with Washington. In the 1850s, over twenty-one thousand new miles of railroad track were laid, linking cities and markets from the East Coast to the Mississippi River. A trip from New York to Chicago that had taken three weeks by water could be made in only three days by train. Railroad expansion continued throughout the century.

By the 1870s, trains traveled on seventy thousand miles of track, connecting the continent from the east to the west. The impact on business was profound; railroads linked distant cities, created new markets, and provided everyone from shippers, distributors, and wholesalers to retailers and consumers with quick, dependable, all-weather transportation of everything from raw materials to finished goods.[3] Other innovations, including the typewriter in 1868, the cash register in 1879, and the harnessing of electric power, accelerated the growth of factories and businesses. In the context of these changes, the local artisan and small independent or family-run enterprise had more difficulty competing.

In the midst of this sweeping transformation, women's lives changed as well. Some women left home and became members of the new industrial workforce; others, primarily members of the rising middle class, stayed home, but also became consumers. Beginning in the 1830s, some states passed legislation that gradually dismantled women's legal disabilities. By 1880, married women in most states could keep property in their own name, they could buy and sell property independently of their husbands, and they could negotiate contracts on their own. Unlike Elizabeth Murray, who had had to negotiate a prenuptial agreement in order to keep her property and run her business on her own when married, now women entrepreneurs could carry on business freely and independently of their husbands. The married women's property acts nudged women legally and economically closer to men.

While legal reforms redefined women more equally with men, cultural norms increasingly asserted marriage and motherhood to be women's appropriate roles. Paradoxically the heightened emphasis on domesticity enabled women to move beyond the boundaries of the home and enter into the public sphere. The opening of female academies and seminaries, such as Mt. Holyoke, introduced young middle-class women to the opportunities of education while preparing them for their future jobs as wives and mothers. Wrapped in the banner of domesticity and moral superiority, women left the comfort of their homes to uplift the world, leading them to become involved in reform work, particularly temperance and antislavery.

Meanwhile, domesticity provided women with valuable training for entrepreneurship. Author and educator Catharine Beecher defined "housewives" as managers of their homes and families. Her books, *Treatise on Domestic Economy* and *The Domestic Receipt Book*, conceptualized the home as a business, and were widely read by middle-class women. Men often agreed that the home was the domestic equivalent of a business. Well-known author T. S. Arthur likened domestic duties to business responsibilities in his short story, "Sweethearts and Wives," which editor Sarah Josepha Hale published in the popular

Godey's Lady's Book. Not surprisingly, many housewives defined themselves as managers of their homes. As they kept precise account books, balanced the family budget, and managed the daily operation of their homes smoothly and efficiently, they gained valuable business experience. As a result, they were often prepared, rather than helpless, when widowhood thrust them into entrepreneurship.[4]

While most women defined their public lives around domesticity, in 1848 a small group of women met in Seneca Falls, New York, to discuss the issues of women's rights. The famous Declaration of Sentiments produced by the conference's participants became a manifesto for nineteenth-century women's grievances and goals. Its clarion call for autonomy and opportunity made it unmistakably clear that women's economic independence was a crucial demand. In the Civil War era, women's access to higher education, the professions, and other public activity expanded. Some forged careers in teaching and nursing, a smaller number broke into the male-dominated profession of medicine, a few even entered the law, while many got involved in social reform.

As women in this period from 1830 to 1890 increasingly claimed their place in the public sphere, women entrepreneurs conducted business in a context that was both different from and similar to that of their predecessors a century before.

Rebecca Lukens (1794–1854) never expected to be an iron manufacturer (color-plate 3). But in 1825, at the age of thirty-one, while other young women of her economic class settled into a life of domesticity, she inherited her family's iron mill. The first woman iron manufacturer in the country, Rebecca was one of the pioneers of early industrialization in America.[5]

Born in 1794 to Quaker parents, Isaac and Martha Pennock of Chester County, Pennsylvania, Rebecca absorbed the Quaker respect for woman's intellect and initiative. Her childhood was a combination of joyful freedom, as she rode horseback and explored the countryside of her home, and apprenticeship for a future of domesticity. Under the strict watch of her mother, she learned sewing, cooking, spinning, and quilting, and helped her mother raise her eight younger siblings. While her mother was a traditionalist, her father was a visionary. In the years after the Revolution, he astutely anticipated the importance of manufacturing to the future of the new nation. Perhaps he had heard about the first steamboat, which sailed in 1787 on the Delaware River near Philadelphia. Shortly before the birth of his daughter, he took a bold step: he gave up farming, the business of his family for several generations, and started a slitting mill in Chester County, where he manufactured iron products including iron tires, hoops for barrels, and rods for blacksmith shops.

While her father ran the mill and her mother managed the household, twelve-year-old Rebecca attended boarding school with other young girls. She studied a range of academic subjects from math to chemistry that had suddenly become available at the female academies and seminaries that sprang up to educate young women for a new

Rebecca Lukens, a successful iron manufacturer and industrial leader during the antebellum period (detail of colorplate 3)

age. Rebecca thrived in school, recalling her years as a student as some of her happiest: "I always look on this period of life with pleasure," she later wrote.[6]

Having experienced the thrill of education, Rebecca returned home "with regret" to resume her responsibilities as the eldest sibling. Blessed with an active mind, Rebecca found the small town stifling after her years of education. "For a long time I felt lonely and isolated," she complained. "I had no companion to mingle my thoughts with."[7] But she found something to occupy her intellectual energies, as her attention quickly turned to her father's new project. Isaac Pennock converted a sawmill on his 110-acre estate on the Brandywine River into an iron mill—the Brandywine Iron Works and Nail Factory.[8] The future of river travel would depend on iron production from such mills.

Rebecca was captivated by the new project, watching as iron arrived by horseback or wagon at the new mill. Her father encouraged her interest in his iron mill and took her with him on a business trip to Philadelphia. The trip was a turning point in Rebecca's life; she met Charles Lukens, a young doctor and fellow Quaker, and fell in love. The restraints of her proper Quaker upbringing had not prepared her for the power of her attraction to this "tall and commanding" young man. In her eyes he was "manly and remarkably handsome," with his hair "the deepest shade of black, his eyes Hazel," while the "suavity of his manner" and the "thrilling sound" of his voice made him utterly irresistible. Charles was overcome as well. He wooed Rebecca with poetry, confessed to her that he had "never before felt the witchery of female power," and offered to "love and cherish thee as the first, best gift of heaven."[9]

In 1813, at the age of nineteen, Rebecca Pennock married the twenty-seven-year-old Charles Lukens, a young man who resembled her father in important ways. Just as Isaac Pennock had abandoned farming for iron manufacturing, so Lukens, in the midst of the nation's expanding economy after the War of 1812, seized the opportunity to enter the iron business; he gave up his medical practice to become a partner in his father-in-law's Federal Slitting Mill, under the new firm name of Pennock and Lukens. A few years later, having mastered the iron business under the tutelage of his father-in-law, Charles and Rebecca moved to the Brandywine estate. She settled down to homemaking and child rearing, while he leased the ironworks from Isaac Pennock for $420 a year and set to work as his own iron manufacturer.

But the duties of the home were not so separate from those of the family business for the young Mrs. Lukens. At every turn she was at her husband's side. When he purchased new nail-making machines, he explained to her how nails were cut from the ends of the iron sheets. When he rebuilt the mill and installed a larger waterwheel, she understood the mill was constantly breaking down and required an owner's special care.

But Charles had even bigger goals. The new nation was growing and he wanted to be part of it. Factories sprang up to manufacture machine-made products. Territories being settled west of the Allegheny Mountains created new markets for manufactured products, while the Louisiana Purchase promised future economic expansion. Roads and canals were built to reach the new markets, and steamships transported raw materials and manufactured goods. Charles knew that steam power would fuel this new industrial age; when he described his plan to adapt Brandywine to make iron boilerplates for steam power, Rebecca shared his dream.

Charles reconverted the Brandywine mill to produce iron plate. His timing was perfect. His charcoal iron boilerplates were ideally suited to the high-pressure strains of steamships and locomotives. In 1818 his mill was the first to roll iron boilerplate, and his reputation soared as he received orders from steamboat manufacturers. The year 1825 promised even greater success. Just when the Schuylkill Canal connecting Philadelphia and Reading and the Erie Canal linking Buffalo to Albany were completed, Charles was commissioned to produce the sheet iron for the nation's first ironclad steamship. In November 1825, the *Codorus* set sail on the Susquehanna, girded with iron plates rolled at the Brandywine mill. Charles Lukens's dream of manufacturing iron for the new industrial age had become a reality—one he did not live to see. He had died a few months earlier after a brief illness.

Pregnant and in the midst of her child-rearing years, thirty-one-year-old Lukens inherited her husband's dream and was determined to make it her own. She faced enormous odds. Charles's dying wish was that she take over the mill. "[H]e wished me to continue and I promised him to comply," Lukens recalled.[10] But her husband died without a will to affirm his wishes. In addition, Isaac Pennock, who had died the year before, left an ambiguous will that promised the mill to his daughter but gave immediate control to his wife until her death. Rebecca's mother did not make it easy. Ever the traditionalist, she believed the mill was no place for her daughter. Meanwhile the mill was practically bankrupt; Charles had died with bills unpaid and orders unfilled.

Undeterred by financial, legal, or family obstacles, Lukens forged ahead, bolstered by her Quaker belief in female intelligence and initiative. She was determined to set the Brandywine Iron Works and Nail Factory back on course and to pull herself and her children out of poverty. But she could not do it alone. She turned to a few supportive men, two of whom were willing to supply her with iron and charcoal on credit, and her brother-in-law, Solomon Lukens, who took over the daily operations of the mill. Meanwhile, Rebecca took over the commercial end of running the mill. It was a demanding responsibility, one that would have been a challenge for any man of the day, but was particularly so for a widow with young children. In an era when women of her class increasingly made their lives within the privacy of the home, Lukens spent her days in the mill. While other women spent their time in the kitchen, she oversaw the hot furnaces of her mill; while other women managed a family budget, she kept careful business records, accounting for the purchase of coal and iron, the repair of

waterwheels, and the sale of iron nails and boilerplate; while other women kept husbands and children happy, she maneuvered in a world of men, trying to satisfy suppliers, customers, and laborers; and while other women increasingly found time for leisure activities, Rebecca Lukens put in long days at the mill, from seven o'clock in the morning until late in the afternoon, before returning home to her domestic responsibilities.

It is not certain how she managed to care for her children, one of whom was born just a month after her husband's death. But she did not ignore her domestic duties; indeed, she found great pleasure in them. Away from the hot furnaces of the mill, she kept a comfortable home with attractive furnishings and a large kitchen hearth, told her children stories, tended her garden, and recorded her favorite recipes. These were the private delights of a woman publicly known for her success in a man's world. At first glance, Lukens seemed to live a life of contradictions. In an age when women were increasingly expected to devote their lives exclusively to home and family, her daily life contradicted this emerging ideal of proper womanhood. As a young widow and mother who spent her day running an iron mill, she deviated sharply from the ideal of femininity.

Yet, while Rebecca Lukens may have been doing a man's job in a man's workplace, she was doing it as a woman. To Lukens, her iron manufacturing company was simultaneously more and less than a business. Quite simply, it was an extension of her family responsibilities as well as a deviation from them. Driven by her promise to her dying husband and her responsibility to her children, she embarked on the life of an iron manufacturer, determined to take over her husband's business and make it profitable. Lukens was so successful at her task that in less than ten years, she had paid off all of the mill's debts and the balance due on her father's estate.[11]

The constant demands of managing the mill were made even more challenging by a steady barrage of uncontrollable obstacles. The mill required costly and time-consuming repairs. If the waterwheel broke, she had to close the mill. Transportation, so important

VIEW OF LUKENS' ROLLING MILLS, COATESVILLE, PA. U. S. A. *about 1870*

The Lukens Rolling Mill in Coatesville, Pennsylvania, ca. 1870

to the smooth functioning of her business, was inefficient and unpredictable. Until the railroad made its way to the Brandywine Valley in the mid–1830s, Lukens had to depend on rivers and roads to transport goods. But wagons had to travel rough roads that were often impassable in the spring, while boats had to navigate dangerous rivers that were closed in the winter. Moreover, Lukens had to rely on the Brandywine River to power her mill. Like any river, the Brandywine did not provide a steady flow of water; when it ran low, she had to shut down her mill.

The promise of profits from iron manufacturing attracted competitors into the industry and threatened Lukens's dominance on the Brandywine. Several built mills upstream from her. One company even sued her for raising the level of her milldam. Perhaps the men who ran it believed that a young widow with children would meekly back down. But they picked the wrong woman. While Lukens was ordered to lower her dam six inches, she confidently stood up to the men who had chosen to challenge her, fortified by her Quaker commitment to fairness in commercial transactions. Her warning to them revealed that she was not only propelled by her Quaker convictions but also acutely aware of the gendered nature of her competition. "Men," she declared, "I have something to say to you. You have started out in business taking unfair advantage of your neighbor, and, mark my words, you will never prosper."[12]

The opening of the Housatonic Railroad in 1834 promised Lukens greater economic opportunity. The impact of the railroads on the growth of the nation's economy cannot

"If the men had some of the energy of that . . . lady, . . . California would have been a prosperous state."

Juana Briones

Though she never learned to read, Juana Briones (ca. 1802–89; seen at right in a drawing by Robert Gebing) was a shrewd businesswoman. In the 1820s, as the first female householder in Yerba Buena, now San Francisco, she took advantage of the commercial opportunities available to her in this pioneer community. Since her husband drank rather than provided for his family, Briones's commercial endeavors enabled her to support herself and her children. She raised cattle, sold produce, ran a tavern, and provided tailoring services–all valuable commodities and commercial services for the region's settlers as well as sailors docked in San Francisco Bay.

In 1844, Briones left her husband. For three hundred dollars, she purchased La Purisma Concepcion, a rancho in what is now Palo Alto, in Santa Clara county (see map, above right). While the previous owner had been unable to manage the land, Briones turned the impressive tract of 4,440 acres into a thriving rancho, where she raised cattle and horses and farmed the land. Moreover, in an age when most of the Californios–as the original Hispanic inhabitants of northern California were then known–lost their land, Briones protected her land with patents from the United States, which also enabled her to sell and lease her land at will.

Briones blended kindness with a hard-driving will to succeed. She was a skilled midwife, who provided medical

care to anyone who sought her help, regardless of their financial circumstances. She sheltered sailors from impressment and cared for indigent Indian children, but demanded their labor in return. Loved for her charity, she was deeply admired for her accomplishments. As one sailor explained: "If the men had some of the energy of that buxom, dark-faced lady, California would have been a prosperous state, even before it was annexed."[1]

[1] Florence M. Fava, *Los Altos Hills: the Colorful Story*. Woodside, Calif.: Gilbert Richards Publications, 1976, pp. 36–37.

be underestimated, for trains radically transformed the distribution of goods and markets. They provided dependable year-round transportation unavailable on roads and rivers, and they opened new markets, linking previously unreachable parts of the country. For Lukens, the railroads enabled her to transport her iron plate faster and farther. Orders came in from Boston, Baltimore, Albany, New York City, and even New Orleans. The reputation of her iron mill expanded as she increasingly supplied the iron plate for locomotives and steamboats. By the mid-1850s, Lukens had staked out her position at the very center of the expansion of the nation's economy. She was one of the most successful entrepreneurs in the nation's burgeoning iron industry, a pioneer in the country's rapid industrialization. As the only woman among the twelve iron manufacturers in the country, she was keenly aware of the broad implications of her business. While Elizabeth Murray valued her personal "cherished independence," Lukens saw her enterprise as crucial to the growth of the new nation. "Manufacture of iron is not a mere local or individual interest," she wrote, "but is of national importance."[13]

In the midst of her growing influence and successes, Lukens faced economic crises, first the Panic of 1837 and later the tariff reductions of the 1840s. These were uncertain times for entrepreneurs, and she was no exception. "The difficulties of the times throws a gloom over everything," she wrote in 1837. "All is paralyzed–business at a stand. I have as yet lost nothing but am in constant fear."[14] But while many businesses succumbed to the enormous financial pressures of the day, Lukens made wise business decisions that enabled her mill to weather the economic crises. With a large supply of rolled iron on hand, she temporarily closed down her mill to avoid overstock. Uncertain about which of her customers were financially able to pay her, she directed her agents in New York and other cities not to sell her iron to anyone. Yet, even with her economic survival at stake, she always remained loyal to her workers. Years before, she had constructed a group of stone houses for her mill hands, and through these crises she continued to consider their welfare. Rather than lay them off, she put them to work half-time making repairs on her mill and dam, and paid them for harvesting vegetables and slaughtering hogs on her farm.

Lukens's economic interests thrust her into the midst of the era's political issues. In 1840, the Whig Party held its convention in nearby Harrisburg, Pennsylvania, and nominated Benjamin Harrison as its presidential candidate. Like women all around the country, Lukens got involved in the campaign and threw her support behind Harrison, who favored higher tariffs. In a parade for Harrison, the women of her town carried a silk banner, inscribed with Lukens's words, which called on "freemen" to "rally round brave Harrison."[15] While Lukens joined other women in their new role as participants in a political campaign, she also participated as an iron manufacturer. Motivated by concern for her mill, she led her workmen to rally for the iron tariff during the election. Her slogan for the campaign rang out from her iron mill: "We fondly hope for better days / When every furnace fire shall blaze / And streaming to the midnight sky / Proclaim to all prosperity."[16] Almost a decade before women made their first public demand for suffrage in 1848, Rebecca Lukens understood all too well the connection between politics and her own economic interests as a major manufacturer.

While all entrepreneurs faced the economic uncertainties of the era, Lukens faced the threat of difficult private family matters as well. In 1844, when her mother died, Lukens assumed that the mill would finally be hers. After all, that had been her father's intention as well as her husband's dying wish. But family members challenged her claim and forced her to make substantial payments for the mill. While she paid a steep price for ownership, she had the legal right to fight for and keep her property, unlike most women just a generation before. In the midst of this family controversy over the ownership of the mill, asthma and age began to slow her down and forced her to share the demands of the business. Wishing to keep the company in the family, she turned to her two sons-in-law, Abraham Gibbons and Charles Huston, made them her partners, and turned the responsibilities of management over to them. She also provided generously for her daughters in her will, taking careful steps to insure their financial independence, even in marriage.[17]

Rebecca Lukens died in 1854. Her legacy was profound. She was a shrewd businesswoman who built an iron company near bankruptcy into a business worth over a hundred thousand dollars. The success of her iron mill made her a central figure in the early industrial growth of the new nation. Moreover, it contradicted the cultural assumption that male power and strength were essential to competing in the new industrial economy. Lukens was also a devoted mother, committed to the financial protection of her daughters. And, finally, in an age of heightened domesticity, she was a successful public woman. While leisure, rather than work, increasingly became ascribed to the lives of middle-class women, Lukens found her greatest pleasure in "the power of being useful."[18] In her own words, she revealed her strong identity as an entrepreneurial woman: "I have built a very superior mill, though a plain one, and our character for making boiler iron stood first in the market, hence we had as much business as we could do."[19]

While Rebecca Lukens was a lone woman in the business of iron manufacturing, Lydia Pinkham (1819–83) took a different tack; she made women's health her business. Pinkham turned the intimate experiences of sexual relations and childbearing–essential parts of being a wife and a mother–into a profitable business. She well understood the gynecological and obstetrical pitfalls, from annoying inconveniences to significant pain and serious health risks, that were associated with being a woman in nineteenth-century America. While Rebecca Lukens manufactured boilerplate in her iron mill, Lydia Pinkham brewed and bottled her personal remedy for women's ills in her kitchen and made a fortune promising women that they could find health and strength in her unique concoction of herbs.

Born Lydia Estes, she spent her life in Lynn, Massachusetts, a working-class community north of Boston.[20] Her parents, William and Rebecca Chase Estes, were well-to-do Quakers devoted to reform. These ardent antislavery advocates left the Lynn Friends Meeting when it failed to support abolition. Estes's neighbors included Frederick Douglass and antislavery speaker Abby Kelley, and her childhood home was always open to antislavery activists such as William Lloyd Garrison and Lydia Maria Child. Her grammar school teacher was an abolitionist, who reinforced the antislavery lessons she learned at home.

Growing up in the midst of this antislavery zeal, the passion for reform rubbed off on Estes. She became an antislavery supporter at an early age and joined the Lynn

Female Anti-Slavery Society when she was sixteen. After graduating from the select Lynn Academy, the local academy for girls, Estes decided to teach, like many young, single women of her day; she also helped organize the Freeman's Institute, a reform group open to anyone regardless of race, sex, religion, or political opinions. Estes's allegiance to this credo of inclusion revealed how thoroughly she had absorbed reform values and foreshadowed her commitment, both entrepreneurial and ideological, to improving women's lives.

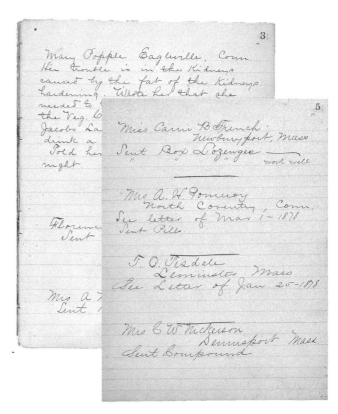

Lydia Pinkham's notes describing ailments of her customers

While working at the Freeman's Institute, Estes, then twenty-four, met Isaac Pinkham, a twenty-nine-year-old widower who had recently moved to Lynn with his five-year-old daughter. At first glance they made an odd pair. She was tall and slim; he was short and stout, and not particularly dynamic or bright. But they shared the same political values that brought them together at the Freeman's Institute, and after a brief courtship they married in 1843. Over the next fourteen years, Lydia Pinkham bore five children, one of whom died in infancy. For three decades, she devoted her life to her family, raising her three sons and one daughter.

One of Pinkham's most important duties as wife and mother was her responsibility for the health of her family. In an age before modern medical science, women grew herbs and prepared remedies on their kitchen stoves. In addition to recipes for stews, puddings, and other dishes, cookbooks of the era often included recipes for botanical medicines. Pinkham often relied on her personal copy of John King's *American Dispensatory*, the fullest listing then available of the medicinal powers of plants and herbs. In addition, she experimented with her own botanical concoctions and recorded her recipes for herbal medicines in a notebook she labeled "Medical Directions for Ailments." Among her collection was her recipe for the cure of "female weakness," a concoction of unicorn root and pleurisy root adapted from *The American Dispensatory* that ultimately became the cornerstone of the Pinkham family's medicine business. But the business of women's health was far from Pinkham's mind during the years she devoted to raising and caring for her family.

Meanwhile, Isaac Pinkham pursued his dreams and schemes; he saw fortune around every corner, but never seemed able to grasp it. For three decades, the Pinkham family lived in economic peril as Isaac tried his luck at a range of occupations including trader, farmer, builder, and produce dealer. At the end of the Civil War, he invested in real estate in Lynn, and in the early 1870s it appeared that his investments were paying off and that financial success was finally at hand. But the Panic of 1873 destroyed these opportunities. As the economy crashed and the nation sank into a financial depression, Isaac fell once

In this 1879 photograph, Lydia Pinkham and her daughters stand before the family home (at right). At left, the Pinkham men are seen in front of the first laboratory of the Lydia E. Pinkham Medicine Company.

again into debt and faced the threat of jail. He never recovered from this last fiasco in an endless string of financial failures; he spent the rest of his life a weak and ruined man.

But Isaac's failure opened the door to opportunity for the Pinkham family. Over the years, Lydia had earned a reputation with neighboring women in Lynn for her home-brewed cure for female weakness. Now, in the midst of this most recent family economic crisis, her medicine also offered a way out of the family's money problems. When a group of women traveled from Salem to Lynn to purchase six bottles of Lydia's medicine for five dollars, her son Dan recognized a business opportunity. "Mother, if those ladies will come all the way from Salem to get that medicine, why can it not be sold to other people—why can't we go into the business of making and selling it, same as any other medicine?"[21]

Dan was right. The time was ripe for marketing his mother's home remedy. Doctors, who had little of therapeutic use to offer patients, resorted to calomel, a mercurial compound that caused bleeding, blistering, and even death when given in excess. Many patients, aware of the dangers of this widely used medicine, sought alternative botanical therapies. Herbal remedies, with such names as "Vegetine" and "Wright's Indian Vegetable Pills," may have had little therapeutic value, but at least they were painless and harmless. Women in particular were eager for these herbal alternatives to traditional medicine. At a time when labor and delivery occurred more often at home than in hospitals, and before antisepsis and the widespread use of anesthesia, everyone knew that childbirth was painful and often life-threatening. Expectant mothers lived in dread of a life of gynecological problems if they survived delivery. Herbal medicines promised women a healthy, painless route back to health.

Pinkham was not the first to market an herbal remedy to women in the Boston area. In the 1830s, one Mrs. Elizabeth Mott built a women's-health business that combined bathing, mild exercise, and herbal remedies with frank and practical medical advice. Her book, *Ladies' Medical Oracle: or Mrs. Mott's Advice to Young Females, Wives, and Mothers*, provided women with information on gynecological problems in a language that they understood, while her therapeutic system of European Vegetable Medicine and her Medicated Shampoo Baths offered women a regimen of hydropathy and botanical therapeutics.[22]

A half-century later, Pinkham followed in this tradition of marketing women's health. She took the traditional female approach, relying on herbs, cooking, and healing to carve a niche in the male-dominated field of medicine. Still, she adopted bold marketing practices to build her business. Officially launched with the registration of her label and trademark with the United States Patent Office in 1876, the Lydia E. Pinkham Medicine Company was a one-product enterprise built around Pinkham's Vegetable Compound. The business began modestly, with Pinkham preparing the medicine at home as she always had done. From her local suppliers of botanical roots and herbs, she purchased the ingredients—unicorn root, life root, black cohosh, pleurisy root, and fenugreek seed—all of which were believed to alleviate gynecological problems from painful menstruation to the threat of miscarriage. In her kitchen, Pinkham measured, soaked, and mixed the herbs, percolated them in cloth bags, added approximately 19 percent alcohol as a preservative, and then strained the liquid into glass bottles. While the Pinkhams were active temperance advocates, Pinkham included alcohol in her Vegetable Compound because she believed it was therapeutically useful as well as a necessary preservative. In the midst of the growing temperance crusade, even the influential Woman's Christian Temperance Union agreed.

In addition to preparing the Vegetable Compound, Pinkham was a master at public relations (colorplate 6). As a married woman who survived childbirth five times, she understood firsthand women's most intimate fears about their health. She encouraged her customers to write to her about their health problems, and diligently answered their letters, responding frankly to intimate questions about women's physiology and health. Her message was simple and appealing: women held the key to their own health. All they needed to do was adopt a healthy regimen of mild exercise, a nutritious diet, and hygiene; wear loose-fitting clothing; and take her Vegetable Compound when needed.

Pinkham's advice connected her to the broad popular health movement of the day, which sought alternatives to the harsh therapeutics and surgical practices of regular doctors. More specifically, her advice placed her squarely within the tradition of nineteenth-century women's health reform. Her message echoed the views of women's health advocates, including female doctors, nurses, educators, and social reformers, who

Ledgers from the Lydia E. Pinkham Company and packaging for Pinkham's Vegetable Compound

"A woman best understands a woman's ills." Advertisements such as this one from 1893 traded on Lydia Pinkham's special bond with her female customers.

believed that women were inherently neither weak nor sickly; that a regimen of prudent diet, exercise, and cleanliness could insure women a life of health and strength.

Moreover, Pinkham's message crossed class lines and appealed to a diverse group of women throughout the country, from society matrons to farmwives to young girls in the industrial workforce. They all depended on the dialogue she encouraged and they trusted her with their most intimate problems. Ultimately, Pinkham received so many letters–up to one hundred a month–that she organized and supervised a Department of Advice to answer them all. "I have doctored for several years with no success" was a typical complaint of her customers. "By all means avoid instrumental treatment. . . . Use the

Compound faithfully and patiently," was a common response.[23] Women rewarded her with their loyalty and eagerly bought her Vegetable Compound.

While Pinkham was the heart and soul of the business as well as the producer of the Vegetable Compound, the Lydia E. Pinkham Medicine Company was a family business from the start. Everyone had a role. Two of Pinkham's children, Charles and Aroline, provided the small but crucial amount of capital needed to get the business started. Their wages enabled Pinkham to convert her cellar kitchen into a factory and to purchase the herbs, alcohol, bottles, and other equipment needed for production. One son, Will, helped write the advertising copy and peddled the medicine in the Boston area, while another son, Dan, sold it in New York City. Even Isaac participated, packing pamphlets for Dan and Will to distribute.

Business began slowly. Despite constant door-to-door peddling of pamphlets and medicine, Will and Dan often sold only a bottle of medicine a day. But in 1876, Will took a chance and paid sixty dollars, the family's entire advertising budget, to buy a full-page advertisement in the *Boston Herald*. It was a risky step because it left no money to cover the cost of printing pamphlets. But newspaper advertising, not pamphlets, was the surest way to sell patent medicine in the late nineteenth century, and Will's ad in the *Herald* gave the family the break it needed. A few wholesalers put in orders for the Vegetable Compound and the Pinkhams poured their new profits into more newspaper advertising. Meanwhile, in New York City, Dan used his winning personality to convince Charles N. Crittenton, then the major patent-medicine dealer of the day, to sell the Vegetable Compound through his wholesale markets. Crittenton provided important cash and credibility, enabling the company to attract other wholesalers and to pay for more advertising.

In 1879, Dan came up with a new marketing idea: incorporating a picture of his mother in the advertising. Sixty-year-old Pinkham, pictured sitting erect and appropriately attired in black silk and white lace, was the symbol of healthy womanhood—calm, content, dignified, and strong. Her image was a clear message to all: Lydia Pinkham, strong and healthy, was a woman to trust and so was her medicine. The strategy was an immediate success. Less than a year later, the Pinkhams were offered one hundred thousand dollars to sell their business and the new trademark with Pinkham's face. They turned down the offer and the company continued to flourish. It was the right decision, for just two years later, in 1881, the company had annual sales of almost two hundred thousand dollars.[24]

In the midst of this business success tragedy hit. Dan developed tuberculosis in 1879. No amount of rest or therapy, not even Pinkham's own remedies, could save him; he died in 1881, a month before his thirty-third birthday. Shortly after Dan's death, Will came down with tuberculosis, and he died two months after Dan, at the age of twenty-eight. Pinkham never recovered from the loss of her sons. Spiritualism, rather than the day-to-day matters of her business, increasingly captured her attention. In the winter of 1882, she suffered a stroke, which she survived, but during the following months she became infirm. She died on May 17, 1883, at the age of sixty-four. By the time of her death, her business had an annual gross income of about three hundred thousand dollars.

Behind the success of the business was a woman who skillfully touched the deepest concerns of the women of her day for the well-being of their families and themselves. From her kitchen stove, Lydia Pinkham captured the spirit and urgency of women's health reform, and turned her personal remedy for women's ills into a thriving business. Marketing the promise of health and strength, Pinkham became a national symbol of women's well-being, an enthusiastic advocate of self-medication rather than reliance on doctors, and a successful entrepreneur.

∽ While Lydia Pinkham built a business around the most intimate details of women's private lives, Ellen Demorest (1824–98) made a fortune catering to women's desire to appear fashionable in public. Following in the tradition of Elizabeth Murray and other eighteenth-century she-merchants, Ellen Demorest made her way among the thousands of women dressmakers and milliners in the nineteenth century. Beginning as a modest milliner in upstate New York, she established an empire in the female-dominated fashion industry in New York City and became the arbiter of style for women.

Unlike Rebecca Lukens or Lydia Pinkham, Demorest built her business with her husband. They made an ideal team. While most female entrepreneurs were independent proprietors struggling simply to support themselves, Demorest rose to the top of the fashion industry alongside her husband. Her story reveals that marriage did not always hinder, but could sometimes help a woman in business. And as an enterprising woman in an era of great social change, her story also illuminates the close connection between business and reform that characterized the lives of many successful entrepreneurs, women and men, of the day.

Ellen Curtis was born on November 15, 1824, in Schuylerville, New York, the second of eight children.[25] Her father, a farmer and the owner of a men's hat factory, made a living in both agriculture and industry. Ellen benefited from the expanding educational opportunities for young girls, attending first a local school and then the all-female Schuylerville Academy. When she was not in school she spent much of her free time watching the fashionable women who strolled through the nearby resort town of Saratoga Springs.

Curtis's years of closely observing women of style left their mark. When she finished school at eighteen she set her sights on becoming a milliner. It was not an unreasonable goal. Like dressmaking, millinery was work that offered young women of her era the opportunity for independence and creativity, and at the same time it was an acceptable enterprise for a woman. It demanded the traditionally feminine skill of sewing, and it catered to a female clientele. Along with dressmakers and seamstresses, milliners were the backbone of a female economy. Owned and serviced by women for women,

"Happy as pigs in the clover"
Hannah, Mary, and Margarett Adams

Like so many daughters of New England farm families, Hannah and Mary (see colorplate 4) and Margarett Adams (see the portrait on this page) learned the traditional domestic tasks of sewing and needlework. Imbued with the spirit of independence and the belief in the virtue of hard work, they turned their sewing skills into a thriving business in Manchester, New Hampshire.

After education in the local schools, the sisters set out to learn the needle trade. All became proficient in millinery and dressmaking, and the youngest, Mary, apprenticed herself to a tailor to learn cutting, a skilled craft then typically reserved for men. In the late 1830s, the sisters set up a shop on the outskirts of Manchester. It began as a very modest venture. They bought materials—thread, buttons, trim, and lining—in limited amounts sufficient to cover their immediate needs. Their weekly earnings ranged from six to twenty dollars, and their annual profits rarely surpassed six hundred dollars.

But over the years their business grew to become a successful enterprise. They concentrated on the lucrative area of men's tailoring, expanded their customer base beyond neighbors to include male tailors, brought in several young girls as apprentices, and purchased a sewing machine. By 1858, their net worth exceeded four thousand dollars. Their careful record keeping for all the tailoring orders they completed is easily seen in the daybook pages shown at right.

As the business grew and thrived, the self-named "Manchester sisterhood" developed an independent spirit that conflicted with contemporary filial demands made on adult daughters. When their mother asked them to come home to care for her, these enterprising young women challenged her to reject the "dreadful doctrine that your daughters were born slaves to serve you until they are married."[1]

The Adams sisters delighted in the success of their enterprise. They exemplify the respect for independence, work, and business that inspired New England farm women of their day. As Hannah explained: "We are as happy as pigs in the clover; nothing to do but to work & of that we are overrun."[2]

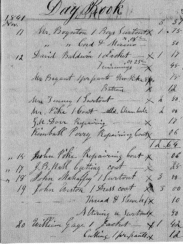

[1] Hannah, Margarett, and Mary Adams to their mother, Elizabeth Adams, Manchester, [no month] 23, 1842, Adams Family papers, private papers of Jo Anne Preston.

[2] Hannah Adams to Capt. Edmund and Elizabeth Adams, Nov 14, 1841, Adams Family papers, private papers of Jo Anne Preston.

businesses in this female economy formed a separate commercial community apart from the mainstream industries run by and for men.[26]

Millinery and dressmaking were at the top of this female economy; and most milliners worked their way up a hierarchy, toiling for five years or more before they advanced to the upper echelon of trimmers. Curtis's mother, ever conscious of status and reputation, did not want her daughter to face the drudgery and low status of an apprenticeship. Her father, supportive of his daughter's desire to enter the family trade, provided the capital and credit to set her up in her own shop in Saratoga Springs with the assistance of an experienced milliner. Curtis brought her years of watching the ladies of fashion in Saratoga Springs to her new venture and was an immediate success. From there it was a quick climb, first to Troy, a prospering millinery center where she studied dressmaking, and then to New York City.

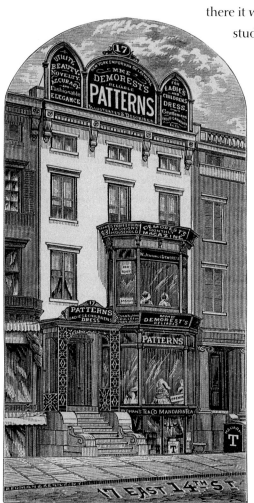

In the 1850s, New York was a city on the move, rapidly emerging as the center of the nation's developing garment industry. The earliest retail clothing stores and department stores, including Brooks Brothers and Lord and Taylor's, opened elegant shops on Broadway, which was undergoing a transformation from an avenue of homes to a commercial street of shops. Eager to make her mark, Curtis settled in the Williamsburgh section of Brooklyn. Through business connections, she met her future husband, William Jennings Demorest, a dry goods merchant from Philadelphia, who had established a fashion emporium named Madame Demorest's, after his first wife, Margaret Poole Demorest. But when Curtis met William Demorest, he was a thirty-five-year-old widower with two young children, bankrupt from the crash of 1857. After a brief courtship, they married; and at the age of thirty-four she became not only a wife but also, instantly, a mother of two. A year later she gave birth to a son, then in 1865, at the age of forty-one, a daughter.

Ellen Demorest settled into her role as the woman behind Madame Demorest's fashion emporium. Strategically situated near other fashionable stores on Broadway, the shop catered to wealthy, fashionable women. With her years of millinery experience and attention to style, the new Madame Demorest was well prepared to provide her sophisticated clientele with the look and quality they demanded. Her sister, Kate, also a skilled needlewoman, worked with her in the shop, which freed her to go home to her children as needed. It was an ideal arrangement—one that enabled Demorest to balance her public position with her private role as a wife and mother.

Exterior of Madame Demorest's Emporium, 17 East 14th Street, New York City, 1874

While Ellen Demorest developed a loyal New York City clientele, her husband introduced a women's fashion magazine, *Mme. Demorest's Quarterly Mirror of Fashions*, to market the clothing and reputation of Madame Demorest's well beyond Broadway (colorplate 5). *Mme. Demorest's Quarterly Mirror of Fashions* not only included the customary color plates of

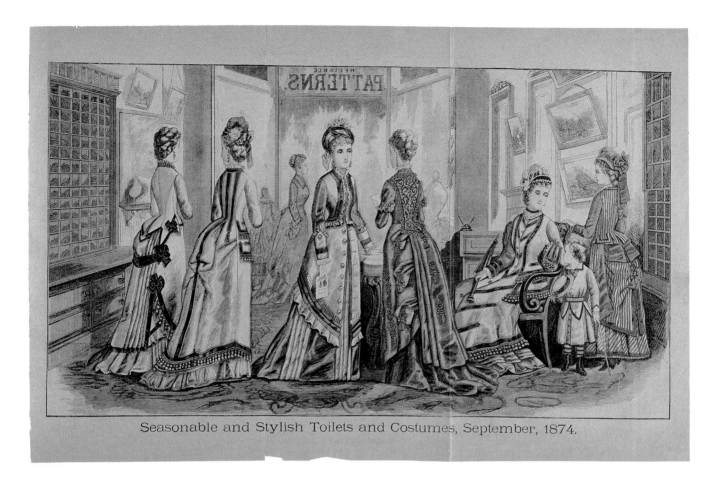

Seasonable and Stylish Toilets and Costumes, September, 1874.

elegant women in fashionable attire; it provided its readers with tissue-paper patterns of the fashions. In an era when women's clothing was complicated and elaborate, when the very cutting of a dress pattern was an intricate and difficult task, patterns were beginning to transform the fashion industry. Stylish dress designs relied on skills well beyond the ability of a typical seamstress who did straight sewing or stitching of hooks and eyes. They demanded the experience, patience, and precision of cutters, who took their place at the very top of the dressmaking hierarchy. The typical dressmaker who had achieved the status of cutter relied on the complicated, time-consuming "pin-to-form" method. First she draped and pinned paper or inexpensive fabric to her customer's body; next she cut the fabric or paper to create a pattern; she then basted the pattern to create a lining or model for the finished garment. Next, the customer tried on the basted garment and the dressmaker fitted it to her body precisely. Only then was the dressmaker ready to cut the costly fabric for the outfit itself.

Paper patterns promised to simplify this elaborate and expensive process. William Demorest had gotten into the pattern business in the mid-1850s, selling patterns for a woman's "under wardrobe" at Madame Demorest's. A decade later, Ebenezer Butterick began producing patterns for women's clothing. The launching of *Mme. Demorest's Quarterly Mirror of Fashions* enabled William Demorest to expand his pattern business to a national market. By including a paper pattern between the covers of the *Mirror of*

Interior of Madame Demorest's Emporium, 1874

Fashions, he introduced the affordable, easy-to-use innovation to every subscriber. His timing was perfect. He introduced Demorest paper patterns to women just as the sewing machine was becoming a common fixture in middle-class homes. The sewing machine first became available in 1846, when Elias Howe of Massachusetts patented his invention. In 1851 Isaac Singer patented an improved machine with a foot-operated pedal. The machine, which made sewing faster and easier, became increasingly popular in the next few decades among housewives as well as dressmakers. In 1870, 95 percent of all dress-making establishments in Boston used sewing machines.[27] By the time the Singer Manufacturing Company introduced an electric-powered machine in 1889, the sewing machine had become a universal item in households from New York to California.

Health !! Comfort !! Convenience !!

MME. DEMOREST'S

HANDY SKIRT SUSPENDERS

Ladies' and Children's.

Attaches all the skirts together at the bands, without buttons or sewing, and suspends them from the shoulders, thus relieving the back and hips.

Are adjustable in length, very durable, and more indispensable than any other article of dress.

| 4 Sizes for Ladies, | - | - | 50 Cts. each. |
| 4 Sizes for Children, | - | - | 37 Cts. each. |

Address, *MME. DEMOREST*,
838 Broadway, New York.

Warranted to give satisfaction. Sold everywhere, or mailed post free on receipt of price.

Skirt suspenders were among the numerous fashion innovations Demorest developed for her customers

Just as the sewing machine turned any housewife into a seamstress, paper patterns turned the same woman into a dressmaker, enabling her to cut her own intricate outfits like the expensive custom-made clothing worn by wealthy women of style. Meanwhile, articles in the *Mirror of Fashions*, such as "Hints in Regard to Dress-Cutting and Fitting," gave women sewing tips and encouraged them to believe they could do it all themselves at home. "[T]here is a delightful satisfaction," wrote one very grateful reader, "in being able to serve myself."[28]

Along with the sewing machine, Demorest's paper patterns played an important role in the democratization of women's fashion, making style available to middle-class women around the country. But the skilled dressmaker was the victim of all this change. As the art of dressmaking gave way to the precision of mass-produced paper patterns, the sophisticated dressmaker found her talents and experience less marketable. The lowly seamstress and the novice housewife could follow a paper pattern and make an intricate outfit much like one made by the experienced dressmaker. It was difficult to escape the hard reality: the democratization of fashion was directly tied to the decline of the skilled dressmaker.

Readers of the *Mirror of Fashions* proclaimed that they were delighted to be "emancipated . . . from dependence upon milliners and dressmakers."[29] They clamored for the Demorest paper patterns. They willingly paid eighteen cents for a blouse pattern, seventy-five cents for a trimmed cloak, one dollar for a dress, and five dollars for a complete set of fifteen patterns. Tinted paper, another of William Demorest's creative marketing ideas, added glamour to the patterns and heightened their popular appeal. While William Demorest dominated the business end—publishing the magazine, running the factory, and overseeing the finances—Ellen Demorest contributed her creativity. With an eye to outfitting the entire family, she started lines of children's and men's clothing, an original idea for the time. Her scouts in Paris and London constantly sent information to her on the latest fashions. In her Emporium on Broadway, Ellen Demorest, her sister Kate, and an ever-growing team of designers made expensive wardrobes for her wealthy clientele. In a fashion era dominated by the controversial corset and crinoline, Demorest offered her customers welcome innovations without rejecting the dictates of style. She introduced a corset widely hailed as the most comfortable on the market; she created a small hoop skirt that was easy to manage and inexpensive; and she developed her Imperial Dress–elevator, an undergarment with strings women used to raise and lower their skirts as they cleared sidewalks, gutters, and puddles.

The Demorests had found an ideal formula for success. The elite Emporium, combined with their inexpensive paper patterns and popular fashion magazine, allowed them to dominate the fashion industry from top to bottom. Their fashion empire expanded even during the years of the Civil War. Ellen gained widespread praise and publicity in 1863 when she designed the trousseau for the future bride of P. T. Barnum's circus star, Tom Thumb. The following year William purchased the *New York Illustrated News*, merged it with the *Mirror of Fashions*, and created *Demorest's Illustrated Monthly Magazine and Mme. Demorest's Mirror of Fashions*. The new publication appeared monthly, priced at three dollars a year. Every subscriber received an engraving suitable for hanging in their parlor and a dollar package of patterns. Each issue arrived with a paper dress pattern stapled inside. William Demorest offered premiums to readers for bringing in new subscribers. Three new subscriptions earned a reader a photograph album; thirty–five subscriptions earned her a sewing machine.

William's plan made *Demorest's Monthly* an overnight success. The magazine joined a growing list of women's periodicals, including *Harper's Bazaar*, *Hearth and Home*, and *Home Companion*, and enabled the Demorests to expand and profit from an emerging women's-information revolution. Even with stiff competition from a host of new women's magazines, *Demorest's Monthly* reached a hundred thousand households by the summer of 1865, bringing Demorest patterns and fashion ideas into households well beyond a local market. Meanwhile, a network of three hundred shops, many using the label "Mme. Demorest's Magasin des Modes," showcased and sold the Demorest paper patterns to customers around the country.[30]

As the nation tried to heal in the years after the Civil War, Demorest built on her reputation as the arbiter of women's fashion to help create a national fashion culture for women. Her Emporium became the place to shop for society brides, who flocked there to purchase trousseaus costing thousands of dollars and complete wardrobes with hundreds of items for up to twenty thousand dollars. At the same time, her fame spread overseas: her designs were featured at the Paris Exposition, *Demorest's Monthly* began publication in London, and international stars toured the United States in her fashions.

The Demorests' fashion empire continued to grow, even during the financial crisis of 1873. The year before, they had introduced sized–and–notched paper patterns for women and children. Even though Butterick had introduced the same innovation several years before, the Demorests proudly announced their new patterns to subscribers as "Something New."[31] By the mid–1870s, their business ventures had reached a peak. Fifteen hundred women worked as Demorest agents around the country. In 1876 alone, the very year that Lydia Pinkham launched her medicine company, the Demorests distributed three million paper patterns. Participating in the Centennial Exhibition in Philadelphia that year, their display of hundreds of paper patterns as well as a dress-cutting system and a drafting tool won them awards and recognition. Their international reputation expanded as well. Ellen Demorest made annual trips abroad for fashion openings and they won top awards for their designs at expositions. Offices in Europe, Canada, and Cuba distributed the Demorest patterns in French and English to an international market.

At every turn, as the Demorests built their fortune, profit went hand in hand with their principles. They were social reformers involved in the major causes of the day, including abolition and temperance; as well, Ellen took a special interest in improving women's lives. From the very beginning, they brought their reform zeal to their business. In the midst of the national crisis over slavery, they took a bold and courageous step. In an effort to promote racial integration, they hired African American women, treating them as equals with their white employees. All workers, regardless of race, sat together in the workroom, received the same pay, and were invited to the same company social events. If customers objected, regardless of how wealthy or influential, the Demorests told them to go elsewhere.

The Demorests' business and reform interests became inextricably linked in 1860 when Jennie June Croly became chief writer for *Demorest's Monthly*. Croly shared the Demorests' deep commitment to social reform, particularly women's rights, and she turned *Demorest's Monthly* into a vehicle to promote a range of causes on behalf of women, including exercise, hygiene, education, and the importance of useful work. "What Women Are Doing," her regular column, claimed to take "note of every woman rancher, banker, dentist or businesswoman of any sort who came to light in a distinctive way in any part of the country."[32] Several years later, in 1868, Croly and Demorest continued their shared commitment to women's reform, founding Sorosis, the pioneering New York City woman's club. Through her relationship with Croly and her Sorosis club work, Demorest broadened her involvement in women's causes. Her concern for promoting women's career opportunities led her to become treasurer of the New York Medical College, a school dedicated to training women in homeopathic medicine and supported by Elizabeth Cady Stanton and other leaders in the women's rights movement. Her interest in temperance and the welfare of women and children led her to become board chairman of a temperance refuge in the city, the Welcome Lodging House for Women and Children.

In 1872, Demorest combined her efforts on behalf of women with her own entrepreneurial goals and launched a new business, the Woman's Tea Company. It's goal was twofold: to make money by importing and distributing the very best tea, and to provide dependent women, primarily widows and single women, with a respectable means of self-support. Tea, after all, was a ladylike and refined commodity suitable for any respectable woman to sell. To launch the Tea Company, Demorest joined with Susan A. King, a businesswoman who had made her fortune buying and selling New York City real estate. William Demorest, who also dabbled in real estate, met King and introduced

Demorest's prize-winning display at the Paris Exposition, 1878; at the time, her Emporium of Fashion, located next to the American Consulate in Paris, was France's only source for sized patterns.

her to his wife. Each was thrilled to meet another entrepreneurial woman who wanted to help others become more independent. Demorest and King first set up a house to aid "fallen women," but they had a grander idea: to establish an international tea-trading business and to employ women exclusively to sell the tea. As King made clear, their goal was economic–not political–independence for women. "The dollar has carried me all around the world," King declared. "What do I care for the ballot? But now mark my words, if ever women do get the right of suffrage it will be through their showing the ability to win the dollar, and win it just as men do."[33]

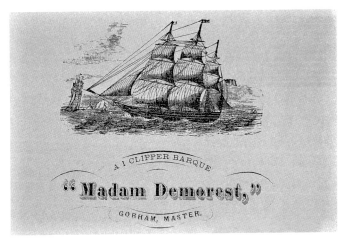

Ellen Curtis Demorest and Susan King founded the Woman's Tea Company to import Mandarin tea from China in their clipper ship, the Madam Demorest.

   After two years of careful planning, they launched their tea company in 1872. Backed by half a million dollars, King set sail on their clipper ship, the *Madam Demorest*, to purchase tea in Japan and China. The Woman's Tea Company turned Demorest and King into merchants, an unusual commercial role for women of the day. While women had long been accepted as retailers, especially in dry goods, men dominated the role of merchant. Trading in foreign goods was not deemed proper work for a lady. Given the

The Wages of Friendship
Elizabeth Keckley

Elizabeth Keckley (ca. 1818–1907) learned to read, write, and sew while she was a slave. But it was her skill as a dressmaker that attracted the attention of wealthy St. Louis women that enabled her to earn the $1,200 required to buy freedom for herself and her son in 1855. In 1860, she established a bustling dressmaking business in Washington, D.C., with parlor, private fitting room, and upstairs workroom. Among the prominent women attracted to her successful dressmaking establishment was the wife of Jefferson Davis, who was soon to become president of the Confederacy.

In the winter of 1861, when newly elected President Lincoln arrived in the nation's capital, Mary Todd Lincoln went directly to Keckley and hired her as her private dressmaker. The business relationship developed into a personal one as Keckley became maid, travelling companion, and confidante to the First Lady. Wishing to share her good fortune, Keckley founded the Contraband Relief Association, an organization of African American women who helped former slaves settle in the nation's capital, a cause to which Mary Lincoln contributed two hundred dollars.

In 1868, however, *Behind the Scenes*, a book published under Keckley's name, exposed intimacies about the

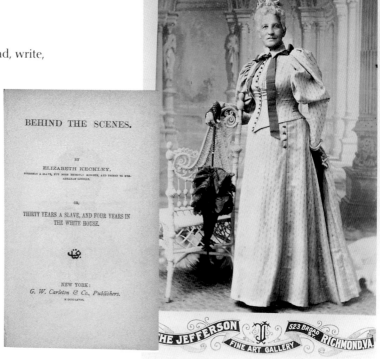

Lincoln family and destroyed her relationship with the First Lady. As a result, Keckley's dressmaking business suffered a rapid decline, which revealed her dependence for economic security on Mary Lincoln and other influential white women. She also lost the respect of many in the African American community, who viewed her as a traitor to the Lincolns. Once well-know for her dressmaking skills and her own understated good taste, Elizabeth Keckley died in obscurity at the Home for Destitute Women and Children, an institution she had helped found. ✎

popular resistance to female merchants, it is not surprising that Demorest attracted public attention and curiosity in her new position as a tea trader. "The American tea trade is threatened with a monopoly by a firm of ladies," fretted one New York newspaper. "Woman has resolved she will no longer be only a tea-drinker; she aspires to be a tea-trader."[34] Public opinion did not faze Demorest and she and King moved forward with their enterprise to give business opportunities to respectable, needy women. The tea was sold in Madame Demorest's emporium where customers enjoyed sipping tea while trying on outfits. Wealthy families ordered tea for their households while fashionable clubs and hotels put in thousand-dollar orders. By 1873, their clipper ship was paid in full and women agents sold tea throughout the country.

By the mid-1870s, Demorest had reached the peak of her power and prestige. But she and William never patented the Demorest paper pattern. For two successful entrepreneurs, this curious oversight had profound financial implications. In the 1880s, the enterprising Ebenezer Butterick patented his own paper patterns and emerged as a formidable competitor. Meanwhile, the Demorests, now in their sixties, were less interested in business and more concerned about reform. They sold their pattern business in 1887 and devoted themselves to social causes. Demorest continued her work on behalf of women's reform, while her husband focused on temperance. When Ellen Demorest died in 1898, at the age of seventy-three, she was no longer a reigning fashion entrepreneur. Having failed to protect legally their paper patterns, she and her husband left their innovation vulnerable to competitors. So to future generations, Butterick, not Demorest, became the name associated with tissue paper patterns.

Still, the Demorests built a fashion empire that had an enormous impact during their lifetime. The combination of the paper patterns, their national network of agents, *Demorest's Monthly*, and the Emporium of Fashions made Demorest fashions available to both working women and the elite. While fashion had once been exclusively a luxury of the wealthy, the Demorest enterprise reached up and down the social ladder. Linking self-interest with women's interests, Demorest not only democratized fashion, she also gave hundreds of needy women a respectable way to achieve economic independence. Her contributions did not go unnoticed. "No woman in this country has done more than Mme. Demorest to secure the best interests of her sex," proclaimed one New York reporter in 1866. "She has proved, in her vast business transactions, the capacity of woman to care for herself; and she has been instrumental in placing many others on the path of prosperous trade which leads to independence."[35]

⟨⟩ While Ellen Demorest's paper patterns shaped the way women dressed during the Civil War, Martha Coston's pyrotechnic night signals literally influenced the events of the Civil War. Her red, white, and green flares, visible for miles in the dark, were used by the Union forces for maritime communication. Unlike Demorest, who never patented her paper patterns, Martha Coston (1826 (?)–1902 (?)) aggressively protected her flares with patents.[36]

Martha Coston never intended to become an entrepreneur. Born in Baltimore, Martha Hunt and her mother moved to Philadelphia after her father died. When she was only fourteen, she met nineteen-year-old Benjamin Franklin Coston, and they fell in love. Two years later they eloped. Martha Coston left her home and family in Philadelphia, and went off with her young husband to make a new life in Washington, D.C. Benjamin Coston was an inventor whose technological innovations had already caught the attention of the United States Navy. His reputation as a brilliant nautical engineer thrust him into the social circle of Washington's public leaders, and Martha became acquainted with distinguished individuals including Henry Clay and Dolley Madison.

While the young couple made the rounds of the capital's social elite, Benjamin directed a pyrotechnic laboratory for the navy, and Martha settled down to childbearing and child rearing. She had four sons in five years and was blissfully happy. Even with their active social life, her happiest moments were their quiet nights at home. "My husband's inventions were of absorbing interest to me," she recalled, and she loved to sit with him as he pored over his work "to cheer, encourage, and look after his personal comfort." But then tragedy struck; her husband, to whom she was "the very queen of women," died after a brief bout of pneumonia.[37] Within the year, her mother and second son died as well. Martha Coston was suddenly a widow with three young children to support.

Out of personal crises and the need to care for her children, the one-time loving helpmate to her husband became an independent-minded entrepreneur in her own right.[38] Martha Coston was not the first to turn adversity into success. A generation before, Rebecca Lukens, widowed and with children to support, turned her husband's iron mill into a thriving iron company. For Coston, Lukens, and many other women, it was widowhood or other personal crises, not any political drive for equality, that propelled them out of the comforts of domesticity and onto uncharted terrain. Forced to support themselves and their children, they ran businesses beyond the boundaries of women's traditional sphere, proving that enterprising women could compete as equals in industries dominated by men.

Like Lukens, Coston proved herself a resourceful businesswoman as she perfected her husband's pyrotechnic devices. But it was not an easy road. Coston encountered obstacles at every turn as she sought to rebuild her life. She began as a poor widow, left penniless by her husband's business partners and a dishonest relative. Like other widows and single women of her day who studied law or business to protect their inheritances, Coston suddenly discovered her dire "need of a better understanding of my business affairs."[39]

But Coston had two important advantages: knowledge and social contacts. Her shared moments with Benjamin in his study were suddenly invaluable. Having watched and listened attentively while he worked, she could read the diagrams and interpret the charts for his night signals, which she found in a box of his papers. She also understood the significance of his invention. She knew that once they were perfected, the multicolored pyrotechnic flares would be indispensable for maritime communication and safety. While sailors used flags to communicate in daylight, it was impossible to communicate in the dark. Her husband's night signals promised a way to communicate ship-to-shore and ship-to-ship at night and in the fog.

Martha Coston took it upon herself to develop, perfect, and, ultimately, market her husband's invention. This was a bold endeavor, particularly in an era when popular opinion viewed innovation and the assertiveness and daring it required as manly

qualities, inappropriate for a lady. Years after she had successfully patented and sold her pyrotechnic night signals,
Coston reflected in her autobiography on the hypocrisy
and discrimination she encountered from men who
resented her success. "We hear much of the chivalry of
men towards women; but let me tell you dear reader, it
vanishes like dew before the summer sun when one of us
comes into competition with the manly sex."[40] Moreover,
maritime technology was well beyond the boundaries of
women's proper sphere. And Coston quickly learned that
despite the ingeniousness and utility of her night signals,
the navy, with a few exceptions, was a bastion of traditional manliness. "It was a most bitter thing to find in that
lofty institution of our country, the Navy, men so small-
minded that they begrudged a woman her success."[41]

As she embarked on her mission to perfect her
husband's night signals, Coston looked for ways to overcome the prejudice against a woman doing man's work.
She played it safe by downplaying her gender. Aware that
it would be difficult to find pyrotechnic experts willing to
work with a woman, she "opened communication with
several of them, under a man's name, fearing they would
not give heed to a woman."[42] In 1859 she obtained a
patent for the signals under her husband's name, even
though she perfected and implemented the flares. In part,
this was a strategic decision that enabled her to benefit
from his reputation. But in a year when only five women received patents, and these
were for domestic items such as a nursing bottle and a muff, Coston's application for a
nautical device in her husband's name avoided undesirable controversy and demonstrated her willingness to accept prevailing social conventions.[43]

Just as Coston pragmatically concealed her gender, she was a realist who knew that
she could not succeed without help. With an eye to gaining support for her endeavor,
she turned to her social contacts. The influential Washington friends she met when her
husband was alive were a powerful group able to help her in many ways. They
protected her from social ostracism; the secretary of the navy promised to test her signal
flares when she was ready; in 1859 her friend John Quincy Adams signed her patent
application; and in 1867, Samuel F. B. Morse lent his prestige as the inventor of the tele-
graph to her efforts, declaring her "the accomplished inventress."[44]

As promised, the navy tested her night flares and hailed the results. It was an
important achievement, for Coston emerged as a credible inventor in her own right. As
one naval officer remarked: "Madam, your husband's mantle has fallen upon your fair

*Portrait of Martha Coston
from her autobiography,*
Signal Success, *which was
published in 1886*

shoulders."[45] But when the navy wanted to purchase her flares, Coston was caught completely off guard. After a decade of work, Coston had succeeded in perfecting the signals and patenting them, but she had no idea of their worth in the marketplace. She quickly learned that it was one thing to be an inventor and another to be an entrepreneur. "So intently had my mind been concentrated on the one object of perfecting the signals, that I had never given their pecuniary value a thought," she explained in her autobiography.[46]

Suddenly Coston had to become a businesswoman, but she was a quick learner. She settled on a price of six thousand dollars for three hundred sets of flares, contracted with her manufacturer in New York to produce the signals, and formed the Coston Supply Company. With an eye to international expansion, she took out patents for her night signals in a number of European countries, including England, France, and Denmark, and then sailed to Europe to market her signals. In the midst of this flurry of business activity, she began to observe the culture of the commercial arena. Self-interest, she observed, "seems to be the custom in the business world."[47]

Though Coston was a novice in this world of business, her entrepreneurial consciousness blossomed. While marketing her signals in Europe, she saw a lucrative market in the mounting sectional tension at home. "The thought occurred to me that in case of war, what a valuable auxiliary my signals would prove for the Navy!"[48] Eager to seize the opportunity for profit, she sailed "at once for home" to market her patent to Congress. And she was not afraid to defend herself against unscrupulous competitors. When she learned of a plan to infringe on her patent, she confronted her rivals in person. One can only imagine the expressions on their faces when Martha Coston marched into their business meeting with a senator at her side and a copy of her patent in her hand.[49] It was a bold move, one that her competitors must not have expected from a woman, but it worked and Congress purchased her patent for twenty thousand dollars.

While Coston had wanted forty thousand dollars for her patent, she in any case had made a significant sale, and overnight she became a self-made, financially independent woman. But she was more than a wealthy woman. Her Coston Night Signals played a vital role in the naval battles of the Civil War. In an era when thousands of northern women supported the Union cause in gender-appropriate ways, sewing uniforms, wrapping bandages, and nursing the wounded, Coston made her contribution directly to the military campaign. The Coston signal system gave the Union a crucial advantage over the Confederacy. It enabled Union ships to communicate strategic information long distances as they enforced their blockade of the southern coast; gunboats relied on the flares as they maneuvered along the Mississippi River; and, in December 1862, when the *Monitor*, the ironclad ship that had battled with the *Virginia* earlier that year, began to sink in a storm, the signals enabled Union ships to rescue at least ten sailors from the sinking *Monitor*.[50]

After the war, Coston continued to perfect and market her night signals. She expanded her inventive activities, and in 1871 she patented an improved night signal.

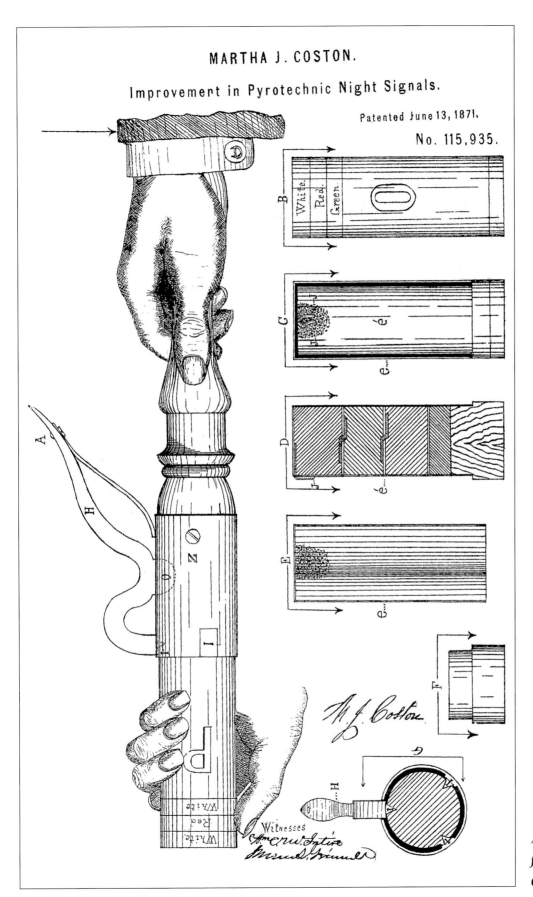

MARTHA J. COSTON.

Improvement in Pyrotechnic Night Signals.

Patented June 13, 1871.

No. 115,935.

A diagram from the patent for an improvement to the Coston flare, 1871

But this time, along with seventy-one other women seeking patents, she claimed the new patent in her own name.[51] This single act reveals the marked change in her identity from a novice in the world of business into a savvy entrepreneur comfortable with her identity as an inventive, daring, and independent businesswoman. Her gradual evolution is a poignant reminder that nineteenth-century women did not become entrepreneurs overnight; for many it was a process of gradual change.

As a successful businesswoman in her own right, Coston looked for opportunities to market her new and improved night signals as the nation sought to heal its wounds. Emphasizing their value to maritime safety in times of peace, she sold the signals to the United States Lifesaving Service, which made them standard equipment at their lifeboat stations.[52] At the same time she looked for new opportunities to publicize the signals. In 1873 she published a technical booklet, *Coston's Telegraphic Night Signals*, to promote her product to maritime experts. And in 1886 she published her autobiography, *Signal Success*, which publicized her signals to a broader audience.

Coston also saw marketing opportunities in the growing women's community of the day. In the decade after the war, women hit their stride, building separate women's institutions–colleges, medical schools, and voluntary organizations–where women could

"The Loss of the U.S.S. Monitor," depicts how a Coston flare was deployed to assist in the rescue of sailors at sea.

known as the domestic arm of the Union army, the Sanitary Commission represented the organized efforts of thousands of women who collected and distributed food, clothing, and medical supplies to the Union soldiers. Bradwell took a leading role in organizing the Sanitary Fair in Chicago in 1865 and became president of the Soldiers' Aid Society, one of the charitable organizations founded in the postwar period.

While Bradwell was one among thousands of women who worked on behalf of the Union cause, when the war ended she became a pioneer, blazing her own path. In 1868 she began publishing the *Chicago Legal News*. She was determined that her newspaper be one that "every lawyer and business man in the Northwest ought to take."[58] In addition, she and her husband started the Chicago Legal News Company, a printing, binding, and publishing business. Thanks to James, who completely supported his wife's new endeavors, Myra won the right from the Illinois legislature to run both businesses free of the legal disabilities of a married woman. But while she was able to get around the restrictions of coverture when it came to carrying on business, she was not so successful when it came to practicing law.

Ever since the early years of her marriage, Bradwell had read law with James, hoping one day to join him in practice to "work side by side and think side by side."[59] In an era when there were only twenty-one law schools in the country, when standards of legal training were informal, when most aspiring lawyers relied on the apprenticeship system for their training, Myra's experience reading law with James met the prevailing criteria for practicing law. In order to practice law with her husband, Bradwell petitioned the Illinois Supreme Court in 1869 to be admitted as an attorney. To Bradwell, her petition already had precedent. Arabella Mansfield had recently been admitted to practice law in Iowa, making her the first woman admitted to practice in the country. But the Illinois Supreme Court rejected her petition, claiming that under the common law of coverture she had no independent legal existence apart from her husband and therefore could not practice law.

Myra Bradwell, 1889

Bradwell did not walk away. She returned to the court with an Additional Brief in which she argued that the married woman's property acts of Illinois permitted women to own property, enter into contracts, and therefore practice law. In addition, she reminded the court that the legislature had already agreed to allow her to publish the *Chicago Legal News* "as if she were AN UNMARRIED WOMAN."[60] Finally, she pointed to the recently passed Fourteenth Amendment, arguing that it protected her right as a citizen to carry on a trade or profession in any state.

The Illinois Supreme Court remained unpersuaded. Ignoring the issue of whether a married woman could legally enter into contracts, the court held that "the sex of the applicant, independent of coverture, is as our law stands now, a sufficient reason for not granting this license." But the court went further. Hoping to settle the question of women in the legal profession once and for all, it articulated a jurisprudence of separate spheres that defined women as naturally unsuited to practice law. Simply put, it argued that "God designed the sexes to occupy different spheres of action, and that it belonged to men to make, apply, and execute the laws."[61]

With the support of leading suffragists of the day, including Susan B. Anthony and Elizabeth Cady Stanton, Bradwell appealed to the United States Supreme Court, arguing that the newly passed Fourteenth Amendment to the United States Constitution guaranteed her the right as a citizen to practice law. But the Supreme Court refused to overturn the state court decision. Far from being the path-breaking decision Bradwell and her supporters had hoped for, *Bradwell v. State of Illinois* reinforced the jurisprudence of separate spheres; it turned the issue of women lawyers over to the state legislatures and state courts. Today, well over a century later, the decision remains an important symbol of the barriers that impeded nineteenth-century women's entrance into the law.

Despite their disappointment with the decision in *Bradwell*, women did not give up their crusade to gain admission to practice law. Throughout the rest of the nineteenth century, they went state by state articulating a competing jurisprudence of integration. In 1873 the Illinois legislature became one of the first to pass a statute to permit women to practice law. By the turn of the century, it was clear that the jurisprudence of separation represented the old order; in contrast, the jurisprudence of integration had become the dominant perspective, as most state courts began to admit women to practice law at their own discretion. After 1920, with the passage of the Nineteenth Amendment giving women the right to vote, the remaining state, Delaware, finally amended its constitution in 1923 to allow women to practice law.

Although Bradwell had been repeatedly denied entry into the legal profession because she was a woman, she understood, more than any man, how to squeeze profit from the very profession that excluded her. Her *Chicago Legal News* was the right enterprise for the time. The legal profession as we know it today was just emerging in the post–Civil War era. While apprenticeship was the dominant mode of training for the law, beginning in the 1870s education in law schools gradually became the more rigorous, formal, and prestigious path into the profession. From 1870 to 1890 the number of law schools rose from 31 to 61—nearly double in twenty years. By 1910, the number had doubled again; there were now 124 law schools. By 1917, law schools had opened across the country and all but seven states had at least one. Several cities had more than one; in the Midwest, Chicago had nine and, farther west, St. Louis had four. The increase in the number of law schools created a rapid growth in the law student population: from 1,653 in 1870 to 4,518 in 1890. Meanwhile, the number of lawyers more than doubled from 40,731 in 1870 to 89,422 in 1890.[62]

These aspiring lawyers were an exploding market for the *News*. Seizing the moment, Bradwell set out to make the *News* indispensable to them. Her first step was to market

Masthead of the Chicago Legal News *for 1887;* Bradwell founded the newspaper in 1868 and published it until her death in 1894.

The Empress of Journalism
Mrs. Frank Leslie

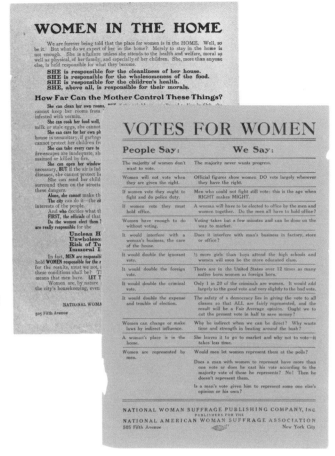

Mrs. Frank Leslie inherited her husband's bankrupt publishing business, turned it into a profitable enterprise, and became one of the major publishing entrepreneurs of her day. Born Miriam Folline in 1836, her private life was as colorful as her public life was successful. She was an actress for a while, had several affairs, was married four times, and had no children. Her first marriage, when she was seventeen, was to a twenty–seven-year-old jeweler with whom she was having an affair; it was annulled after two years. Her last marriage, at age fifty–five, was to the brother of writer Oscar Wilde; it lasted barely one year. Her most enduring marriage–her third–was to Frank Leslie, whom she met while she was married to her second husband, Ephraim George Squier.

During her marriage to Squier, she began her career as a writer and editor for Frank Leslie, who made her editor of several of his magazines. The couple fell in love, then divorced their spouses and married each other in 1874. Miriam Leslie settled into the luxury and social whirl that befit her new position as the wife of a wealthy, successful publisher. She entertained royalty, wore expensive jewels, and took extravagant trips. But her lavish lifestyle collapsed when Frank Leslie died, leaving her a widow with a business that was $50,000 in debt.

Legally changing her name to "Frank Leslie," she immediately took over her husband's business and began returning it to the powerful position it once held in the publishing world. Her success can be attributed to a combination of her business acumen, hard work, and fortunate timing. First, to get her business back on its feet, she borrowed $50,000 to pay the company's creditors. Then, when President Garfield was shot, she seized the opportunity to profit from the event. The detailed stories and vivid illustrations of the assassination and its aftermath that she published attracted nationwide attention; the expanded readership that resulted enabled her to pay all her

debts. Leslie then set out to reorganize and rebuild the business. She hired new writers, upgraded the paper stock, cut the number of periodicals in half, and ultimately re-established her husband's publishing empire. Under her skillful management, it reached a circulation of 250,000, brought her an annual income of $100,000, and earned her a reputation as the "Empress of Journalism."

Mrs. Frank Leslie lived a uniquely independent life for a woman of her day. Without children of her own, she sought to extend that independence to other women: when she died in 1914, she left almost half of her two million–dollar fortune to suffrage leader Carrie Chapman Catt to further "the cause of Woman's Suffrage." The National Woman's Suffrage Company, financed by her bequest, produced what were popularly known as "rainbow" flyers (shown here), which publicized the cause of women's right to vote. ✎

the *News* as the key to staying up-to-date on the latest legal news in Illinois. For Illinois lawyers this was an appealing message. They often had to wait three to five months after the Illinois legislature passed a law for the state to publish it. The only alternative was to travel to the capital to read the originals. Bradwell solved the problem. She secured for the *News* the right to publish all statutes immediately after each legislative session. In addition, she traveled to Springfield herself to examine the precise wording of the statutes before she published them. Lawyers who subscribed to the *News* read the latest laws in a timely fashion, confident that they were correctly printed. No Illinois lawyer could compete in the rapidly expanding legal profession without following Bradwell's legal updates in the *News*.

To prove her point, Bradwell printed a story about a Chicago lawyer who supposedly won the sizable sum of $750 because he followed the *News*. This attorney, Thompson, had apparently asked a judge to order the losing party to pay his legal fees. The judge refused, seeing no precedent for such a ruling. A few days later, as the story went, Thompson returned to the courtroom with the latest issue of the *News*, which recorded a statute passed just three days before establishing that the losing party should be responsible for legal fees. The judge awarded Thompson his $750 and declared, "Mr. Thompson, you are indebted to Mrs. Bradwell for this!"[63] By reporting the incident, Bradwell skillfully created demand for her paper and demonstrated that it was indispensable reading for every Illinois lawyer. Within a few short years, one could find the *News* in every legal office in Illinois.

Bradwell did not stop there. Building on the same model that brought her success in Illinois, she arranged with the United States Supreme Court and the lower federal courts to print federal court decisions around the country in the *News*. Her resourcefulness turned the *News* into a paper with a national reputation. As the most widely read legal paper in the country in an era of rapid growth of the legal profession, the *News* was certainly good business. Meanwhile, Bradwell worked hard to manage every facet of the *News*. To control the weekly publication and yearly binding of the paper, she ventured into the printing and bindery business.

Like the *News*, these ventures quickly took on a national scope as she capitalized once again on the lack of speedy communication of legal decisions, this time in state and federal courts. At the request of lawyers and judges around the country, the Chicago Legal News Company expanded its publishing efforts, and began to print statutes and judicial decisions of other states. In addition, Bradwell printed standardized legal forms that she designed herself, as well as legal stationery, law books, and lawyers' briefs. Bradwell's ingenuity and exhaustive efforts turned the Chicago Legal News Company into an empire in the legal publishing business. Her capabilities were so well known that in 1876 the young New Hampshire Supreme Court asked her to compile and publish all of the cases and opinions from its first six years in existence.

Nothing seemed to get in her way. Though she was a dedicated advocate for women's rights, the rights of workers took a backseat to her own business interests. She was firm and unbending when her typesetters struck and demanded that she pay them for the printing of blank pages. Rather than negotiate with the Typographical Union, she defended herself vociferously in the pages of the *News*. Turning a deaf ear to the demands of her workers, she claimed that she would never pay them "FOR WORK THEY NEVER DID" and hired nonunion workers to print the paper.[64] Within a week, the typesetters came back to work without any pay increase.

Even the infamous Chicago fire of 1871 did not stop her. In fact, while other professional careers were completely destroyed, Bradwell benefited from the tragedy. The fire destroyed the offices of most lawyers in the city. Almost everything in Bradwell's office burned, including her library of two thousand books. Only the subscription book of the *News* survived the fire. Aware that lawyers would be even more dependent on the *News* in this time of crisis, she took a train to Milwaukee, had the *News* printed there, and published it on schedule three days later. In the midst of the chaos and ruin, Bradwell's quick action and determination made the *News* the symbol of reliability and stability. Since most Chicago lawyers had lost everything–records, books, entire offices–they needed the *News* more than ever. Bradwell urged publishers to advertise in the *News*, she encouraged lawyers whose libraries had been totally ruined to continue their subscriptions and to buy back issues as well, and she persuaded the Illinois legislature to make the *News* the official publisher of all court records, including land title notices that had been destroyed in the fire.

This was a significant business accomplishment, for it expanded the readership of the *News* beyond the legal profession to anyone who owned land in Cook County. It was also an impressive moral victory, for the lawyers who had so recently excluded her from the bar, claiming that "it belonged to men to make, apply and execute the laws," were now dependent upon her for their professional lives. While most Chicago lawyers faced financial ruin, Myra Bradwell expanded her publishing empire, bought a large mansion on Lake Michigan, and emerged as one of the most well-known individuals, man or woman, in the legal community throughout the United States.

Bradwell did not hesitate to use her power and prestige. While she was a shrewd businesswoman, she was a passionate reformer as well. In her deft hands, the *Chicago Legal News* was much more than a successful business venture; it was a powerful political tool, which she skillfully used to forward her agenda of professional and social reform. The legal profession was the focus of much of her reformist zeal. Having been unfairly excluded from the legal profession solely because she was a woman, Bradwell used the *News* to argue for admission standards based exclusively on merit. She emphasized the importance of intellect and integrity, condemning such unethical behavior as bribery and drinking. And she particularly chastised divorce lawyers. In an age when women lacked child custody rights and property rights, Bradwell well understood that divorce could destroy the lives of wives more than husbands.

Bradwell also focused on a number of reforms that expanded well beyond the legal profession. Having competed successfully with the male legal establishment, she was not afraid to tackle the business giants of the day, and she urged the passage of laws regulating railroads and other big corporations. She also voiced her support for controversial social issues including temperance and prison reform. In 1875, she came to the aid of her friend and neighbor, Mary Todd Lincoln, whose son, Robert Todd Lincoln, had had her incarcerated on a claim of insanity. Without any defense, the widow of the former president was sentenced indefinitely to Bellevue Place, an asylum "for genteel women" in Batavia, Illinois. Desperate to be freed, Mrs. Lincoln managed to sneak a letter out to Bradwell, who immediately came to her rescue. In the pages of the *News*, she published stories of Robert Lincoln's misconduct and brought the press corps with her for an interview with the clearly sane former first lady. For Robert Lincoln, a respected attorney, the publicity was embarrassing, and in just a few months he begrudgingly relented and allowed his mother to be freed.

More than for any other issue, Bradwell used the *News* to fight for women's rights. A friend of suffragist Elizabeth Cady Stanton, she was an ardent woman suffragist and a leader in the suffrage movement in Illinois, serving on the executive committee of the state Woman Suffrage Association. Her most passionate concern was women's legal status. With the help of her husband, a member of the Illinois legislature, she crusaded against women's legal disabilities. In the pages of the *News*, she called for laws to give married women the right to their earnings and equal guardianship of their children and to give widows an interest in their husbands' estates.

The issue closest to her heart was women's right to earn their livelihoods in the occupations of their choice. Having been denied admission to the office of notary public as well as to the legal profession because she was a woman, Bradwell was determined to reform the laws to give women equal access to occupations of their choice. Merit, she claimed, rested on the abandonment of all sex prejudice. Bradwell and her husband were an influential team. Women won equal guardianship of children in 1873; they became eligible for the office of notary public in 1875; and they gained admission to the Illinois bar in 1872. Though this was the most personal of victories for Bradwell, she refused to reapply for admission; however, she became an honorary member of the Illinois State Bar Association in 1872 and served as vice president for four years. Meanwhile, Bradwell had cleared the path for other Illinois women to enter the practice of law, one of whom was her daughter, Bessie, who graduated at the top of her class at Union College of Law (Northwestern) in 1882.

Finally, in 1890, the Illinois Supreme Court, acting on Bradwell's original application, admitted her to the Illinois bar; and in 1892, she was admitted to practice before the United States Supreme Court. By this time Bradwell was close to the end of her life; two years later she died of cancer at the age of sixty-two. When she died she was possibly the most well-known woman lawyer in the country.

Bradwell played a major role in opening the legal profession to women. By the time of her death, the United States already had more than two hundred women lawyers, and by 1900 it had over one thousand women lawyers. Locally, she helped make Illinois, and

Chicago specifically, a mecca for women lawyers. By 1920 there were more women lawyers in Illinois than in any other state in the country, and more in Chicago than in any other city.[65] Meanwhile, Bradwell's daughter Bessie took over the *News* and the Chicago Legal News Publishing Company, and continued the tradition of providing legal information and social commentary to the legal community.

But while Bradwell is most remembered as a pioneer woman lawyer, she was an astute, resourceful, and successful businesswoman as well. She built a remarkably influential publishing business geared to a specific market, the legal profession. In an age of big business and the rise of corporations, the *Chicago Legal News* played a major role in the evolution of law from a personal and informal occupation of solo practitioners to a formal, hierarchical profession. The *News* was a successful business enterprise in this era of exploding business ventures. But it was far more than a profit-making venture to Bradwell; it was a personal passion as well. It embodied her crusading spirit and social goals. In the *Chicago Legal News*, Bradwell made business, law, and the advancement of women inseparable. She stands as an ideal example of the enterprising woman who skillfully blended profit and principles.

"My father," recalled Hetty Green (1834–1916) after she had become a financial power, "taught me never to owe anyone anything, not even kindness."[66] Edward Robinson taught his daughter well. Following his advice, Henrietta Howland Robinson Green, nicknamed "Hetty," rose to prominence as the richest woman in the world in the late nineteenth and early twentieth centuries. While her hundred-million-dollar fortune made her the thirty-fourth wealthiest individual ever, her frugal lifestyle and beliefs earned her a more enduring reputation as the "world's greatest miser."[67] Behind her money and reputation, however, is the story of a woman who had to battle the conventions of male-dominated society to amass her enormous fortune. The story of Hetty Green reveals the way in which the aggressive, hard-nosed, frugal qualities demanded of a successful financier clashed with prevailing ideas about female sentiment and women's inability to manage money to create a character that was more myth than reality.

Henrietta Howland Robinson was born and raised in New Bedford, Massachusetts, in the heart of the nineteenth-century whaling industry.[68] Her mother, Abby Slocum Howland, was one of two heiresses (along with her sister, Sylvia Ann) to the Howland fortune. The Howlands, who could trace their lineage back to the *Mayflower*, built their fortune in the whaling industry through the efforts of Isaac Howland, Jr., and his son-in-law, Gideon Howland. In an age when Quaker families who reigned over New Bedford's whaling industry practiced parsimonious habits and intermarried to avoid sharing wealth, Hetty grew up in a family where control, force of will, and money were intertwined.

Hetty was in a unique position in the Howland family. When her younger brother died in infancy, she became the sole heir to the Howland family fortune. Gideon, Hetty's grandfather, had two daughters, Sylvia Ann and Abby. Both women were invalids, though Abby was more physically capable than her sister. Edward Mott Robinson of Rhode Island chose Abby to be his wife. He saw his first bit of the Howland fortune when, shortly after their marriage, his new father-in-law, Isaac Howland, Jr., passed away and Edward joined the Isaac Howland firm. With Howland's death, Edward Robinson inherited a substantial sum that represented a fine beginning to the fortune he was to amass in his own name.

Due to her mother's poor health, Hetty spent her early years living with her grandfather and aunt, Sylvia Ann. They sent her first to a Quaker school in Sandwich, Massachusetts, and then when she was fifteen, to a ladies' finishing school in Boston run by Reverend Charles Russell Lowell and his wife, Anna Cabot Lowell. While Hetty received the proper education for a young girl of her social class, it was the business education she received at home that captivated her. With both her grandfather and father suffering from failing eyesight, Hetty "read aloud to them the financial news of the world. In this way I came to know what stocks and bonds were," she recalled, "how the markets fluctuated, and the meaning of bulls and bears."[69]

Like the families of Rebecca Lukens and Lydia Pinkham, Hetty's Quaker family imbued her with business principles and a belief in women's abilities. She, too, accompanied her father on his business expeditions. She spent many days along the New Bedford harbor, where she grew accustomed to the rough language and manners of the sailors and watched her father handle business transactions and manage his employees. By the time Hetty left home for school in Boston, she was already different from her female classmates. She knew "more about these things than many a man that makes a living out of them."[70] And her father, known for his tight-fisted business practices, had become the role model for the future female financier.

Thanks to Hetty's father's financial cunning, the Howlands avoided the decline in the whaling industry in 1861. Isaac Howland's company was dismantled in 1862, just in time to preserve its substantial assets. While the Civil War and new possibilities from kerosene cut whaling revenues almost in half between 1860 and 1865, the Howland family fortune was spared.[71] When Hetty's father died in 1865, he left Hetty, his only heir, $1,000,000 outright and an additional $4,000,000 in a trust fund.[72] The death of her aunt, Sylvia Ann, just a few months after her father, made Hetty an even wealthier woman. Her inheritance of $1,132,929–half of her aunt's estate–promised Hetty an additional annual income of $65,000. By all standards, she was now a very rich woman, whose inheritance promised her a lifetime of comfort and independence. But Hetty wanted more than a life of wealth and leisure. She had learned too well the financial lessons of her father and grandfather. It was capital–as much as she could get her hands on–that she wanted.

Robinson's quest for capital led her to contest her Aunt Sylvia's will. In a widely reported and acrimonious lawsuit, she contended that she had prepared and her aunt had signed a second will, leaving all of Sylvia's money to Hetty. Although experts such as Louis Agassiz and Benjamin Peirce of Harvard University testified to the veracity of the competing wills, Hetty lost her case. Instead, she earned a reputation as a relentless businesswoman.

Ironically, just as her public life was being tarnished by images of greed, Hetty's private life was following a more traditional path. In 1865, shortly before her father's death, he introduced her to Edward Henry Green, a man in his mid-forties, and himself a millionaire. Green, a native of Bellows Falls, Vermont, had spent years in the Philippines amassing his fortune, mostly through trade. He and Hetty quickly became friends. They married in 1867 and moved to London, where Green directed a number of banks. Over the next few years Hetty gave birth to two children, Edward Henry in 1868 and Sylvia Ann in 1871, and settled down to the responsibilities of motherhood, while continuing to pay attention to her fortune. With her husband's advice, she made a lucrative decision to invest heavily in the U.S. dollar while she was abroad.[73] Despite Hetty's wealth, Edward assumed a husband's traditional financial role, covering all of the family's living expenses, while Hetty did not spend a cent of her rapidly accumulating fortune. With a family and a fortune of her own, this was a happy time in Hetty's life.

Hetty and her family returned to New York City in 1874, where she devoted her attention to building her fortune. While she made millions, she eventually discovered that Edward was secretly borrowing against her holdings and making bad investments, all against her orders. To Hetty this was an intolerable breach of trust and the marriage ended after Edward went bankrupt in 1885. Still, they remained friends and reconciled in 1898, though they never lived together again.

Wealthy investor Hetty Green could often be seen walking to her Wall Street office.

Meanwhile, Hetty put into practice the lessons of her girlhood and rapidly emerged as a powerful financier. She was well prepared to compete in the financial capital of the world. Reared in a mercantile, Quaker family by tight-fisted men and frail women, she strongly identified with her grandfather and father who had run their whaling ventures. She was an anomaly in late-nineteenth-century America: a wealthy woman with the skills and experience to invest wisely. She was an independent financier, but unlike famous financiers like J. P. Morgan, she had no corporation, sold no products, and relied on private banks to hold her investments. She stayed away from the traditional stocks in industrial enterprises and invested instead in government bonds, railroads, and real estate.[74] Her strategy was to buy low and to sell high, and she always held sums of cash for buying and lending when the markets fell. She was remarkably successful. As an

Dancing Mistress at the Million Dollar Tango Ball
Hetty Green

By the end of Hetty Green's life, her reputation for having great wealth had seeped into the American consciousness. In an age when tremendous fortunes were made, she inspired the words to two songs, each of which revealed both the nation's love of money and just how deeply Green's reputation as "the Richest Woman in the World" had established itself in popular culture.

"At the Million Dollar Tango Ball" (1914) placed Hetty Green in company with the new captains of industry, the lone woman among the wealthiest men in America. The lyrics place us at the ball:

> Given by the millionaires at Wall Street Hall,
> John D. Rockefeller sold the tickets by the score,
> Andrew Carnegie was taking tickets at the door.
> Hetty Green was Dancing Mistress of the floor,
> Vanderbilt was playing every rag encore.[1]

Another song, "If I Were Just as Rich as Hetty Green" (1905), reflected on what one would do if in possession of all of Hetty Green's money. The humorous words reveal contemporary thought about a number of social concerns: the wealthy should balance their personal luxuries with philanthropic deeds; prohibition should be eliminated; and all eligible young bachelors should marry. The dreamer muses that she or he would . . .

> . . . own a house in town and in the country.
> I'd build another just between the two . . .
> Each day I'd give the poor a thousand dollars,
> A diamond ring to every little queen—

> O you bet your life that I would go the limit,
> If I were just as rich as Hetty Green.
> I'd build the U.S.A. a mighty Navy,
> So she could be the ruler of the sea.
> I'd fill the land with many books and papers,
> Like philanthropic Andrew Carnegie. . . .
> For every man of twenty-eight unmarried,
> Ten thousand dollars he would have to pay . . .
> Ah, believe me there would be no single ladies,
> If I were just as rich as Hetty Green. . . .
> I'd first take off the law of prohibition,
> And let them have high license in this town. . . .
> Just one saloon in town and let me own it,
> Then I'd be as rich as Hetty Green.[2]

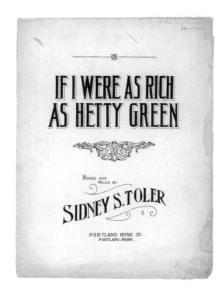

[1] Words and music by James White
[2] Words and music by Sidney S. Toler

entrepreneurial woman, her fortune grew from twenty-six million dollars to over one hundred million dollars between 1885 and her death in 1916.

Perhaps precisely because of her enormous success in the world of finance, an arena dominated by powerful men, Green attracted attention. Her behavior was often eccentric and misunderstood. She wore plain, old clothes, probably a product of her Quaker upbringing and the frugality she learned as a child, and she quarreled with shopkeepers over even the smallest of purchases. When her son injured his knee, her decision to seek the services of a charity clinic was viewed as heartless and miserly, even though there was little then that even the best physicians could offer; indeed, it was not until years later that doctors finally advised medical attention.

While her critics decried her as stingy and strange, the reality was that Green earned her reputation as much because she breached the boundaries of proper womanhood. Not only did she make enormous sums of money, she behaved like a man in doing so. "She was absolutely fearless and . . . relentless toward those who tried to take advantage of her," explained a close friend who adored her.[75] In an age when women of means took pains to dress fashionably and behave modestly and graciously in public, Green's behavior was deemed totally unacceptable for a woman of her class. No one, not even her family and closest friends, denied that her behavior was often unconventional.

But those who knew Green best adamantly refuted her mean and miserly reputation. "Much has been printed about my mother that is untrue," explained Edward, the very son she was accused of neglecting when he injured his knee. "No one was ever more misjudged," echoed a family friend, who described her as a "gentlewoman" with a sweet smile and a twinkle in her eye.[76] Beyond those closest to her, many women admired Green for her accomplishments and viewed her as a role model. The popular *Woman's Home Companion* sought Green's expert advice. In an interview for the magazine Green extolled the value of a business education for all women and girls. Drawing on her childhood experiences, she explained to the magazine's readers that "American women would be much happier" if they learned the principles of business in girlhood.[77] While some knew Green as "the Witch of Wall Street," the readers of the *Woman's Home Companion* were proud to call her "the Richest Business Woman in the World." Meanwhile her friends never forgot that the "World's Richest Woman" was "kind" as well.[78]

By the time of Hetty Green's death, a younger generation of women entrepreneurs was embarking on business ventures for the twentieth century. Yet, as this new generation of women launched their new ventures, many capitalized on the gendered conventions of the nineteenth century. Continuing to build businesses that catered specifically to women, they expanded beyond the separate corner of the business world created by nineteenth-century women entrepreneurs to claim a broad territory of women's enterprise in the twentieth century, run by women for women.

1893 Panic of 1893
• World's Columbian
Exposition, Chicago
• Sears, Roebuck and Co.
established

1896 Plessy v. Ferguson
legalizes "separate but equal"
doctrine
• National Association of
Colored Women founded

1901 U.S. Steel
Corporation founded
• President McKinley
assassinated; Theodore
Roosevelt assumes presidency

1904 Helen Keller
graduates from Radcliffe
College

CHAPTER THREE

"A field that is their own province"

HELENA RUBINSTEIN

1890–1960

FASHIONING THE BUSINESS OF BEAUTY

In 1915, the noted author Edna Ferber introduced the American public to Emma

McChesney, successful businesswoman. In the early 1910s, readers followed the life of

Emma McChesney, first in stories in *Cosmopolitan* and *American Magazine* and then in a three-volume

trilogy.[1] Emma was a compelling character for her time. Her ambition, willingness to take risks, and

ability to understand just what the female consumer wanted catapulted her to the top of the

Featherloom Petticoat Company. She helped transform the ladies' undergarment company into an

influential enterprise with a national reputation and along the way she became a co-owner of the firm.

But life had not always been so easy for Emma. Married at eighteen, a mother shortly thereafter,

she divorced her husband when she was twenty-six and set out on her own to support herself and her

---

1908 Muller v. Oregon limits women's hours in the workplace

1914 World War I begins in Europe
• First national celebration of Mother's Day
• Panama Canal opens
• Federal Trade Commission established to prevent unfair business competition

1920 Nineteenth Amendment gives women the vote
• League of Women Voters established
• First commercial radio station, WWJ, Detroit

1929 Stock market crash; Great Depression follows

son. She went to Featherloom, where she worked her way up from stenographer to traveling salesperson to secretary of the firm and, ultimately, to her position of ownership. Along the way she encountered sex discrimination. Some people treated her with suspicion as she traveled unescorted on trains and slept alone in hotels, and she constantly confronted the cultural view that a woman simply could not comprehend business. As one influential businessman explained when he opened important negotiations with her: "A lady as charming as you can understand nothing of business."[2] Emma also struggled to be both breadwinner and caregiver to her son; she agonized over the loss of independence she would face if she chose to remarry. She worked hard and at one time even traveled alone to South America, an unusual and daring business trip for a woman in the 1910s. There she completed a lucrative transaction, which turned Featherloom into an international firm; and she returned to marry the boss and run the company.

The popularity of the fictional Emma McChesney revealed a stunning reality for a new century: the notion of the successful businesswoman had seeped into the popular culture and captured the public imagination. Emma epitomized the optimism that emboldened women as they entered the twentieth century. She mirrored women's aspirations for public lives and their belief that a companionate marriage of equals would enable them to balance career and family. Meanwhile the growing numbers of businesswomen around the country and the founding of the National Federation of Business and Professional Women's Clubs in 1919 revealed that Ferber's Emma McChesney reflected fact as well as fiction.[3]

For the most part, women entrepreneurs continued to find their best business opportunities in areas that catered specifically to women. Many clustered in the traditional areas of dressmaking and millinery, while others marketed hair products and cosmetics. This was a familiar pattern. Owned and run by women for women, the fashion and beauty industries brought the female market into the twentieth century. But the enormous demand by women for cosmetics and clothing was unprecedented and created an explosion of the fashion and beauty business in the early twentieth century, and women entrepreneurs transformed the beauty business into big business.[4]

Despite the major crises of the century–World War I, the Great Depression, World War II, and the Cold War–women entrepreneurs in fashion and beauty continued to turn fledgling companies into thriving corporations. As the beauty business became a national industry, many women entrepreneurs could not keep up. Others–including Elizabeth Arden, Helena Rubinstein, and Estee Lauder–achieved fortunes to rival those of many successful businessmen and proved their ability to compete as equals in the competitive world of capitalism. As they created businesses that catered to women, they proved their equality with men, achieved power and fortune, and expanded the boundaries of their gender roles without rebelling against them. At the same time, the growth of the fashion and beauty industries left an indelible mark on American culture and capitalism. These industries, founded by women entrepreneurs for women consumers,

(page 74)

Madam C. J. Walker at the wheel of her Model A Ford, in 1912; she is shown in front of her Indianapolis home, with her niece and two co-workers.

took their place in the mainstream of American business and became a cornerstone of the American economy.

⟨⟨ The dawn of the new century, with its burgeoning consumer culture, was an ideal time for an enterprising woman to launch a woman's business. The emergence of department stores, the institutions of mass distribution for the modern age, accelerated the growth of a mass consumer market. New York City, the nation's largest and most concentrated urban market, was the heart of the consumer revolution that swept the country. Most of the earliest department stores, including Lord & Taylor, B. Altman, Macy's, and Bloomingdale's, opened there. The department store phenomenon spread rapidly—stores opened around the country: Jordan Marsh and Filene's in Boston, Wanamaker's in Philadelphia, Marshall Field's in Chicago, and Bullock's in Los Angeles. Chain stores such as F. W. Woolworth served the consumer in smaller cities and towns, while mail-order houses such as Sears, Roebuck reached the rural market.

A few women stood out among this group of department store entrepreneurs: including Mary Ann Cohen Magnin of San Francisco, Carrie Marcus Neiman of Dallas, and Beatrice Fox Auerbach of Hartford. Scattered around the country, all three were daughters of Jewish immigrants; they not only felt comfortable in the world of commerce but understood the importance of consumption in women's lives.[5]

Mary Ann Magnin was the genius behind I. Magnin and Company of San Francisco. Her reputation as a skillful needleworker made I. Magnin the place to go for lingerie, baby clothes, and bridal trousseaux when it was founded in 1877. Had the store been named a century later, it might have carried her name, but conventional gender restrictions that demanded a private role for women in the late 1800s caused it to be named after Mary Ann's husband, Isaac, even though he took little interest in the business. Nevertheless, Mary Ann Magnin was the power behind the name. She managed all aspects of I. Magnin including buying and inspecting merchandise; further, she prepared her children to enter the business.[6]

Carrie Marcus Neiman, ca. 1890

In 1907, in the midst of a financial panic, Carrie Marcus Neiman, along with her husband and her brother, opened the Neiman Marcus department store in Dallas, Texas.[7] At every turn, Neiman Marcus was a family venture: Carrie Marcus Neiman and her brother did the buying while her husband managed advertising and sales. Combining her careful attention to detail with her eye for fashion, she skillfully appealed to the regional loyalty and tastes of Texas women. Targeting wealthy women who traditionally had their clothing custom-made by personal dressmakers, she offered an alternative—high-styled, ready-to-wear clothing that could be customized by the store's hired dressmaker. In an era when New York City was the fashion center of the country, her goal was "to dress a whole city."[8] When oil made Dallas a wealthy city, the Neiman

Marcus department store was perfectly situated to serve the fashion needs of its newly rich women, and it emerged as the fashion center of the South.

Across the country, the new department stores offered women one-stop shopping for industrial goods. Such savvy businesswomen as fashion designer Hattie Carnegie and cosmetics entrepreneur Elizabeth Arden eagerly turned to the high-end department stores like Neiman Marcus to market their ready-made clothing and beauty products to large numbers of women with money to spend. Meanwhile a flourishing advertising industry sent an urgent message, announced in newspapers and magazines, on billboards, buses, and the radio, that women simply had to have the new products. The consumer craze took hold with the many young women who flooded the cities in search of careers, independence, and excitement. Yet, even as these young women claimed equality with men, they eagerly indulged their cravings for beauty and glamour. Following the exhortations of advertisers that consuming was the foundation of progress, they willingly played their part in the growth of the national economy, buying personal luxuries like lipstick and lingerie along with ice boxes and sewing machines for the home.[9]

The first advertisement for the new Neiman Marcus department store, in Dallas, Texas, 1907

In 1912, *Vogue* magazine suggested that women who wanted to look younger and healthier should use a discreet application of lipstick and rouge. *Vogue*'s endorsement of cosmetics signaled a tidal wave of change. Nineteenth-century women had viewed cosmetics with great skepticism. Respectable women valued natural, not artificial, beauty. They used nothing more than glycerin and rosewater for their personal beauty regimen. Lipsticks and rouges were the questionable paraphernalia of prostitutes and showgirls. But in the second decade of the twentieth century a younger generation of women rejected the prohibitions against artificial beauty, adopted a more youthful and freer appearance, and literally changed the face of American women. They bobbed their hair, replacing the constant care of their long curls with the freedom of a short cut; they shed their multi-layered, floor-length outfits and wore short, loose-fitting dresses; they smoked in public to emulate men; and they began to wear makeup.

In 1920, the year that women won the vote, they spent $129 million on beauty products.[10] And even with their new status as equal citizens with men, they continued to purchase beauty. As a reporter for the *Saturday Evening Post* astutely observed in 1926, the beauty business was like a "husky infant" in the midst of a growth spurt.[11] In 1929 *Ladies' Home Journal* as well as several other popular women's magazines devoted about 20 percent of their advertising space to cosmetics alone.[12] By 1930 retail sales of cosmetics had mushroomed to $336 million, irrefutable proof that the beauty business was well on its way to becoming big business.[13]

While the beauty business was the ideal new industry in the era of the New Woman, it was also firmly rooted in the historic tradition of a separate female sphere. Helena Rubinstein urged women to enter the cosmetics business precisely because it was a woman's enterprise that provided unique opportunities for women. Echoing nineteenth-century ideals about womanhood, she explained: "Here [women] have found a field that is their own province–working for women with women, and giving that which only women can give–an intimate understanding of feminine needs and feminine desires."[14] Within this separate sphere of women's business, the beauty industry crossed lines of class, ethnicity, and race.[15] Women like Elizabeth Arden, Helena Rubinstein, and Martha Matilda Harper built companies that catered to wealthy and middle-class white women, but among them, both Arden and Harper were poor Canadian immigrants, while Rubinstein was a Jewish immigrant from Russia.

Meanwhile, African American entrepreneurs built thriving beauty businesses that sold hair and skin products to women of their race. Among the first generation of African Americans born into freedom after the Civil War, Annie Turnbo Malone and Sarah Breedlove Walker were pioneers in the black beauty business. Each was an extremely successful entrepreneur; indeed, they were identified in the black press in 1919 as the founders of "the two most lucrative business enterprises conducted by colored people in America."[16] Focusing on women of their race, Walker and Malone carved out a special market within the arena of women's business. Through their hair products designed specifically for black women, they reshaped the beauty business to address the unique needs of beauty, respect, and uplift for African American women. They restricted their advertising to the black community, relying on black newspapers and magazines to spread the word. Finally, they hired hundreds of black women to sell these products door-to-door. This was an era in which the motto of the National Association of Colored Women–"Lifting as We Climb"–made manifest the connection between economic and social reform. African American women created institutions to improve the education, health, and economic conditions of their race. Walker's and Malone's beauty businesses embodied the goal of uplift by offering black women beauty as well as the opportunity to realize economic independence.

Women like Walker and Arden were among the most successful female entrepreneurs of the day. By the mid-1910s, Walker's beauty business had annual gross sales of $275,000; by the 1920s, Arden had a multimillion-dollar business.[17] Moreover, both had risen from poverty. Not only were they testimony to the vitality of the beauty industry, they stood as proof that the era of the "self-made man" included women, white and black.

⤬ Throughout her childhood, into young adulthood, Sarah Breedlove Walker (1867–1919) plunged her hands into hot soapy water, washing clothes simply to survive. At the age of fifty-two she strolled into the Fifth Avenue showroom of Tiffany's to adorn her once-blistered hand with a 3.38-carat solitaire diamond ring. She had come a long way.[18]

Though she would become the wealthiest African American—man or woman—of her time, Sarah Breedlove Walker never forgot her humble beginnings. While the early years of Reconstruction held out hope for a better future for African Americans, the economic and social realities of life in the rural South offered little hope of escape from her impoverished roots. She spent her earliest years in overwhelming poverty, living with her parents and older brother and sister in a dirt-floor shack along the Mississippi River Delta in Louisiana. Her parents, recently freed slaves, struggled to survive as share-croppers. Young Sarah Breedlove worked from sunup to sundown in the fields, helping her parents pick cotton. When a yellow fever epidemic claimed both their lives, seven-year-old Breedlove began a quest for safety and security.

At first, Breedlove lived with her older sister and husband, working as a washer-woman to contribute to the family economy. But the cruelty of her sister's husband was intolerable, and at the age of fourteen she left, married Moses McWilliams, and estab-lished a home of her own. When she was seventeen, she gave birth to her only child, a daughter she named Lelia. Like so many other African Americans of her day, however, she suffered from the unchecked violence against blacks in the post-Reconstruction South. Her newfound stability was suddenly cut short when her husband was killed a few years later by a lynch mob.

Barely twenty years old, Sarah Breedlove was a widow with a young child to sup-port. Impoverished and uneducated, she moved to St. Louis, where her brother lived, hoping to find better economic opportunities. For almost two decades she worked as a laundress, earning enough money to send Lelia to the all-black Knoxville College in Knoxville, Tennessee. But she never stopped looking for a way out for herself. "I couldn't see how I, a poor washerwoman, was going to better my condition," she remembered.[19]

She had few options. Her lack of education precluded her from becoming a teacher or a nurse like the female graduates of black colleges. And she lacked the financial resources, skills, and social connections to become a seamstress, milliner, or caterer. A second marriage, this time to an unfaithful, unemployed alcoholic named John Davis, was a failure. To add to her worries, she began to suffer from serious hair loss, a common phenomenon among black women of her day. It was a symptom of a combination of poor health and hygiene, low-protein diets, damaging hair treatments, and stress. In seeking to forestall or to prevent the further loss of hair, she found a way out of her poverty.

She turned first to Annie Minerva Turnbo Malone, already a successful black hair-care entrepreneur in St. Louis.[20] The two women had much in common. Malone also grew up poor and parentless during Reconstruction. In the 1890s she began to experi-ment with ways to manage black hair and by 1900 she had developed a series of prod-ucts including oils and shampoos as well as a pressing comb and iron. Her most popular product was her Wonderful Hair Grower. In 1902 she moved to St. Louis to market her hair-care system. With demand for her Wonderful Hair Grower too high to meet on her own, Malone looked for agents to sell her product door-to-door. Hundreds of African American women, searching for a way to earn more money than the few dollars a week they made as domestic servants, responded eagerly to the call. One such recruit was Sarah Breedlove.

As she went door-to-door promoting Malone's hair-care products, Breedlove quickly saw the advantages of striking out on her own. Motivated by her drive for independence and greater financial opportunity, she began to experiment with her own hair treatments and finally claimed that she had developed a unique formula inspired by God. His inspiration, she claimed, came in the form of an unusual dream. "In that dream a big black man appeared to me and told me what to mix for my hair. Some of the remedy was from Africa, but I sent for it, mixed it, put it on my scalp and in a few weeks my hair was coming in faster than it had ever fallen out."[21] The dream was a brilliant marketing device, linking the power of God's influence with the allure of distant Africa. With it Breedlove justified selling a product that was probably a variation on Malone's Wonderful Hair Grower rather than anything truly original.

When her brother died in 1905, Sarah moved with Lelia to Denver, Colorado, to live with her sister-in-law and four nieces. With meager capital—one dollar and twenty-five cents—and a labor force consisting of Lelia and her extended family, she began to lay the groundwork for her own hair-care business. But she was still an agent for Malone. She invested the first twenty-five cents of her capital in business cards that announced to the African American women of Denver that she was bringing Malone's products to their city. Gradually, however, she built her own hair-care business. First she turned to the African American press, a vehicle she would rely on for the rest of her life. For five cents a line, she advertised her introductory offer in *The Statesman:* special rates at her "hairdressing parlor" where she would "demonstrate her ability to grow hair."[22] Her enthusiasm and commitment to her work were infectious. Customers gravitated to her and she gradually made the transition from washerwoman to hair-care entrepreneur.

Just as she seemed on her way to financial independence, she married her third husband, Charles Joseph Walker, whom she had known in St. Louis. The relationship revealed how a marriage could both help and hinder a woman in business. On the one hand, Sarah Breedlove Walker benefited from her husband's experience as a newspaperman. His ideas for promotion and his familiarity with advertising and mail-order procedures were important contributions to Walker's burgeoning venture. But his "narrowness of vision," as she described his modest goals, threatened to stifle her far greater ambitions for financial success. He was satisfied making ten dollars a day; she was not.[23] Finally, in 1912, Sarah Breedlove Walker left the marriage and struck out on her own.

Nevertheless, during the early years of the marriage she made great strides in Denver. She changed her name to Madam C. J. Walker; the initials and the title of Madam conveyed dignity and respect in an era when whites asserted their superiority by referring to blacks by their first name. She severed her ties with Malone and began to sell her own hair-care formula, Madam Walker's Wonderful Hair Grower. With her husband, she embarked on a marketing plan that included aggressive advertising in the local African American press; pictures of herself on her products, making her a familiar face in African American homes; and a mail-order business that brought her products into those homes, first in the southern and eastern states and then throughout the country. At the same time, she traveled around Colorado selling her products door-to-door and teaching her "Walker system"–shampoo, pomade "hair grower," vigorous brushing, and heated iron combs–to aspiring "Walker agents." In 1907, after an extended road trip that took her throughout the South, Walker earned over thirty-five hundred dollars.[24] In an era when most women of her race earned eight to twenty dollars a month as domestic servants, she had achieved an unimaginable degree of financial success.

But Walker was unwilling to stop there. With an eye to expanding her growing mail-order business, she moved to Pittsburgh, the home of the steel industry, where railroads and shipping lines promised easy access to national transportation. Newly arrived, she turned to the institutions that formed the city's vital African American community. Church and civic leaders endorsed her as "a hairgrower . . . with no equal . . . and a thorough-going business women."[25] She spoke in homes, women's clubs, and churches, promoting her vision of beauty and self-improvement. She founded a beauty school, naming it Lelia College after her daughter, to train women in the Walker method. Once again, she touched a nerve among African American women. Those seeking to improve their hair care bought her products, while those seeking economic opportunity eagerly entered Lelia College to become Walker agents. Meanwhile, Walker's income climbed to almost eight thousand dollars in 1909.[26]

With her Pittsburgh business well established and in Lelia's hands, Walker set her sights on further expansion. She moved this time to Indianapolis, where a central location and a vast railroad network guaranteed easy transportation for her mail-order business. Moreover, the city lacked hair parlors for its growing black middle class. She built a plant to manufacture her products and made Indianapolis the headquarters for the Madam C. J. Walker Manufacturing Company. As her business grew rapidly in the next few years, Walker continued to travel around the country and into the Caribbean and South America, selling her products and training others to become her agents. By 1913, she was making more than three thousand dollars a month, an astounding amount that far exceeded the average American worker's annual income of eight hundred dollars. "I think you are the money making wonder of the age," exclaimed her close friend and lawyer, F. B. Ransom.[27]

Walker's lifestyle began to reflect her financial success. She moved to New York City, joining the thousands of new arrivals relocating from the South to the heretofore predominantly white community of Harlem. She purchased and remodeled a luxurious townhouse at the center of Harlem. While the move made her an instant leader in Harlem's thriving social and intellectual community, it still kept her reputation within the boundaries of the African American community. But that changed quickly when

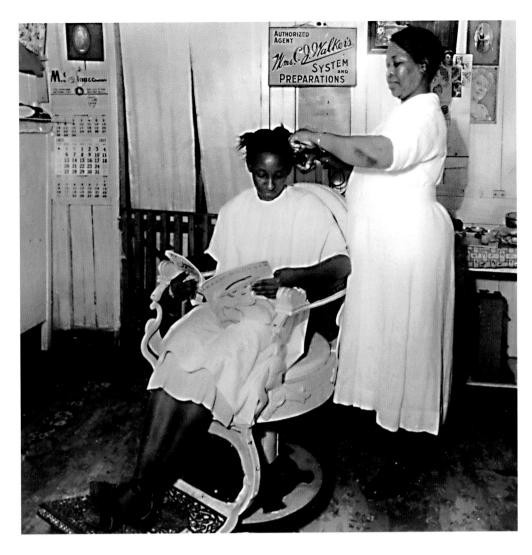

A Walker agent at work

Walker built a thirty-four-room mansion in the exclusive Westchester County community of Irvington–on–Hudson, where powerful families such as the Rockefellers, Astors, and Vanderbilts had estates. Walker's astounding fortune and plans to move upstate instantly captured the attention of her wealthy neighbors. "Hair Grower on Negro's Heads and Oil Magnate Will Be Neighbors if Plan Goes Through as Arranged," announced the local newspaper.[28] It seemed an impossibility. The common opinion, according to a *New York Times* reporter, was quite simple: "No such woman of her race could afford such a place."[29]

Walker was indifferent to the skepticism of her wealthy white neighbors. She understood the power of her impressive wealth, new as it was in contrast to her established Hudson River neighbors. Exhausted and suffering from hypertension and kidney disease, she wanted a place where she could rest and enjoy the fruits of her lifetime of hard work. With a chauffeur, gardener, and two housekeepers, she settled into her luxuriously decorated mansion. With annual earnings reaching well over a quarter of a million dollars she bought expensive jewelry, automobiles, and other trappings of wealth that epitomized entrepreneurial success.

But to Walker, her new home on the Hudson was testament to more than her personal success. It was a public symbol of black pride and possibilities. She built it, she explained, "to point to young Negroes what a lone woman accomplished and to inspire them to do big things."[30] Her friends in the black press echoed her message. Her striking success, claimed one reporter, was proof that "all of the brains, executive ability and business acumen are [not] lodged in white craniums."[31]

Walker was committed to the welfare of her race long before she had become a symbol of black business success. From the very beginning, her drive for self-improvement was linked to her commitment to race improvement. And at the heart of her crusade for race betterment was her concern for black women, her struggle "to build up Negro womanhood."[32] Her commitment to African American womanhood took many forms. In the early days, she marketed her hair products as a key to uplift for black women. Every purchase of her Wonderful Hair Grower not only put pennies in her own pocket; it opened the doors to opportunity for its purchasers. To be sure, she faced opposition from some members of the black community who believed that she was discouraging race pride by encouraging black women to strive for the shiny, straight hair of white women. But Walker saw it differently: healthy hair and a neat appearance were the keys to self-confidence, greater respect, and ultimately more opportunity.

Walker's concern for the women of her race was most fully embodied in her creation of Walker agents, a business practice that expanded black women's opportunities for self-improvement while advancing Walker's own entrepreneurial efforts. On the one hand, the Walker agents were a central part of Walker's ingenious business plan. Along with her advertising and mail-order business, the Walker agents helped transform her business from a local venture into a vast nationwide enterprise. It was a simple system that foreshadowed the emergence of the modern direct-sales method more familiarly known as pyramid organization or multilevel marketing. The system was quite simple: agents recruited and trained other women, thereby multiplying the sales force while they spread the product to more and more consumers.[33]

At the same time, Walker's agents formed the centerpiece of her efforts to improve economic opportunities for the women of her race. From her own experience she understood all too well that the instruction she offered in the Walker method gave many poor black women the crucial education and job training they needed to lift themselves out of their endless cycle of poverty. A properly trained Walker agent earned the right to demonstrate and sell Walker products in return for a commission. Motivated by the opportunity to make more money, hundreds of black women, from laundresses and cooks to teachers and nurses, eagerly earned diplomas at Lelia College in Pittsburgh or apprenticed under existing agents. Dressed in long black skirts and white blouses, Walker agents were models of respectability and industriousness as they combed their neighborhoods selling Walker products. By the 1910s, thousands of Walker agents were

Madam C. J. Walker's first home in Delta, Louisiana (above); Walker agents at Villa Lewaro, Walker's mansion in Irvington-on-Hudson, New York (left)

making up to forty dollars a week each, a considerable sum compared to the dollar a day a black women earned washing laundry in the South.[34] Ultimately Walker challenged her agents to adopt her belief in the importance of charity. Organizing them into local clubs, she encouraged them to contribute a portion of their earnings to black causes. The message was inescapable: philanthropy and business were intimately connected.

As business grew, Walker expanded her philanthropic efforts. She supported a number of educational projects, including schools run by or for black women and scholarships at Tuskegee Institute; she gave sizeable contributions to the NAACP; and, contributing money and time, she passionately supported federal antilynching legislation. In recognition of her financial fortune and her philanthropic generosity, the National Negro Business League (NNBL) declared her "the foremost business woman of our race" in 1914.[35]

A Walker beauty parlor in
Harlem, New York City

Walker traveled a long and difficult road for most of her life. Not only did she overcome poverty, lack of education, and racial discrimination, but she surmounted resistance within the African American community as well, particularly among male leaders
with traditional ideas about womanhood. For years, Booker T. Washington, the most
powerful black man of the era, rebuffed her before finally inviting her to speak at a
meeting of the NNBL. Her speech was a passionate endorsement of the American dream.
Proudly presenting herself as an example of individual success, she challenged her
African American sisters to seize the American dream for themselves. "I had little or no
opportunity when I started out in life. . . . I had to make my own living and my own
opportunity. But I made it. That is why I want to say to every Negro woman present,
don't sit down and wait for opportunities to come, but you have to get up and make
them!"[36]

When Walker died in 1919, no one could deny her accomplishments. As an African
American businesswoman, she carved out a distinct arena of the marketplace–the
women of her race–and built her fortune selling healthy hair and hope for tomorrow to
them. She was a brilliant entrepreneur, who used modern techniques of advertising and
marketing to turn her very modest local venture into a national and international business. In doing so, she was a pioneer in the creation of a national mass market beauty
industry affordable to all women.

As a black woman who lifted herself from poverty to wealth, Walker left a profound legacy. The Associated Press declared her "the wealthiest negro woman in the United States, if not the entire world."[37] Her millionaire status, more myth than reality, revealed that she had become a powerful symbol of the fruits of ingenuity and hard work. As the *New York Post* announced, she stood as proof that the people of her race "may rise to the most distinctive heights of American achievement."[38] But Walker never forgot her roots: at every turn, she linked beauty and business to black philanthropy. "I am in the business world, not for myself alone, but to do all the good I can for the uplift of my race," she once explained.[39] To many of the leaders in the African American community, she more than accomplished her goal. As W. E. B. DuBois proudly proclaimed, she was one of a "few persons to transform a people in a generation."[40]

Like Madam C. J. Walker, Elizabeth Arden (1878?–1966) rose from poverty to make her fortune in the burgeoning beauty business of the first half of the twentieth century. Unlike Walker, who never forgot her roots, Arden left home and never looked back. And while Walker made "the uplift of my race" a cornerstone of her business, Arden had no such altruistic goal. Her sponsorship of charity luncheons and balls were as much self-promotion as they were philanthropy. In striking contrast to her African American counterpart, Arden was driven by her single-minded goal "to be the richest little woman in the world."[41]

In the spirit of the personal makeovers she popularized and profited from, Arden cast off the birth name "Florence Nightingale" (given to her by her mother, who admired the famous nurse), and made herself over as the elegant-sounding "Elizabeth Arden." In doing so, she rose from poverty to make a twenty million dollar fortune.[42] While Walker may have become the wealthiest black businesswoman of her day, Arden's fortune far exceeded Walker's or that of any other contemporary beauty entrepreneur. Her success not only revealed the advantages of her race; she ultimately defined the pinnacle of success for every entrepreneur, white or black, male or female, in the beauty industry of the early twentieth century.

Florence Nightingale Graham was the fourth of five children born to tenant farmers in Woodbridge, Ontario.[43] Her mother died of tuberculosis when Florence was a young girl, and she grew up in poverty. When the family economy declined, she dropped out of high school and, rather than marry, went to Toronto to find a job. Like many young women of her generation in Canada and the United States, she headed to the city to find work, opportunity, and independence. Jobs were opening to women and Graham tried several of them. She began as a student nurse in a Toronto hospital but, while her mother may have admired the courageous Florence Nightingale of the Crimean War, her daughter found nursing depressing. She left after barely three weeks and moved on to a series of jobs including stenographer, dental assistant, and bank teller.

Nothing satisfied Florence Graham's appetite for success, and in 1908 she moved to New York City, where her brother lived. She found work in Eleanor Adair's beauty salon, where wealthy women paid high prices for facial treatments. She learned how to give facial massages and quickly developed a loyal clientele of Adair customers. Driven by a passion for independence, she left Adair in 1910 and went into business with Elizabeth Hubbard, who sold skin-care products. Together they opened a salon, named "Mrs. Elizabeth Hubbard's," on fashionable Fifth Avenue. But Graham chafed under the restrictions of part-ownership, and the two women soon parted ways. Graham stayed in the Fifth Avenue salon while Hubbard moved down the block. She scraped the gold-lettered "Hubbard" off the shop window and replaced it with "Arden," from her favorite Alfred Lord Tennyson poem, "Enoch Arden." With the stroke of a gold-leafed brush, Florence Graham reinvented herself as "Elizabeth Arden."

With a new name that she believed evoked the refinement of the clientele she hoped to attract, the newly incarnated Elizabeth Arden set out to make it on her own. She borrowed six thousand dollars from her brother and invested it in her shop, transforming it into a luxurious salon with oriental rugs, antique furniture, and crystal chandeliers. To enhance the femininity of her salon she created a lush environment of pink, which eventually became her signature color. Her customers entered the salon through a bright red door with an elegant brass nameplate. The red door, unmistakably yet tastefully visible from the street, became her trademark and adorned the entryway of every salon she opened over the years (colorplate 10).

But the pampering and indulgence Arden offered her customers contrasted sharply with the hard work and personal sacrifice that defined her daily life. From nine in the morning until six in the evening, she catered to her customers. To save money, she arrived at work at seven to clean the salon, and she stayed late to mix batches of her face creams and to balance her books. Her hard work paid off; in six months she had made enough money to repay her brother.[44]

Arden's success was the result of more than hard work and a burning passion to achieve. An astute businesswoman, she seized on women's growing desire for freedom, beauty, and sex appeal in the era of the New Woman. But she was not alone. Helena Rubinstein, Arden's greatest competitor, arrived in New York just a few years after Arden. With a few jars of a special face cream she brought from Poland, she set up her own exclusive beauty business on Fifth Avenue, not far from Arden's. Referring to each other as "that woman," the two competed fiercely for decades as they turned the beauty business into one of the major consumer industries of the twentieth century.[45]

From the very beginning, Arden developed a creative marketing plan that capitalized on the culture's growing emphasis on youthfulness and beauty. She set her sights on two distinct groups of women: the middle-aged, who sought to recapture their youthful look; and the plain-looking or unattractive, who hoped to find beauty in a bottle. Through clever advertising she linked beauty to women's rights, subtly evoking the emerging feminist rhetoric of the day. "Every woman has the right to be beautiful," her ads asserted. The well-heeled, middle-aged women who marched down Fifth Avenue on behalf of women's suffrage could not miss Arden's barrage of advertisements

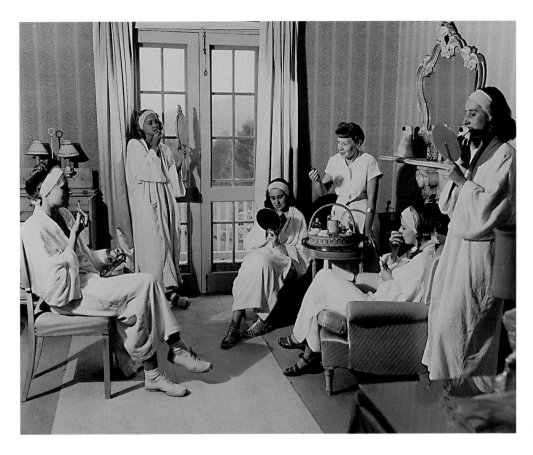

Guests at Elizabeth Arden's
Maine Chance spa

in *Vogue* and other upscale ladies' magazines exhorting them to "grow more beautiful as you grow older."[46] Not coincidentally, in 1920, the year that women finally won the right to vote, Arden could not keep up with the growing demand for her beauty products.[47]

With the modern woman as her loyal customer, Arden brought new ideas to the beauty industry. Early on, she introduced science into her business, hiring a chemist to do what others claimed was impossible—create an alternative to the thick, greasy face creams women wore at night. The new concoction—Venetian Cream Amoretta—was light, fluffy, and an immediate success. She adapted the principles of diathermy—the application of heat to body tissue via electric current—into a beauty device of papier-mâché and tin foil that she called the "Vienna Youth Mask." Her Intracellular Mask used short-wave radiation to "revitalize the blood."[48] Arden never stopped introducing new ideas. She created cosmetics to match a woman's clothing rather than her skin tone and she encouraged the everyday use of mascara and eye shadow. In the first quarter-century of her business, Arden developed a product line of over one hundred items in almost six hundred shapes and sizes.[49]

Arden's business grew quickly; the year 1915 was a turning point. Arden opened a salon in Washington, D.C., to serve the hostesses of the nation's capital. She also began a wholesale business, producing and distributing her products to upscale department stores around the country. And she married, taking barely an hour off from work for the ceremony. From the beginning, the childless marriage was more a friendship than a

Helena Rubinstein with her employees among flowers used to produce her cosmetics, 1925

relationship of love, and it ended in divorce years later. A second marriage in 1942 lasted only a year.

Arden's first marriage had a profound effect on her public life. In several significant ways, her first husband, Thomas Jenkins Lewis, provided an inseparable link between her private life and her growing business. He was the bank official who processed her loan for the Washington, D.C., salon, and he built and managed her wholesale business. In his skillful hands, the wholesale business grew from a modest thirty-thousand-dollar-a-year venture to a colossal success that grossed four million dollars in 1929.[50]

While Lewis managed the wholesale operation, expanding the business into department stores throughout the country, Arden's sister Gladys led the direct-sales effort. She traveled around the country with specially trained representatives who demonstrated the Elizabeth Arden product line in department stores. But rigid guidelines modified this mass-marketing campaign. Unlike the thousands of Walker agents who sold Walker's products door-to-door, the "Arden girls," as they were called, went only to the most fashionable department stores, such as Neiman Marcus, that carried the Arden line. And while Walker agents carefully cultivated an image of respectability, the meticulously groomed Arden girls, "trained to a perfection of smart hauteur," deliberately exuded an aura of glamour. This sales force was an expensive but worthwhile investment. Annual salaries and expenses ranged from five thousand to eight thousand dollars, but a week-long visit by an Arden girl to the Elizabeth Arden counter at a department store could earn that store up to six weeks' worth of sales.[51]

It seemed that Arden had found the formula for success. Throughout the 1920s, she expanded her business, opening new salons in Boston and San Francisco, as well as in cities where the wealthy congregated including Palm Beach, Florida, and Newport, Rhode Island. She also set her sights on the international market, selling her products in the exclusive Harrod's department store in London and the Galeries Lafayette in Paris. By 1925 her business was grossing two million dollars a year; by 1929 it was grossing eight million dollars a year.[52] While others predicted financial disaster for her at the start of the Great Depression, Arden boldly rejected a fifteen-million-dollar offer for the purchase of her business, expanded to a seven-floor salon on Fifth Avenue in 1930, and went on to

open new salons in Los Angeles, Palm Springs, and Miami Beach. By 1935 she owned twenty-six salons worldwide and employed one thousand workers.[53] A decade later, she owned twenty salons in the United States alone and fifteen others internationally.[54] A few ventures failed, including a fashion boutique and a radio show, but she wisely cut her losses quickly. Meanwhile, Maine Chance, her get-away spa, succeeded, attracting a distinguished clientele, including Claire Booth Luce and Mamie Eisenhower to the woods of Maine to spend hundreds of dollars for a week of pampering. In addition, Arden owned a stable of racing horses that brought her more fame and fortune: her picture appeared on the cover of *Time* magazine and one of her horses won the Kentucky Derby.

Elizabeth Arden with one of her winning race horses.

Elizabeth Arden built her business by selling the possibility of youth and beauty. She was her own best advertisement. Blessed with beautiful skin, she always looked younger than her actual age. To her eager customers, Arden's radiant complexion was visible proof that the Arden line of beauty products worked. Dressed in her signature color of pink, to enhance her glowing skin, Arden defined ideal femininity. And like Ellen Demorest a century before, she brought the rituals of female culture to her workplace. Work stopped daily at 3:00 PM in every Arden factory and office while her employees enjoyed tea.[55]

But behind Arden's feminine image was a hard-nosed, tough-minded entrepreneur who was as "fragile as a football tackle."[56] She expected perfection from her workers. "I only want people around me who can do the impossible," she claimed.[57] Despite her ritual of afternoon tea, she was an unpredictable, demanding, and relentlessly competitive employer. As a result, while some employees remained devoted to her for decades, many left. "Work for Elizabeth Arden and live in a revolving door," became a common warning.[58] Arden's intensely competitive spirit spilled over into her private life as well. When she divorced Lewis because of his infidelities, she offered him a meager settlement of twenty-five thousand dollars, and then only after he agreed not to work anywhere else in the cosmetics industry for five years. Five years later, Lewis went to work for Arden's archrival, Helena Rubinstein. Not to be outdone, Arden hired a dozen employees away from Rubinstein.

Ultimately, Arden thrived on the competition. While Rubinstein and such others as Estee Lauder and Hazel Bishop also made fortunes in the cosmetic industry, "[Elizabeth] Arden," observed one contemporary, "made the cosmetic industry."[59] From her Venetian Cream Amoretta and three-room salon on Fifth Avenue, she built a multimillion-dollar business with over fifty salons around the world and a cosmetics line of more than three hundred products. It is no exaggeration to say that Arden was more than the most successful woman entrepreneur of her time. In the view of the *New York Times*, "she was a sociological and historical phenomenon."[60]

When her long-lasting, kissable lipstick hit the market in 1950, Hazel Bishop (1906–98) became a household name. Following in the footsteps of Elizabeth Arden, Bishop entered the cosmetics industry but took her own unique path. Unlike Arden, who developed her business out of a service tradition based on beauty and pampering, Bishop was a professional scientist who applied chemistry to cosmetics. And while Arden made her fortune by selling fantasy and glamour, Bishop built her business by selling practicality and convenience. Finally, unlike Arden, who kept tight control of her business, Bishop placed her trust in others, ultimately losing her business to a man whose help she sought.

Hazel Bishop learned about business at home.[61] Her father was a manufacturer and small business owner who taught her the importance of advertising. Her mother managed her husband's businesses and instilled in her daughter the value of entrepreneurship. "Open your own business," she advised her young daughter, "even if it's a peanut stand."[62] As a young woman, however, Bishop wanted to become a doctor. Unfortunately the crash of 1929 coincided with her graduation from Barnard College and derailed her plans for medical school. Instead, she took night classes in chemistry at Columbia University and found a job during the day, first as a chemical technician at the Columbia University Medical Center and then as an assistant to a dermatologist. While the crash of 1929 ended Bishop's dreams of medical school, World War II opened up new opportunities. Like other women who found employment in jobs formerly monopolized by men, Bishop was hired as a chemist in the oil industry. First she worked at Standard Oil, where she discovered the cause of oil deposits on the superchargers of war-craft engines. While thousands of women worked on assembly lines to build warplanes, Bishop helped develop a special gasoline to fly them. Then she continued her research on oil products at another oil company.

In her spare time, Bishop directed her scientific expertise to women. It was a short route from chemistry to cosmetics. "I am a woman," she told *Business Week*. "If you are an organic chemist and a woman, then cosmetics attract you."[63] And as a woman in the male-dominated science of chemistry, she believed she had special insights into

Economics of Luxury
Martha Matilda Harper

By turning hair care into a thriving business, Martha Matilda Harper (1857–1950) pulled herself out of poverty. Born in Ontario, Canada, Harper spent her childhood away from home in domestic service. She learned about the physiology of hair and the value of hair tonics while working for a doctor. In 1882, hoping to improve her life, Harper moved to the bustling city of Rochester, New York, with sixty silver dollars, a jug of her hair tonic, and its formula. She worked as a domestic servant by day and at night mixed hair tonic, which a neighbor then sold door-to-door.

In 1886, she took a risk that would change her life: she invested her entire savings of 360 dollars to open a salon. Harper was a savvy entrepreneur from the very start. Locating her salon strategically in Rochester's premier commercial building, she trademarked a logo–the horn of plenty–that conveyed a message of abundance and success. Her long, healthy hair (seen in the photograph at right) hung to the floor; it was Harper's first and best advertisement for her hair tonic.

Like Elizabeth Arden, Harper focused on luxury and personal pampering to attract a wealthy clientele. With every shampoo she gave a head and shoulder massage. So her customers could relax as they received hair treatments and massages, she designed the first reclining chair for hair care in the United States. Wealthy Rochester women as well as leading suffragists such as Susan B. Anthony became loyal customers.

While Harper offered luxury to wealthy women, she offered economic opportunity to poor women. As demand for her products and services spread, she developed a unique method of business expansion, licensing shops to domestic servants who duplicated precisely her hair care methods, customer services, and products in shops around the country. The franchise–re-created in over three hundred Harper salons around the country–was Harper's legacy to American business. ✍

women's needs. "Women have an insight and understanding of cosmetology a male chemist can never have," she explained.[64] "Does a man, for instance, know what happens to makeup under the hot beach sun?"[65] And she knew firsthand about the embarrassment of lipstick on coffee cups and cigarette butts as well as the inconvenience of reapplying lipstick numerous times in a day. As a woman trained in chemistry but raised to love business, Bishop set out to develop a product to solve the problem. After two years and over three hundred experiments in her kitchen, Bishop finally developed a product she believed women could not refuse, a smear-proof, long-lasting lipstick.

The time was right for Bishop's ingenious and practical innovation. Women had grown accustomed to cosmetics during the war. Many viewed makeup as essential and lipstick, in particular, as indispensable. As women took over men's jobs in the war industry, they wore makeup to highlight their femininity and to reassure an anxious nation that women who built bombers were still ladies. Linking beauty with patriotism, private industry supported women's demand for makeup during the war, offering charm classes and providing beauty salons and cosmetic stations. The popular *Business Week* magazine supported the trend, claiming that "Miss America's part in winning the war should not include sacrifice of lipstick, eye shadow, or any of her bottled beau-catchers."[66]

After the war, as women returned to the home and settled into domesticity, they continued to use makeup to enhance their femininity. By 1948 an estimated 80 to 90 percent of adult women wore lipstick.[67] But as they retreated into the privacy of their homes, the patriotic justification for cosmetics gave way to a more personal rationale: namely, to enhance their allure and attraction for their husbands. At the same time a new generation of teenage girls began to wear makeup. In a 1949 survey of high school girls in Florida, teens identified over forty different lipsticks as their favorites.[68] This widespread use of lipstick among adolescent girls promised a new market for the cosmetics industry. Accompanying the postwar growth of lipstick consumption, however, was a growing recognition that lipstick was a not a problem-free product. Any woman who wore it knew that it smeared, left stains, and constantly needed to be reapplied. Even teenagers complained that it "comes off too easily." Readers of *Woman's Home Companion* were advised to apply special preparations both under and over their lipstick "to help it stay put and not smear."[69]

Bishop hoped to solve these problems with her long-lasting lipstick. Recalling her parents' advice from childhood to "offer the customer what she wants," Bishop set out to market her product.[70] She found a lipstick manufacturer and, with the help of a lawyer she met through her mother, she formed Hazel Bishop, Inc., and raised the capital to launch her product. She began locally. First she turned to her alma mater, where she introduced her lipstick at a fashion show for the Barnard College Club in the fall of 1949. Then she convinced the owner of her neighborhood drugstore to carry her lipstick. His supply sold out in a matter of days. After she splashed a tube of lipstick across a full-page newspaper advertisement, she averaged sales of three hundred lipsticks a day in one city drugstore alone.[71]

Despite these sales, the local demand was not enough to keep Hazel Bishop, Inc., going. Bishop was rapidly losing money and after only three months it was clear that she had to devise a different strategy. She turned to the well-known New York advertising agent Raymond Spector to popularize her lipstick the way he had popularized the Lone Ranger. Under Spector's direction, Hazel Bishop, Inc., launched a $1.5 million advertising campaign in 1950. It was an aggressive move; no other cosmetics firm had ever devoted as much money simply to advertise a lipstick. And Spector was aggressive about distribution as well. He was the first to distribute a major lipstick to big syndicated stores like Woolworth's and Kresge's which sold low-cost items. Yet, while other lipsticks sold for fifty cents, Hazel Bishop lipstick retailed on nearby shelves for one dollar and ten cents.[72]

The Hazel Bishop advertising campaign successfully combined sex and romance with economy and practicality. The most famous ad pictured a man and a woman sharing a passionate kiss, with the text, "it stays on YOU not on Him!" The message of female sexual assertiveness went even further with the suggestive promise to women that Hazel Bishop's lasting lipstick would stay on "until *you* Take It Off!"[73] Bishop eagerly promoted the sexual message on her own. Questioned about whether her lipstick was "really kissproof," she teased a reporter at *Business Week*: "How kissproof it is depends on the degree of friction." One can only imagine the private fantasies of the *Business Week*

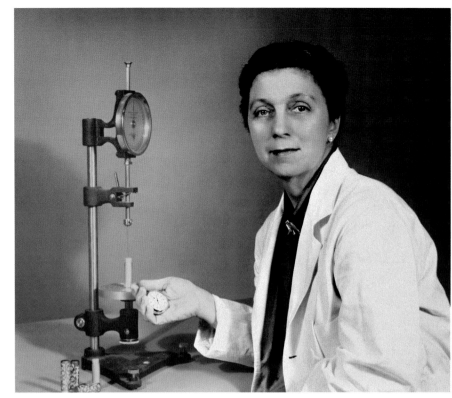

Hazel Bishop, chemist and beauty-products entrepreneur, who developed "kissable lipstick," ca. 1950

reporter when she coyly explained to him that "a woman would just as leave go out without a dress on as without lipstick."[74]

Bishop's new marketing campaign also emphasized economy and practicality. Advertisements praised women as thrifty and smart for buying Bishop's long-lasting lipstick. And her product line reflected this practical approach. Unlike her competitors, who offered many shades of lipstick, Bishop's lipstick was available in only seven different colors. And while her competitors evoked fantasy with such lipstick names as "Burning Embers" and "Fragile Passion," Bishop took a no-nonsense approach, describing her lipsticks simply as she saw them—"pink," "dark red," etc. Moreover, while her competitors emphasized their own glamour and sophistication, Bishop portrayed herself as a professional chemist with the same beauty needs as the everyday woman.[75] This practical approach mirrored the simplicity of her life. In sharp contrast to Arden's lavish lifestyle, with her multiple residences, expensive furnishings, and race horses, Bishop lived with her mother in an apartment in New York City and had one indulgence: hats.[76]

Bishop's practical approach and Spector's aggressive advertising paid off. Her kissable lipstick became an overnight sensation; its popularity also launched a frenzy among cosmetics firms. By 1951, more than thirty lipsticks purported to be indelible, and by 1954 more than fifty made the claim. The fad attracted the attention of *Consumer Reports*, which tested thirty-one such products in 1951 and supported the Hazel Bishop claim to "indelibility."[77] Despite all the competition, Spector's aggressive advertising made Hazel Bishop lipstick the one to beat. By March 1951 it was racing to the top of the charts, with sales second only to Revlon's. In 1953, the once-failing Hazel Bishop, Inc., sold over ten million dollars' worth of lipstick. As Bishop's lipstick threatened to overwhelm the market, Revlon launched a fiercely competitive "lipstick war."[78]

But as Bishop's long-lasting lipstick captured one-quarter of the lipstick market, a drama was unfolding behind the scenes between Bishop and Spector.[79] The same aggressive promotion approach he had used to catapult the kissable lipstick into its dominant position in the cosmetics market enabled Spector to overpower Bishop and, ultimately, to take over her company. In desperately trying to save her failing company, Bishop had entered into an unfavorable agreement that permitted Spector to take all profits from the company to cover an unlimited advertising budget and gave him shares in the company as well. In just a few short years, Spector had taken advantage of the contract to manipulate and buy out the majority stockholders. To stop him, Bishop sued, but ultimately she settled in 1954, selling Spector her remaining 8 percent of the company and agreeing never to sell her products under her own name. As Bishop walked away from Hazel Bishop, Inc., forever with a cash settlement of two hundred and fifty thousand dollars, the annual sales of the company topped ten million dollars.[80] The press responded sympathetically to Bishop. Headlines like "The Smear Behind That No-Smear Lipstick" and "Spector of Wealth Haunts Adman Spector" portrayed Bishop as the unfortunate victim of the greedy and scheming Spector. She was "the plucky gal who started it all and was then prevented from finishing her own exciting story."[81]

The advertisement (1950) that established the Hazel Bishop brand of lipstick

Bishop continued to believe in the opportunities chemistry offered women. "Cosmetic chemistry is a wonderful field for women," she explained just three years after she left Hazel Bishop, Inc.[82] She returned to the chemistry lab, where, once again, she applied her scientific expertise to the development of products for everyday use. They included a leather cleaner called "Leather Lav," a spray to relieve tired feet, and a solid perfume stick she named "Perfemme." Ever the entrepreneur, she founded three separate companies to market her new products. In the 1960s, Bishop moved into financial circles, becoming a stockbroker for Bache and Company, then later a financial analyst who specialized in cosmetics and health securities. Her advice was highly valued, particularly as the fragrance industry blossomed. In the 1970s Bishop taught the business of cosmetics to students at the Fashion Institute of Technology in New York. And in 1980 Revlon, once her fiercest competitor, recognized her remarkable accomplishments in business, in finance, and in academics and appointed her to the institute's newly endowed Revlon Chair in Cosmetics Marketing. Bishop died in 1998 at the age of ninety-two. She never married and had no children; still she left a legacy more indelible than her long-lasting lipstick. A chemist and an entrepreneur, her story is poignant testimony to the possibilities and pitfalls confronting women in business.

While some enterprising women made their fortunes in the new beauty business, others found success in the more traditional arena of women's fashion, dressing the modern woman for the new century. Among these fashion entrepreneurs, three women, Hattie Carnegie, Lane Bryant, and Ida Rosenthal, were quintessential examples of the American dream of success—for women. All three were Jewish immigrants who left their homes in Eastern Europe and settled in the Lower East Side of New York City in search of opportunity. They brought with them the values of their Jewish culture that encouraged women to work in the practical world, earning money to support the family, while men immersed themselves in the world of ideas. And each discovered a unique way to satisfy the female consumer in the early twentieth century.[83]

The daughter of poor Jewish immigrants, Hattie Carnegie (1886–1956) founded a women's fashion company that brought her wealth, status, and nationwide fame. In an era that valued assimilation, she shed her ethnic identity completely and became the model of sophisticated American style. Society women clamored for a "little Carnegie suit," while those who could not afford her originals still strived for the "Carnegie look." In the first half of the twentieth century, Carnegie made a fortune as the arbiter of style and taste for the American woman.

Hattie Carnegie rose from obscurity. The second of seven children, she was born Henrietta Köningeiser in Vienna, Austria.[84] When her family's home burned down, her father immigrated to New York City and sent back money until the family could afford to come over in 1892. They settled in the Lower East Side of Manhattan, the neighborhood for thousands of immigrant Jewish families. It was also the location of the notorious tenement housing that photojournalist Jacob Riis had so powerfully portrayed in his 1890 book, *How the Other Half Lives*, exposing a neighborhood of misery, poverty, and despair. Hattie attended public school until her father died when she was thirteen. With her family in financial crisis, she turned to jobs then available to young Jewish immigrant girls. She worked briefly pinning hats in a millinery workroom, as a messenger girl at Macy's, and in a wholesale dress house.

Even as a young girl, Hattie Köningeiser had style and self-confidence. She did not hesitate to tell her boss in the dress shop why an outfit did not sell. Though skeptical of her opinion and annoyed by her nerve, he took her advice and Köningeiser's redesigned dress was a great success. Meanwhile, Köningeiser wore the three blouses and one skirt that composed her entire wardrobe with such flair that she could not be ignored. With her blond curls, striking blue eyes, and slim waist, she caught the attention of a Jewish seamstress in the neighborhood, Rose Roth. Roth offered to design dresses for Köningeiser, hoping that her striking appearance would draw customers to Roth. It was an ingenious arrangement: Köningeiser gained a brand-new wardrobe, which she wore with such style that customers, including well-known actresses, flocked to Rose Roth's showroom.

In 1909 Köningeiser and Roth went into business together, opening a custom-made dress and hat shop.[85] Though their shop was a modest venture on East Tenth Street,

Köningeiser had great ambitions. With poverty and despair surrounding her, she believed passionately that she could achieve the American promise of upward mobility. In an overt expression of her desire for wealth and success, she changed her last name to Carnegie, deliberately choosing to embrace the name of one of the wealthiest men in America. Thus her first business, in partnership with Rose Roth, was called "Carnegie–Lady Hatter." Their business grew quickly. By 1913 they had capital of one hundred thousand dollars and were able to move to a more desirable location on West Eighty–sixth Street. Though they were near fashionable Riverside Drive, their shop, on the second floor directly above a delicatessen and a Chinese restaurant, was far from elegant. But nothing, not even the pungent smells of food, could keep women out of Carnegie–Lady Hatter. Socialites, including Mrs. Randolph Hearst, climbed the stairs of the odorous building to buy Hattie Carnegie's creations.

By 1918, with a growing clientele of wealthy women, Carnegie bought out her partner and renamed her business "Hattie Carnegie, Inc." While she could neither sew nor draw a pattern, she had other talents–especially an uncanny eye for style and enormous self-confidence. She began to frequent expensive hotels and restaurants, looking for trends and inspiration. In 1919 she took her first of what would become hundreds of trips abroad, where she adapted the ideas and models from the haute couture of Paris into a uniquely American style. Her outfits, which began at seventy–five dollars, struck just the right balance to satisfy the tastes of America's society women: they were simple but stylish, understated but elegant, neat but luxurious. They were always very feminine and appealed to women of all ages. It was not long before women of fashion clamored for what became popularly known as the "little Carnegie suit."

Hattie Carnegie, dean of American designers, set fashion standards for her time.

By 1923 the "Carnegie look" had become the symbol of high fashion. With capital of $426,000, Carnegie moved from her second-story showroom above the delicatessen and Chinese restaurant to a chic townhouse on East Forty–ninth Street. This became the heart of her retail business, where she sold dresses trimmed in mink, spangled cocktail suits, velvet evening gowns, and, of course, her little Carnegie suits. Carnegie expanded her line to include furs, jewelry, lingerie, hats, perfumes, and accessories–the idea was to provide an entire look, her signature Carnegie Look. In 1925 she struck a deal with the California department store I. Magnin to establish a joint line of clothing. The arrangement put Carnegie's clothing within easy grasp of the Hollywood elite, so that she influenced the fashion worlds on both coasts. It also made Carnegie the first custom designer to branch out beyond the high–end custom line into ready–to–wear attire.

By the end of the 1920s the Carnegie Look had become the standard of elegance and style for fashion-conscious women. Carnegie's customers were socialites and celebrities, including the Duchess of Windsor, Tallulah Bankhead, Claire Booth Luce, and Norma Shearer. They thought nothing of paying seven hundred dollars for a wool dress and fur-trimmed coat. Money was no object for actress Joan Crawford, who wired Carnegie with the simple request: "Send me something I'd like."[86] Another customer bought twenty-two thousand dollars' worth of Carnegie's creations and paid for them with a single check. By 1929, before the economic crash, Carnegie was a model of the successful self-made woman. She earned a half-million dollars annually through her agreement with I. Magnin and had overall yearly sales of three and a half million dollars.[87]

Neither the economic depression of the 1930s nor World War II slowed Carnegie down. When the Depression began to cut into the sales of her expensive lines, Carnegie opened a wholesale business called "Spectator Sports." This new branch of the business manufactured moderately priced clothing to be sold in retail stores around the country. It was an immediate success and quickly became one of the most profitable branches of her business. In 1941 she broadened her market even further, opening the Jeune Fille department, which sold an affordable line of clothing to younger women. This was an innovative and deliberate attempt to attract the daughters of wealthy families who would eventually marry and "have checkbooks of their own."[88] During World War II it was impossible to ignore Carnegie's influence over the fashion world. The little Carnegie suit had become such a classic expression of American fashion that the United States Army called on Carnegie to reinterpret it for the Women's Army Corps [WAC] uniform. In Carnegie's skillful hands, the wartime Carnegie Look became the symbol of patriotic womanhood.

Hattie Carnegie receives the Neiman Marcus Distinguished Fashion Service award (1939) from Stanley Marcus, nephew of Carrie Marcus Neiman.

Carnegie emerged from the Great Depression and World War II a wealthy and influential woman. She received the United States Army's highest civilian award for designing the WAC uniforms, and in 1948 she won the coveted Coty American Fashion Critics Award. Meanwhile, Hattie Carnegie, Inc. was a multimillion-dollar business, with $6.5 million in annual sales and more than one thousand employees. Her retail shop spanned an entire block between Forty-eighth and Forty-ninth Streets in the fashionable Park Avenue neighborhood. She sold dresses for hundreds of dollars at a 60 percent markup; hats were available for hundreds of dollars as well. She also sold furs. A simple suit was featured with eight hundred dollars' worth of mink accessories. In addition, Carnegie sold costume jewelry, handbags, sweaters, scarves, bed jackets, lingerie, and even chocolates from Paris. And with an eye to cornering the beauty business as well, she inaugurated her own cosmetics line, competing directly with Helena Rubinstein and Elizabeth Arden.

Over sixteen thousand women had charge accounts with her, most of whom spent between three thousand and thirty thousand dollars each year.[89] Those who did not live in New York City thought nothing of ordering sketches and fabrics for outfits by telephone. For those who could not afford Carnegie's most expensive creations, there were made-to-order dresses with the "Hattie Carnegie" label in stores throughout the country.

Carnegie's own lifestyle mirrored the sophisticated, indulgent luxury of the Carnegie Look. She owned a townhouse on Fifth Avenue and a farm in New Jersey. She had silk sheets and a mink coverlet on her bed, gold faucets in her bathroom, and antiques from France that "would make a curator's mouth water."[90] She played poker and gin rummy weekly with New York City society women on her own illuminated card table, which supposedly enhanced her concentration.

Carnegie's private life also reflected sophisticated independence. She was divorced twice before she finally settled down to marry her childhood sweetheart when she was in her forties. Her third husband, John Zaft, was an executive in the movie industry who spent most of his time in Los Angeles. As a result, Carnegie's third and final marriage was a model for the future, anticipating by several decades the dual-career, commuter marriage of the late twentieth century.

By the end of World War II, Carnegie was a remarkably successful entrepreneur, a model of the self-made woman. Her success was due to a number of factors beyond her keen sense of style and her ability to translate it to the American woman. Family played a major role. Behind the scenes, Hattie Carnegie, Inc., was a family business. One brother ran the wholesale business, another was responsible for financial matters, while a sister directed the less expensive ready-to-wear line. In addition, ten nieces and nephews worked for Carnegie, the boys in the wholesale department and the girls as models or salesclerks.

Marriage to Zaft was also good for Carnegie's business. Zaft was an insider in the film industry in Hollywood. He worked for Louis B. Mayer, and he was an executive at Fox Films and an agent for top-draw film stars. Carnegie thrived on her husband's Hollywood connections. Film stars were among her most visible and high-paying customers, spending thousands of dollars at the Los Angeles I. Magnin when they did not order custom-made outfits by telephone. Moreover, this was a marriage without children; while most married businesswomen had to find ways to balance child rearing with work, Carnegie escaped this dilemma.

While Carnegie relied on her large, extended family to help her run her business, she succeeded as well because she was a master of assimilation. In an era when ethnic identity was an obstacle to success, and Jews in particular were regarded with resentment and suspicion, Carnegie understood the advantages of blending into the mainstream of American culture. Her decision to change her name from Köningeiser to

Carnegie not only reflected her admiration for a man of enormous wealth and power; it represented a deliberate attempt to shed her Jewish identity. In addition, she took full advantage of her blond hair and blue eyes, which enabled her to distance herself from her Jewish roots and fit in with her elite Anglo-Saxon clientele. Moreover, she preferred to hire attractive blond women to work in her store.[91] Carnegie's trademark Carnegie Look, the very foundation of her business success, was ideally suited to the conservative climate of the postwar era. Arbiters of fashion and social observers defined the genius of the Carnegie Look in its American interpretation of haute couture, that is, its understated elegance.[92] In contrast to the stereotype of the flamboyant clothing worn by nouveau riche Jewish women, the classic Carnegie Look embodied the ideal: the wealthy American woman secure in her social and financial position.

When Carnegie died in 1956, her business was an eight-million-dollar enterprise. But it did not last long after her death. In 1945, as *Life* magazine hailed Carnegie's importance to the business, it unintentionally foreshadowed its eventual decline: "Hattie Carnegie, Inc. is Hattie Carnegie."[93] *Life* was indeed correct. While Carnegie's brothers tried to continue the business, it needed her vitality and personal touch. Hattie Carnegie, Inc., eventually closed in the 1970s.

⌒ While Hattie Carnegie built a business that catered to society women, Lane Bryant (1879–1951) created a fashion empire for society's "forgotten" women, first for the expectant mother and later for the full-figured woman. Born Lena Himmelstein, Lane Bryant emigrated from Lithuania to New York in 1895.[94] Though she began as a poor Jewish immigrant alone in New York, Bryant was a woman for her time. She understood the desire of women of the day for active lives beyond the boundaries of the home. And she knew that many were unwilling to give up their public lives, as their mothers had done, during pregnancy. With an eye to capitalizing on these changing views, and with the courage to take risks and to sacrifice security, she carved out a new corner of the women's fashion industry—maternity wear—and built a thriving business marketing equality and freedom to the pregnant consumer.

Bryant's original plan was far less ambitious. At the age of sixteen she left her home and family and immigrated to New York City, expecting to settle down to marriage and motherhood. Relatives had paid her passage, hoping she would marry their son.[95] But when she arrived in New York she refused to marry the young man. Instead she took a job as a seamstress in a lingerie factory, where she earned just one dollar a week. She had talent and advanced quickly to fifteen dollars a week. Despite her success, at the age of nineteen she stopped working, married a Russian jeweler named David Bryant, became pregnant, and entered a life of domesticity. But sixteen months later, her husband unexpectedly died. Bryant suddenly became a destitute widow with an infant son.

Forced into independence, Bryant drew on the courage and resourcefulness that had sustained her in her early days alone in New York. She sold the diamond earrings her husband had given her when they married, bought a sewing machine, and began her own business as a seamstress in her small apartment on the Upper West Side of Manhattan. Specializing in lingerie and bridal wear, she quickly became popular among young women on the threshold of marriage and motherhood. When an expectant mother expressed the desire to wear something "presentable but comfortable" in public, Bryant, a young mother herself, designed an outfit that became an immediate success.

Bryant's dress, based on a design first worn by Josephine, the small, stout wife of Napoleon, had a high, elasticized waist and an expandable, accordion-pleated skirt. It promised comfort, style, modesty, and flexibility. As the centerpiece of her maternity line, the dress helped transform the "lady-in-waiting," who was secluded at home, into the modern pregnant woman who was active, respectable, and confident in the public sphere. Bryant's design was an innovative and bold fashion statement. It challenged the traditional view that pregnancy belonged shrouded in secrecy and that the expectant mother should retreat to the privacy of the home as soon as her "condition" was obvious.

At first, newspapers refused to accept Bryant's ads. But in 1911 the *New York Herald* cautiously ran an ad in which Bryant declared that the era of confinement was over. The expectant mother "must go about among other people, she must look like other people." Her maternity wear enabled expectant mothers to venture out of the home and "look as other women look," respectable and fashionable. It was a masterful advertisement. It conveyed a clear message to the new generation of young married women: the secrecy and shame of pregnancy were out of fashion; the pregnant woman comfortable and active in the public sphere symbolized the progress and modernity of the twentieth-century woman. While the *New York Herald* may have been hesitant about the ad, young expectant mothers were not. They flocked to Bryant's store and bought out her entire stock in one day.[96]

"Sunshine or Shadows" was Lane Bryant's first advertisement for maternity clothing (1911).

Other life changes accompanied these early years of success. During a visit to a bank to open an account, Lena officially became Lane. As Bryant told the story, a teller misread her signature as "Lane" rather than "Lena," and Bryant was too embarrassed and insecure to correct him. Whatever the case, Bryant's silence suggests her opportunism and quiet understanding that her new name was an Americanized version of the more Jewish "Lena." Though not as deliberately as Hattie Carnegie, Lane Bryant diluted her Jewish identity as she climbed the ladder of success.

In 1909, a second marriage created new business opportunities. Bryant's new husband, Albert Malsin, took over the financial side of the business, introducing a thirty-two-page catalogue that thrust the firm squarely into the mail-order business.

make a place for themselves in the public arena, but apart from men. As the nation's centennial approached, women made plans to celebrate their achievements in a separate Woman's Pavilion at the 1876 Centennial Exhibition in Philadelphia. Coston turned to them for support. In a letter to the *New Century for Woman*, the daily newsletter of the Woman's Pavilion, she explained that she wanted to feature the Coston Night Signals as a woman's invention, even though the U.S. Army and the treasury department already planned to exhibit the Coston Night Signal. "It having been perfected and introduced into public use by a woman," she wrote, it "would be doing her sex an injustice to withhold it from your Department of the Exhibition."[53]

Coston joined a group of about eighty-five women who sought to market their inventions at the Woman's Pavilion.[54] But she was unique. While most of the women displayed domestic devices that were only welcome in the separate women's building, the Coston Night Signals commanded a place in the mainstream of the Exhibition. Thus, she shrewdly planted herself in both arenas. Her sisterhood was a smart business move. The *New Century for Woman* gave her valuable publicity, while her display in the Woman's Pavilion won an award and introduced her night signals to thousands of fair goers, men and women. Almost two decades later, Coston returned to this same woman's community at the World's Columbian Exposition in Chicago in 1893. Once again a separate Woman's Building featured the ingenuity of women and once again women seized the opportunity to market their inventions. Hundreds of fair goers ordered special bread pans, refrigerators, and other domestic items. Meanwhile, Coston's night signals stood out in the Inventions Room as "distinguished and brilliant."[55]

Coston eventually handed over the Coston Signal Company to her sons, who developed new devices and brought the company into the twentieth century. She died in 1902. Reflecting in her autobiography on her accomplishments, she displayed a keen insight into the merits and limits of her accomplishments. She took great pride in her development of the night signals and in her ability to support her children on her own. However, she resented the unfair monetary compensation she received from the government and the prejudice she encountered because she was a woman.

Martha Coston left an indelible mark. Her Coston Night Signals not only helped the North win the Civil War, but they remained standard Coast Guard equipment for decades. Perhaps her contemporary, Ellen Demorest, best captured Coston's significance as an inventor and entrepreneur. In 1876, at the peak of her prestige and before Butterick would overwhelm her own business empire, Demorest praised Coston in *Demorest's Monthly* as "the most remarkable instance of woman's capacity for inventing and producing. . . . She should be as bright as one of her own signals, to guide and encourage other women in business."[56]

⌘ Myra Bradwell (1831–94) is best known today for her unsuccessful bid to become a lawyer. In 1873 the United States Supreme Court in Bradwell v. State of Illinois rejected as a matter of law Bradwell's right as a woman to be licensed to practice law in Illinois.

Many of her contemporaries were well aware of her legal failure. But in her day, Myra Bradwell was better known for her enterprising success as the founder of the *Chicago Legal News*. In an era when the legal profession was growing and the West was expanding, Bradwell used her shrewd business talent to turn the *Chicago Legal News* into the most important legal publication west of the Alleghenies. Like Ellen Demorest, Bradwell contributed to and profited from the expanding information revolution of the day.

And like the successes of Ellen Demorest and Lydia Pinkham, Bradwell's business success went hand-in-hand with social reform. While the *News* was a profitable enterprise, it was also the vehicle for Bradwell's reform agenda. Her loyal readers, so dependent on the *News* for their legal practice, became a captive audience for Bradwell's critical voice. At the heart of her agenda was the reform of women's legal disabilities. But she filled the pages of the *News* with articles on a broad range of issues including temperance, prison reform, government regulation of railroads, and reform of the legal profession. Under Bradwell's skillful direction of the *News*, business, law, women's rights, and social reform all came together, linking financial profit with social reform.

Born in Manchester, Vermont, Myra Colby spent her childhood in western New York with her older siblings, a brother and three sisters.[57] Her parents, Egen and Abigail Colby, were fiercely devoted to the antislavery cause and were close friends of abolitionist Elijah Lovejoy, who was murdered by a proslavery mob in Illinois in 1837. Though Myra Colby was only six at the time, the event became a formative part of her childhood memory. It was but a simple step for the adult Myra Bradwell to make the connection between the injustices of slavery and the legal disabilities imposed on women.

When Myra was twelve, her family continued its westward migration and settled in Schaumberg (Cook County), Illinois. Myra spent her adolescence in much the same way as other middle-class girls of her day. She attended school while living with one of her older sisters in Kenosha, Wisconsin. When a female seminary opened in Elgin, Illinois, in 1851, she returned to Illinois and completed her education there. After graduating, she began teaching, following the respectable path for a young, single woman. In the meantime, she met James Bolesworth Bradwell, a poor law student and son of English immigrant farmers who lived nearby. The Colbys did not approve of the relationship. Myra's brother even threatened James with a shotgun. But Myra was undeterred; she married James Bradwell in 1852 and they moved to Memphis, Tennessee. Together they opened a private academy while James continued to read law and Myra began to raise a family. Shortly after she gave birth to her first child, in 1854, they moved to Chicago, where Myra raised her children and later built her publishing business and established her reputation.

Myra gave birth to three more children between 1856 and 1862, but by 1864 only two had survived. Meanwhile James Bradwell was admitted to the Illinois bar in 1855 and went into practice with Myra's brother, the very one who had chased him out of town just a few years before. During the years of the Civil War, Myra Bradwell joined other women in Chicago to work for the Northwestern Sanitary Commission. Popularly

Meanwhile, Bryant had three children in four years and became a walking advertisement for her maternity creations. By 1917 Bryant had annual sales of one million dollars.

It was a short step from maternity wear to Bryant's next design innovation, a fashionable clothing line especially for full-figured women. Once again, Bryant recognized the needs of women who had been ignored by the fashion industry. "I saw that women of ample figure had no representative at the Court of Fashion," she explained.[97] With an eye to capturing this untapped market, she and her husband set out to create the first line of fashionable clothing for "stout" women, as she referred to them. They took a systematic approach. They measured approximately forty-five hundred full-figured customers and, combining those measurements with statistics on over two hundred thousand women, they developed three general models of stoutness, which became the basis for their new ready-to-wear line of plus-size clothing.[98] For the first time, full-figured women could buy clothing with style.

In a few short years, Bryant's plus-size line was outselling her maternity wear. In 1923 Lane Bryant, Inc. had expanded to seven stores around the country, employed a total of fifteen hundred employees, and had five million dollars in annual sales.[99] In the midst of all this success, Malsin died and Bryant became a widow once again, though this time she was a successful and independent woman of means. She continued to run the business, bringing her sons in to help her.

As her company grew, Bryant never forgot her modest roots. She was a generous and forward-thinking employer who took good care of her workers. Long before comprehensive benefit plans, she offered her workers profit sharing, disability insurance, medical insurance, free hospitalization, and group life insurance. Her generosity extended to her customers as well. She promised a free wardrobe to any woman whose wardrobe was destroyed in a disaster. She stuck to her word. In 1947 she sent new clothing to eighty-five mail-order customers in Texas who lost their wardrobes in a fire. In addition she turned her stores into centers for clothing donated to the victims of World War II. And although she went from Lena to Lane, she never forgot her Jewish roots. She was active in a number of Jewish philanthropies, including the Hebrew Immigrant Aid Society and the Federation of Jewish Philanthropies.[100]

When Bryant died in 1951, Lane Bryant, Inc. had annual sales of forty-five million dollars and was the sixth largest mail-order firm in the country.[101] Paradoxically, while Bryant built her business by promising freedom to the expectant mother at the beginning of the twentieth century, it reached its peak in an era of social conservatism as a new generation of wives and mothers retreated back into their homes.

 Bryant and Carnegie succeeded by helping women to look their best; Ida Rosenthal (1886–1973) built a business that helped women to *feel* their best. The young Jewish immigrant from Russia, born Ida Kaganovich, turned a modest dressmaking venture into the Maiden Form Brassiere Company (renamed Maidenform, Inc., in 1960), ultimately revolutionizing women's fashion from the inside out.

Ida Kaganovich's girlhood in Russia prepared her for a future of entrepreneurial success.[102] Her father, a Hebrew scholar, taught her a respect for learning. But her mother, an astute businesswoman with practical goals, set her daughter on the path to business success. Believing it was never too soon for a young girl to prepare for her future, she arranged for Ida and her younger sister to learn sewing from a local dressmaker, and she bought them a sewing machine that enabled them to begin a small dressmaking business in their home. Ida lived briefly in Warsaw, where she studied math and continued to sew, and returned home an even better dressmaker, with valuable math skills.

Then in her late teens, Ida fell in love with William Rosenthal. The son of a local Hebrew scholar, William Rosenthal had no intention of remaining in his hometown to pursue a life of the mind. Instead, he fled to the United States in 1905 to avoid the Russian army. Ida followed a few months later. Determined to escape the drudgery of factory life, she settled in Hoboken, New Jersey, near an uncle, purchased a Singer sewing machine on credit, and set up her own dressmaking business.

In 1906, as she took her first entrepreneurial step, she also married William Rosenthal. From then on, their lives were inextricably intertwined. Together they turned Ida's dressmaking talents into a thriving business. Their life-long marriage and business partnership were built on mutual respect, a unique allocation of responsibilities, and an uncanny ability to know precisely what the American woman wanted to put between her body and her blouse. Like Ellen Demorest and Myra Bradwell in the nineteenth century, Rosenthal built an enduring partnership with her husband, both in business and in life.

By 1912 Rosenthal's dressmaking business was well on its way. She and her husband had six employees, a group of loyal customers who were happy to pay up to seven dollars and fifty cents for one of her dresses, and a five-year-old son, Lewis, born the year after they married. Both their business and their family continued to grow; in a few years their workforce had more than doubled, they were charging twenty-five dollars for their dresses, and they had a daughter, Beatrice. In 1918 the Rosenthals moved their modest business and their two children to Manhattan, the largest urban market in the country. This move not only placed them in the financial center of the world, it plunged them into the heart of the consumer revolution that was sweeping the country in the early twentieth century.

Rosenthal took advantage of an offer to become the dressmaker for Enid Frocks, an exclusive dress shop on fashionable West Fifty-seventh Street. Then its owner, Enid Bissett, invited Rosenthal to become a partner. This offer entailed a risk: it required that Rosenthal give up her own clientele and invest almost her entire life savings in Enid Frocks. Her family and closest friends urged her to reject the idea, but Rosenthal leapt at the chance. The risk paid off. The business thrived, and Rosenthal was now perfectly situated in the fashion center of Manhattan, designing dresses that sold from $125 to $300.

COLORPLATE 1

Mrs. James Smith (Elizabeth Murray), *1769.*

John Singleton Copley, American (1738–1815)

The Indico Plant.
a.a.a. One of the Pedicules, as enlarg'd in Fig.I.
b.b.b. Bunches of the Seed, as enlarg'd in Fig.II.
The whole Plant is from 4 to 8 Feet in height.

COLORPLATE 2
The process of indigo production. Illustration from Henry Mouzon, Jr., Map of the Parish of St. Stephen's in Craven County (1775)

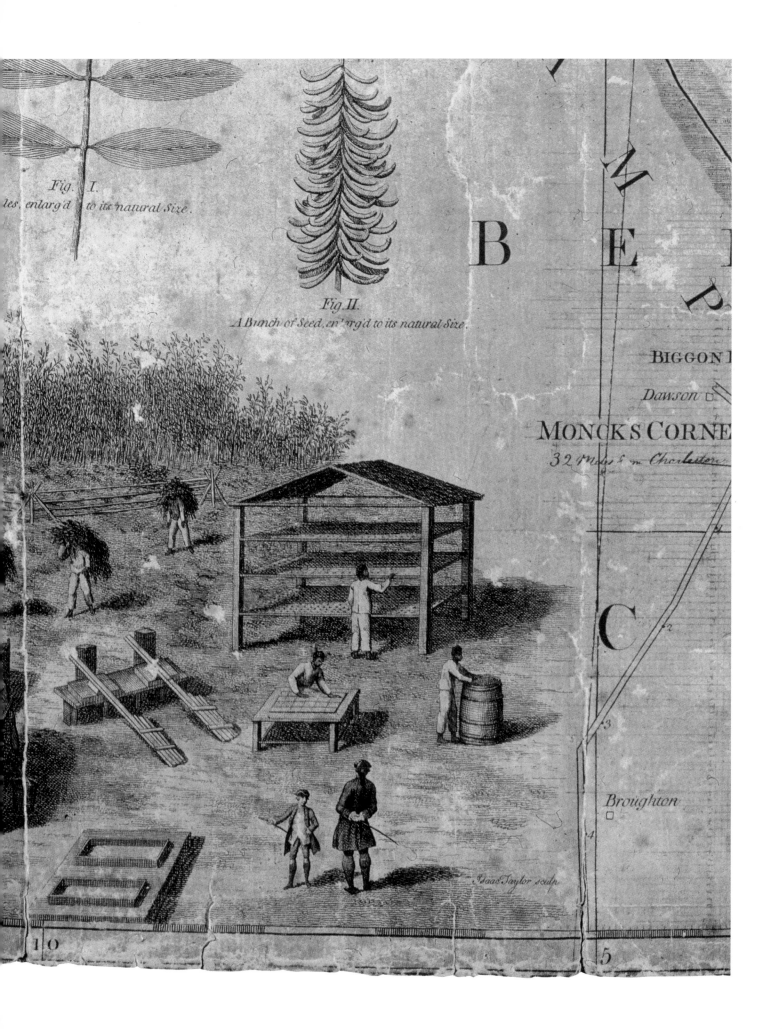

Fig. I.
...les, enlarg'd to its natural Size.

Fig. II.
A Bunch of Seed, en'larg'd to its natural Size.

B E

BIGGON

Dawson □

MONCK'S CORNE

32 Miles to Charleston.

C

Broughton
□

Isaac Taylor sculp.

1 O

5

Colorplate 3
*Rebecca Lukens, the only woman iron manufacturer, is depicted
here holding a purse in one hand and an account book in the other.*

COLORPLATE 4
Hannah Thurston Adams (1809–72) and Mary Agnes Adams (1812–90),
tailors, from Manchester, New Hampshire, holding an account book

✍

COLORPLATE 5
*Demorest's Monthly Magazine (above); three of Madame Demorest's trade cards
(at left and opposite, top and center); packet for Miss C. H. Lippincott's
Flower Seeds (opposite, bottom)*

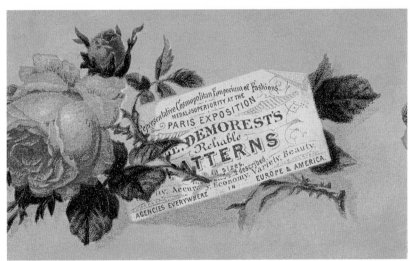

COLORPLATE 6
Lydia E. Pinkham Medicine Company
trade cards (above) and counter card (opposite)

Maggie Lena Walker with neighborhood boys

COLORPLATE 8
"Grapes and Vines" quilt by Marie Webster

COLORPLATE 9(A)

Hearst Castle, San Simeon, California. Julia Morgan, architect

COLORPLATE 9(B)
Asilomar Auditorium, near Monterey, California.
Julia Morgan, architect

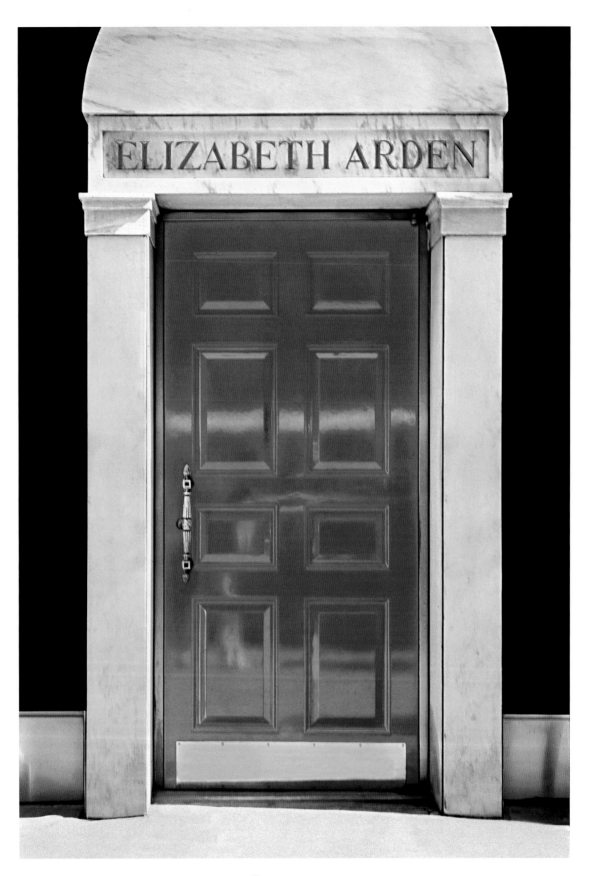

COLORPLATE 10

Elizabeth Arden's signature red door

COLORPLATE 11
Barbie, with creator Ruth Handler
and her husband Elliot, ca. 1961

I dreamed I was a knockout
in my *maidenform* bra

Arabesque*...*new Maidenform bra*...has bias-cut center-of-attraction for *superb*

separation...insert of elastic for *comfort*...floral circular stitching for the most *beautiful* contours!

White in A, B, C cups, just 2.50. Also pre-shaped (light foam lining) 3.59.

COLORPLATE 12
Advertisement from the "I dreamed..."
campaign for Maidenform Company

Rosenthal and Bissett made an ideal team. They shared an appreciation for high standards and an understanding that the key to success was the customer's satisfaction. But they quickly realized that they could not satisfy their customers if their dresses did not fit well. The problem was the boyish, flapper look of the time, which demanded loose-hanging sheaths that looked best on women with flat chests and no hips. Rosenthal watched in dismay as fashion-conscious women tried to reshape their bodies. "It was a very sad story," she recalled. "Nature made woman with a bosom," she explained, "so why fight nature?" [105] Dismissing the dictates of fashion that encouraged women "to look like their brothers," she redesigned the bandagelike undergarment that flattened a woman's chest, making it into a garment having two cups separated with a piece of elastic. She sewed her new design into the dresses at Enid Frocks. [104]

Rosenthal's ingenuity paid off. Women loved the new fit they could get at Enid Frocks, and Rosenthal and Bissett were soon selling the new brassieres separately for one dollar apiece. They named their creation the "Maiden Form Brassiere" to emphasize their rejection of the flat, boyish look of the day. By 1925, just four years after Rosenthal and Bissett went into partnership, the two gave up their dressmaking business to devote themselves exclusively to manufacturing the Maiden Form bra. By 1938 Rosenthal's one-time investment of $4,500 had skyrocketed; the company now had gross earnings of more than $4.5 million dollars. When Bissett left the company because of poor health, Rosenthal and her husband continued to run it on their own.

Ida Rosenthal with her husband, William, the founders of the Maiden Form Brassiere Company

Their marriage was an ideal partnership, both in private and in public. For over fifty years, until William's death in 1958, it thrived on an unconventional allocation of responsibilities, a modern version of the division of labor established by Rosenthal's parents in Russia. William Rosenthal was the creator; Ida Rosenthal took care of business. He put his creativity to work and introduced a number of innovations in brassiere design, including the first nursing bra, the first full-figured bra, and the concept of standard sizes that ultimately became the familiar A, B, C, and D cups. Meanwhile she ran the business, managing sales, finance, and promotions. She had personality and charisma. And though she was a short woman, only four feet eleven inches tall, she was unafraid to take control of a situation by simply commanding her clients to sit down.

Together, the Rosenthals made innovative decisions. In the early years of the business, a seamstress produced about three bras in a day. But unlike women's outerwear, which was subject to the constant demands of changing fashion styles, undergarments, hidden beneath dresses and blouses, were more adaptable to standardized designs. Therefore, to increase output, the Rosenthals adapted production methods used in heavy industry and reorganized bra production so that seamstresses could assemble them from parts. Under a system of division of labor, each seamstress performed a single task—making straps, sewing the backs, stitching the hooks and eyes, and sewing the brassiere together. Though common in heavy industry, this system of mass production was new to the apparel industry.

Creative advertising complemented this mass production. The Rosenthals made sure that Maiden Form bras were marketed everywhere—newspapers, national magazines, radio, the Fifth Avenue bus, and Atlantic City billboards. This aggressive advertising, combined with their innovative bra designs, standard sizes, mass production, and the ideal balance of William's creativity and Ida's business sense, was a formula for success; by the 1930s, the Maiden Form Brassiere Company was the largest manufacturer of bras in the world (colorplate 12).

In the midst of all of this, the Rosenthals raised their children. In the early years of the business, when Beatrice was young, Ida Rosenthal worked at home. She and the other seamstresses worked at their sewing machines in the living room while Beatrice played at their feet. Lewis was older and more independent, but in 1930, while a student at Columbia Law School, he died. The tragedy occurred as Maiden Form was on the brink of national success. In 1938, precisely when Maiden Form's annual gross earnings reached beyond $4.5 million dollars, the Rosenthals memorialized their son by founding Camp Lewis and donating it to the Boy Scouts.

While the tragedy of Lewis's death did not impede the growth of Maiden Form, World War II threatened to do so. Many clothing companies had trouble getting materials such as nylon that the government needed for the war effort. But while other apparel companies slowed down, Rosenthal made Maiden Form indispensable. She convinced the government that the steady delivery of materials to Maiden Form was a vital component of the domestic war effort. In fact, Maiden Form was manufacturing such crucial war items as parachutes and vests for carrier pigeons. But Rosenthal did not stop there: linking patriotism with bra production, she argued that victory for the free world depended on Maiden Form. Here was the full impact of her ingenious business sense. Rosenthal argued that the success of the war effort rested on the shoulders of the thousands of women who flooded the workplace to build the necessities of war—planes, parachutes, ships, and the like. But these new industrial workers could not work effectively when they were tired. The key to avoiding fatigue, she reasoned, was quite simple: an uplift brassiere. Recalling the shortage of fabric during the war, she explained: "We got priority because women workers who wore an uplift were less fatigued than others."[105]

When the war ended women were expected to leave industrial jobs and return to their homes. Precisely at this moment, Maiden Form launched its successful, yet controversial, "Dream" campaign; for twenty-two years the Dream campaign objectified women and emphasized their sexuality while simultaneously addressing their longing for independence and achievement.[106]

Rosenthal continued to run the company after her husband died in 1958. When she died in 1973 at the age of eighty-seven, she left the company in the competent hands of her daughter, Beatrice. But Rosenthal was active to the very end, making international business trips even when she was eighty. She epitomized the independence her Dream campaign promised women, reassuring women through her own example that they could win elections or run their own businesses—as long as they did it in their Maiden-form bras.

No one could deny that women like Ida Rosenthal, Hattie Carnegie, and Sarah Breedlove Walker had amassed grand fortunes by building businesses that catered specifically to women's desire for fashion and beauty. Yet to many their accomplishments were limited because their ventures, directed exclusively at the female consumer, shielded them from competition with men in the mainstream of American business. Reviewing women's entrepreneurial position in 1935, the noted poet Archibald MacLeish observed that there was "no American woman whose business achievement would properly rank with the first or the second or even the third line of male successes." Pointing to Elizabeth Arden, one of the most successful female entrepreneurs of the day, he explained: "Elizabeth Arden is not a potential Henry Ford."[107] To people like MacLeish, women entrepreneurs succeeded because of their natural femininity, not as a result of their business acumen; they created businesses that appealed uniquely to women. It would be up to a different group of women entrepreneurs, those who ventured into male-dominated terrain, to demonstrate that women entrepreneurs could compete as equals with men.

1932 Bonus Army marches on Washington, D.C.
• Radio City Music Hall opens
• Amelia Earhart makes solo trans–Atlantic flight

1933 FDR becomes President
• New Deal begins
• Hitler takes power in Germany
• Oklahoma Dust Bowl

1939 World War II begins
• *Gone with the Wind* opens
• Marian Anderson sings at Lincoln Memorial

1942 Internment of Japanese–Americans begins
• WAAC (Women's Army Auxiliary Corps) established
• Planned Parenthood founded

CHAPTER FOUR

"The cleverest women . . . have entered most of the business fields"

MARION (INDIANA) DAILY CHRONICLE

1890–1960

BREAKING NEW GROUND

If petticoat entrepreneur Emma McChesney represented the successful businesswoman in the fashion and beauty industries, then the fictional Jane Thorndike symbolized the enterprising new woman of the early twentieth century who made it in the mainstream of men's business endeavors. Thorndike was introduced to the public in *Portia Marries*, written by author and lawyer Jeannette Phillips Gibbs in 1926.[1] At the beginning of the story, Thorndike is a young lawyer who has recently opened her own office, hung out her shingle, and is waiting for business to come her way. A lone woman in a male-dominated arena of work, she must overcome the skepticism of clients who are afraid to hire a woman to do a man's job. But she always gets their business, winning them over with her brilliance, no-nonsense approach, and strong work ethic. She builds a thriving business and also

1945 Yalta Conference
• Truman becomes President upon death of FDR
• V–E Day
• United Nations established
• Bombing of Hiroshima and Nagasaki

1947 Truman Doctrine
• Marshall Plan
• Jackie Robinson joins Brooklyn Dodgers
• Hollywood blacklist

1951 First *I Love Lucy* episode airs on television

1955 Rosa Parks starts Montgomery Bus Boycott
• AFL–CIO merger

marries a man who is completely supportive of her work, even when she becomes a mother. The book closes with Thorndike busy in her office and her eighteen-year-old son planning to enter his mother's business.

The character of Jane Thorndike, enterprising lawyer, embodied women's optimistic belief during the Progressive Era of the early twentieth century that they could succeed as equals with men in any type of work. Inspired by their faith in meritocracy, women flooded the public sphere and entered arenas once the province of men.[2] Young women went to college, clubwomen got involved in political and social reform, others entered the professions as doctors and lawyers. African American women opened schools, launched an antilynching crusade, and started businesses beyond the beauty market. Meanwhile, women received over five thousand patents for inventions from dress-making supplies to those in such traditionally male categories as hotel equipment and scientific instruments.[3] In 1920 the Nineteenth Amendment was passed, effectively nullifying many of women's legal disabilities. In their new status as equal citizens with men, women could vote, sit on juries, and own property, regardless of whether or not they were married. Jobs opened for women during men's absence in World War I. While the economic depression of the 1930s forced women into the workplace simply to survive, World War II expanded women's opportunities in the public sphere further than ever before.

In this era of gender equality and expanding opportunities for women, many enter-prising women directed their sights beyond the female-dominated industries of beauty and fashion and ventured into arenas of business dominated by men. As they built their businesses, they capitalized on changing moods in the nation, from the early-twentieth-century concern about unfettered urban industrial expansion, then World War II, and finally the retreat to home and family that characterized the 1950s. Julia Morgan estab-lished a thriving architectural firm in the midst of the Arts and Crafts Movement; in an era of race pride Maggie Lena Walker founded a bank; Olive Beech manufactured military planes during World War II and, after the war, Jennie Grossinger's family getaway grew into a large resort that catered to a growing Jewish middle class, while Ruth Handler manufactured toys for a new juvenile market.

Entrepreneurs like Morgan, Walker, and Beech proved that women had the assertive and acquisitive qualities needed to compete with men in the mainstream of American business. At the same time, others, including Grossinger and Handler, took a different tack. They incorporated the values of home and family into their enterprises. In doing so, they demonstrated once again women's important contributions as producers to the expanding consumer economy. They also revealed the strong influence that women's values exercised outside the traditionally feminine industries.

(page 108)

Olive Ann Beech, CEO of Beech Aircraft Corporation, woman in a man's world, 1964

Yet, in the midst of this progress, enterprising businesswomen continued to encounter obstacles. The very term "businesswoman" was itself misleading. In this new century of supposed equality between the sexes, businesswoman did not convey the female equivalent of the male entrepreneur or corporate executive. Instead, it referred to

Turning Pots—Reaping Profit
Maria Martinez

Maria Martinez (1887(?)–1980), the renowned potter, turned the traditional art of Native American pottery into a profitable enterprise. As a young girl, Martinez learned the craft of pottery making from her aunt. In an era when inexpensive Spanish and Anglo tableware had begun to replace traditional pottery, Martinez continued to make pots by hand, earning a reputation for producing the thinnest, roundest, and most beautiful pots on the San Ildefonso Pueblo, twenty-three miles north of Santa Fe, New Mexico, where she was born.

Martinez' reputation spread beyond pueblo boundaries when the director of the Museum of New Mexico asked her to reproduce the ancient matte-and-shiny, black pottery that had been discovered in an archaeological excavation near San Ildefonso. With her husband, Julian, Martinez developed a technique that perfectly re-created the stark, black-on-black designs that would become the signature of her handmade pots. They were so beautiful and unique that she was invited to display examples at various expositions, including the Chicago World's Fair in 1934.

While profit was not the original motive for Martinez' devotion to pottery, she recognized that the beauty and uniqueness of her work attracted the attention of tourists and collectors and, in turn, she began to wax entrepre-

neurial. At first she sold her pots for the modest price of one dollar; as her son began to market her work, prices rose as high as twenty dollars. But the notion that, by the dawn of the twenty-first century, traditional Native American pottery would become so difficult to find that collectors would willingly pay thousands of dollars for her beautiful handmade pots would have been unthinkable to Maria Martinez. ✐

the growing numbers of women who worked in sex-segregated office positions as stenographers, typists, or clerks.[4] One need look no further than the National Federation of Business and Professional Women's Clubs, where most of the so-called business-women were typists, stenographers, personnel managers, or other office workers. One successful entrepreneur, Mary Foote Seymour, capitalized on this phenomenon, establishing schools, an employment bureau, and the *Business Woman's Journal*, all dedicated to training and placing businesswomen in the expanding field of office work. But as women found new opportunities for work in clerical and office positions, office work emerged as an arena of women's work within the male business world, perpetuating the nineteenth-century pattern of separate spheres for men and women.[5]

Ambitious female entrepreneurs, particularly those with aspirations for business in the mainstream of American enterprise, still found it harder to launch businesses than men. Women continued to have little access to capital and credit, and when they did begin a business, they went bankrupt more often than men and rarely had a second chance. Moreover, women confronted new institutional obstacles. In the first decade of the twentieth century, formal business school education became available at the nation's most elite universities. Most were closed to women, creating a new barrier for women seeking training in business and management. Women tried to keep up. The exclusion of women from the business school at Harvard University led to the founding of the Harvard-Radcliffe Program in Business Administration in 1937. It offered women a valuable one-year program in personnel training. But its female graduates never attained the level of education, training, or prestige of their male counterparts at the Harvard Business School. At the same time, women encountered another impenetrable institution—the large corporations and holding companies that emerged in the last decade of the nineteenth century and set the standard for modern business enterprise in the twentieth century.[6] While women's businesses, indeed most American businesses, continued to be family owned and family run, corporations took business outside the institution of the family, where women could establish a place, and placed it in the hands of stockholders. By selling stock to investors, entrepreneurs could accumulate vast sums of money. With substantial amounts of capital, corporations could invest in major projects and, for the first time in American history, integrate all the processes involved in mass production and mass distribution in a single firm. By the 1910s the corporation had emerged as the modern and dominant form of business enterprise. Corporations took over major industries including railroads, steel, oil, and even food production and became multi-million-dollar enterprises.[7]

As corporations emerged as the most powerful form of modern business enterprise, the industrialists who built them became symbols of the American dream of success. Many began with modest means and went on to make their fortunes as the creators of the nation's first corporations. Industrialists like Andrew Carnegie took their places in the public eye as examples of the popular notion of self-made men. At a time of economic depression, labor unrest, and increasing poverty, they embodied the popular belief in Social Darwinism; their wealth revealed their fitness to rule, while poverty demonstrated one's weakness and inferiority.[8]

Many people argued that women were unfit to compete with men in the harsh world of business. Reinterpreting Victorian ideas about womanhood for a modern age, they used Darwin's theory of the survival of the fittest to argue that women's natural place was in the home as wives and mothers. It was a powerful argument that conflicted with the assertion of women's equality with men and continued to impede women's progress in business; indeed, in public activity in general. The protective labor legislation of the era institutionalized this belief in women's inferiority. Denying women the right to work long hours, at night, and at certain jobs, these laws sought to preserve women's health and strength for domestic concerns. While these laws protected women from some of the harsher realities of the workplace, they also denied women their right to compete in the workplace as equals with men.

It was a complicated time for women, particularly those with ventures in the mainstream of American business. The growing belief in gender equality and the broadening of women's place in the public sphere opened the way for entrepreneurs such as Julia Morgan and Maggie Walker to penetrate traditionally male strongholds of business. However, when measured against the heights of business success attained by male industrialists, even the most successful women entrepreneurs fell short. Simply put, while the rags–to–riches story of Andrew Carnegie earned him the mythological status of "self-made man," the most successful women entrepreneurs–those who rose from poverty to the very pinnacle of fame and fortune–failed to acquire such legendary acclaim.[9]

Still, there was no denying that the twentieth century had launched a new era of opportunity and progress for women entrepreneurs eager to venture into male-dominated arenas of business. Bolstered by the belief in equality and meritocracy, they expanded beyond the fashion and beauty industries and made their way into the mainstream of business enterprise. Even small-town newspapers observed the national trend. "Of recent years the smartest and cleverest women have taken up various kinds of business, have entered most of the business fields and are showing their hitherto latent possibilities in the world from which they were so long barred by custom."[10] From the dawn of the twentieth century through two world wars and waves of economic change, women moved into male-dominated businesses, leaving a feminine imprint and demonstrating new opportunities and obstacles for the enterprising woman.

In the era when enterprising women in the beauty and fashion industries marketed style and glamour, Marie Webster (1859–1956) looked back to a simpler time and built a business on American women's long-held tradition of quilt making. At a time when female entrepreneurs relied on technology and mass production, Marie Webster's business thrived on a deliberate return to the individually handcrafted mode of production in pre-industrial America. Designing her quilts during the Arts and Crafts Movement, which reflected the nation's concern over the loss of nature, Webster built a business that reminded the American family about the simplicity of the past. Finally, Webster proved that women did not always dabble in art as amateurs, as many believed; she moved her art into the marketplace, establishing that she was as serious, productive, and commercially motivated as any man.[11] While her quilts were traditional, her marketing was contemporary; she skillfully promoted her business through department stores, mail-order catalogues, and magazines.

Born on the eve of the Civil War in Wabash, Indiana, Marie Daugherty grew up in a typical middle–class household; her father was a successful businessman and her mother was a skilled needlewoman.[12] As a young girl, she received her basic education at the local public school and learned to sew from her mother. When she was twenty-five she married George Webster, Jr., a businessman like her father, and moved to his hometown of Marion, Indiana, where they had a son. For a quarter of a century she lived a life of domesticity, social activities, and club work like that of many white, middle-class women of her day. But then at the age of fifty, Webster made a quilt that changed her life: this middle-aged wife and mother became an entrepreneur who turned the longtime craft of quilt making into a profitable business.

Webster's timing was perfect. As the nation entered the twentieth century, many viewed the mass production of the era with alarm and yearned for the craftsmanship of the past. The Arts and Crafts Movement, with its emphasis on simple design and natural materials, embodied this nostalgia for a simpler time, untainted by the blight of industrialization. And quilts, once a symbol of the old-fashioned, were making a comeback. In the midst of this rediscovery of handicrafts, Webster sent her quilt off to Edward Bok, the editor of the *Ladies Home Journal*, the most popular woman's magazine of the day. Bok knew simple, good design when he saw it. He was also an astute businessman who was well aware of the growing market for handmade products. He invited Webster to design several quilts for a special issue of the *Journal*. Her quilts, which appeared in the *Journal* in January 1911, were such a success that she faced a sudden and overwhelming demand from *Journal* readers for her quilt patterns. The solution, colored tissue paper patterns, hearkened back a half-century to paper pattern entrepreneur Ellen Demorest, who popularized tissue paper patterns in the 1860s. Webster sold her paper quilt patterns for fifty cents each and launched a budding quilt paper pattern business.

Webster became an overnight entrepreneur and established companies began to capitalize on the growing demand for her quilts. Marshall Field's, Chicago's fashionable department store, displayed them; Bok asked her to design a series of new quilts for the *Journal*; and in 1912 Bok's good friend, Frank Doubleday, founder of Doubleday, Page and Company, invited Webster to write a history of quilts. Her book, *Quilts: Their Story and How to Make Them*, published in 1915, was an instant success. Reviews in newspapers including the *New York Times*, the *Christian Science Monitor*, and the *Chicago Tribune* gave it national exposure and turned Webster into the authority on the history of quilts. Meanwhile, her pastel colors and flowered patterns captured the hearts of the modern consumer tired of the dark colors and geometric shapes of colonial quilts. Capitalizing on the Arts and Crafts Movement, Webster emerged as a leader in quilt design for the twentieth century.

The public could not get enough of the fresh new look of Webster's quilts (colorplate 8). By 1919 she had received over six thousand letters from admirers, mostly women, clamoring for her patterns.[13] Catapulted to the forefront of the national quilt craze, Webster seized the opportunity to turn the popular infatuation with her quilts into a profitable business. For years, with the help of her son and sister, she had produced and sold tissue paper patterns of her quilts. But the explosion of public demand for her quilts inspired her to expand her enterprise. With two friends she created the Practical Patchwork Company in 1921.

To attract a broad market, she expanded her product line beyond paper patterns to include boxed cloth kits, basted quilt tops, and for one hundred dollars, fully completed quilts of any of her designs. She sold her products through mail-order catalogues and retail stores. In addition to the enormous publicity she received in the *Ladies Home Journal* and from her book, she advertised in popular middle-class magazines like *House Beautiful*. But behind the expanded product line and aggressive marketing, the Practical Patchwork Company was really a simple, home-based enterprise. Most of the work occurred in a spare room in Webster's home. Women stitched quilt tops that were sent off to be quilted by women in states throughout the Midwest. Still, Webster brought capitalism to quilt making, turning the quilting bee of colonial America into a cottage industry for the modern age. Moreover, as she moved quilt production into the modern marketplace, she capitalized on her reputation as an expert in the art of quilt design and established herself as a professional quilt maker, the first known to the public by name.

Webster's success attracted competitors who sought to profit from her unique designs. Magazines published her patterns without acknowledging her. Quilt companies sold her designs under different names. And the Stearns and Foster bed company, which created its Mountain Mist label specifically to sell quilt patterns and batting, adopted Webster's Dogwood pattern as its own and marketed it simply as "#29 Dogwood by Mountain Mist/Stearns and Foster." [14]

Yet, nothing seemed to stop Webster. With the success of Practical Patchwork, Doubleday reissued her book in 1926 and again in 1928. In 1929 Webster published it herself, this time with a full-page ad for her patterns on the back. She continued to run her business until the early 1940s. But in the 1930s events in her personal life foreshadowed a change. Her husband died in 1938, and in 1942, when her son moved to Princeton, New Jersey, Webster and her sister followed, leaving Practical Patchwork in the hands of a partner who ran it for a few more years. Though Webster was unquestionably a successful entrepreneur, she was at heart a wife and mother who thrived on a business she built and ran within the context of her family circle.

Webster died in 1956 at the age of ninety-seven, leaving an indelible mark on the tradition of American quilt making. Her pastel floral designs introduced a new aesthetic; her book established a new field of scholarly inquiry; her reputation as an expert in the art of quilt design established a new category, the professional quilt designer. Finally, through her Practical Patchwork Company, she turned patches into profits and helped transform the tradition of American quilt making from craft into commercial enterprise.

℘ While Maria Webster brought an Arts and Crafts perspective to the traditional women's craft of needlework, Julia Morgan (1872–1957) applied Arts and Crafts design to the male-dominated arena of architecture. Morgan preferred to construct rather than to care for a home. A pioneer in a field monopolized by men, she built a thriving architectural firm in which she skillfully combined her background in engineering and classical architecture, her appreciation for the aesthetics of nature and the California terrain, and her sensitivity to women's unique needs, to leave a special mark on the American landscape. The designer of over seven hundred buildings, large and small, private and public, Morgan is best remembered as the architect of the Hearst Castle in San Simeon, California, her largest and most famous achievement.

Julia Morgan grew up in Oakland, California. Her father, a New Englander from Litchfield, Connecticut, dabbled in various business schemes, while her mother, the daughter of a wealthy New York cotton broker, raised her and her four siblings.[15] Like other young girls of her privileged class, Morgan grew up among domestic servants, took music and dancing lessons, and was expected to marry after high school.

But Morgan deviated from the traditional path: her aspirations did not include marriage. Early signs of her architectural talent blossomed in high school, where she excelled in the typically male subjects of physics and advanced math. When she graduated from high school in 1890, eighteen-year-old Morgan insisted on pursuing architecture, and with the encouragement of her mother and the wary acquiescence of her father, she became the first woman to enroll in the College of Engineering at the University of California at Berkeley. There she met the noted architect Bernard Maybeck, who encouraged her to continue her studies at the internationally acclaimed Ecole des Beaux-Arts in Paris. In 1898 Morgan became the first woman to enter the Architectural Section of the prestigious school, where she developed a deep appreciation for classic beauty and symmetry.

Julia Morgan, architect and professional "new" woman

Graduating in 1902, Morgan returned to California to become the first licensed woman architect in the state. The national mood of optimism and expansion at the turn of the century, the concern with urban planning, and the growing popularity of the Arts and Crafts Movement made it an ideal time for a talented young architect. It was not unusual for women to embrace the Arts and Crafts Movement—Maria Webster developed a successful business as a quilt designer, and Mary Chase Perry Stratton established Pewabic Pottery in Detroit, where her unique iridescent glaze became a signature of her Arts and Crafts ceramics. But Morgan set out to bring the Arts and Crafts Movement's emphasis on nature, utility, and harmony to the field of architecture. The timing was right for an ambitious woman like Morgan. She joined thousands of women who entered medicine, law, and other male-dominated professions in the early twentieth century. And she benefited as well from the active community of ambitious, wealthy, and socially connected women who were forging public lives as reformers and social activists. Indeed, Morgan's success as an architect was intricately tied to the growing network of influential women in early-twentieth-century America.

Morgan's earliest jobs came from former college classmates who hired her to design their homes. They were well rewarded for their choice. Morgan's designs combined the classicism of the Beaux–Arts school with the emphasis on nature in the Arts and Crafts Movement. From the exterior her buildings appear classical, graceful, even delicate, while they are firmly supported in reinforced concrete, a building material she had learned about in Paris but which architects rarely used in the United States. Ever faithful to the indigenous habitat of her native northern California, she used local woods and stone to design houses in tune with their natural environment. Her priority was a home's interior, always seeking to design open spaces that took advantage of natural light. Her emphasis on the importance of nature to well-being attracted the attention of women doctors, several of whom hired her to design their homes and offices. And her personal approach–home visits where she sat on the floor with the children–appealed to her clients with families.

Gradually, Morgan expanded her business from private homes to public buildings. In doing so, she contributed to and benefited from the widespread phenomenon of women's "institution building" that was emerging in the vibrant women's movement of the day.[16] With women around the country founding their own clubs and organizations, Morgan was literally in the business of building these institutions. Wealthy women hired her to design clubhouses, retirement centers, settlement houses, and hospitals. In 1904, the women of Mill's College, the only secular women's college in the West, commissioned her to design the school's bell tower. Morgan built a seventy-two-foot structure that combined the beauty of smooth gray walls ascending skyward with the strength of reinforced concrete, her favorite building material. Fortified by this new building material, the bell tower remained unharmed when the San Francisco earthquake of 1906 destroyed most of the buildings in the city. The earthquake brought Morgan more business, including the restoration of the elegant Fairmont Hotel.

Arts and Crafts ceramist Mary Chase Perry Stratton (1867–1961)

Meanwhile, Morgan continued to create spaces that met women's need for female community. She designed numerous buildings for the Young Woman's Christian Association throughout California as well as in Salt Lake City and Honolulu. Her best known YWCA building was Asilomar, the multibuilding conference center she built in the 1910s and 1920s near Monterey, California (colorplate 9B). This large institutional complex, which included an administration building, a chapel, a dining hall, a kitchen, a one-thousand-seat auditorium, athletic facilities, and residential lodges, brought the beauty of the Arts and Crafts style to women's institution-building. Declared a California state monument in 1958, it remained a popular conference center throughout the twentieth century.

Morgan never forgot the needs of the single, working-class women whom the YWCA sought to help. She designed buildings for them that provided such homelike comforts as private kitchenettes and dining areas. Her commitment to creating residences that combined beauty with practicality revealed her respect for the needs of working-class women. However, her careful attention met some opposition: "But these are minimum wage girls," protested some women on the YWCA board, "why spoil them?" Morgan responded simply and directly: "That's just the reason."[17]

As a businesswoman, Morgan combined the same professionalism and special commitment to women that she infused into her designs. The sign on her office door, "Julia Morgan, Architect," announced to all who approached that here was a solo practitioner, a professional woman, making it on her own. And behind the door, Morgan had complete control of her firm. Everyone was on a first-name basis except Morgan. She maintained the highest professional standards and demanded the same from everyone who worked with her. "You worked when you were in Julia Morgan's office," recalled one woman associate. "You worked from 8 to 5 and you didn't stop and you didn't take time off." But Morgan's associates appreciated her demanding standards. "I think anybody that had been trained at Julia Morgan's office was welcome at any other office because probably nobody else would have taken the time to give such a thorough training."[18] Morgan's high standards paid off; she built a thriving architectural firm that demonstrated to even the most skeptical observer that a woman could make it in the male-dominated field. "Not only was she one of the most talented of West Coast architects," recalled a male colleague, "she was also far more accomplished in the area of building technology than any of the men I have known."[19]

Morgan's success was the product of her standards of excellence combined with her unique management style and her deep loyalty to women. She paid high salaries, and she shared profits with her associates before it was a common practice in architectural firms. Unmarried, she treated everyone in her firm like members of her family. Without children of her own, she took a special interest in the children of her associates, giving them gifts and even paying for college tuition or medical expenses when necessary. Within her surrogate family, Morgan never forgot her allegiance to women. She made a special effort to hire women artists and drafters and to train women architects. With women comprising nearly half of her office staff, Morgan's architectural firm was certainly unique for its day.

Skillfully and without fanfare, Morgan marketed herself as an architect who balanced strict professional standards with a special commitment to women. As she designed buildings for Mills College, the YWCA, and influential clubwomen, she gradually emerged as the architect for women in the public sphere. Nothing more clearly reveals the value of Morgan's connection to a women's network than the commission she received in 1919 to build a castle and guest houses for William Randolph Hearst in San Simeon, California. For years, Hearst's mother, Phoebe, had championed Morgan's career. Phoebe Hearst commissioned Morgan to design the outdoor and indoor swimming pools for the family's two-thousand-acre estate, affectionately known as "the Hacienda," outside Berkeley, California. Phoebe Hearst also used her influence as a

Hearst Castle. Photograph
by Victoria Garigliano
(detail of colorplate 9A)

leader in the women's club movement to steer a number of significant projects, particularly YWCA buildings, to Morgan. The relationship between Morgan and Phoebe Hearst
did not go unnoticed by William Hearst. When his mother died in 1919 he turned to
Morgan to design a memorial to her. The project launched a relationship between Morgan and Hearst that lasted the rest of her life and ultimately engaged Morgan in almost a
third of her life's work, including newspaper facilities for the Hearst publishing empire
and palatial buildings for private family retreats.

But it was the Hearst Castle, William Hearst's memorial to his mother, that became
Julia Morgan's most famous creation (colorplate 9A). It was a vast undertaking that con-
sumed her for over twenty years. While she continued her practice in San Francisco, she
spent her weekends at San Simeon where she oversaw an array of highly skilled male
artisans, including stonecutters, woodcarvers, ironworkers, furniture makers, and tile

designers. It was an unusual position for a woman, but not for Morgan. As one of her associates so aptly explained, "Wherever she was, she was boss."[20]

The Hearst Castle at San Simeon was a truly magnificent accomplishment. The central palace rises in twin towers that combine the strength of reinforced concrete with the beauty of its brilliant white stone exterior. Among its many grand rooms are a library, a dining room to serve thirty people, and a private film theater. By 1935 Morgan had designed an estate that includes fifty-eight bedrooms, fifty-nine bathrooms, eighteen sitting rooms, two kitchens, and two libraries. Morgan also designed dazzling indoor and outdoor swimming pools. Built into the side of a steep hill and jutting out beyond the supporting ground, the outdoor pool was a remarkable architectural feat that Morgan accomplished through her use of reinforced concrete.

While the Hearst Castle was a breathtaking architectural project, it was disappointing as a business venture. Originally, Morgan had contracted to receive a 6 percent commission on the cost of the project. But as the costs skyrocketed, Hearst's funds ran out. After twenty-five years of work and over 550 visits, Morgan received only $70,755, a small payment for what had become a nearly $8 million project.[21]

Nevertheless, Morgan had established herself as a remarkably successful architect. While other architects suffered during the economic depression of the 1930s, Morgan's business thrived. It was not until she faced the shortage of labor and material during World War II that she finally slowed down. She retired in 1946 and died in 1957, at the age of eighty-five, after a series of small strokes.

Julia Morgan was a pioneer woman in a traditionally male field. While the Hearst Castle was her most prestigious accomplishment, and catapulted her work into the category of greatness, she was already established as a master of design, from the simplest to the grandest of projects. She was also a remarkably successful entrepreneur who turned her skill in architecture into a thriving business. Although she had no family of her own, she wasn't worried about what would come after her. "[My] work will be my legacy," she said.[22]

⟡ The hospitality industry, though dominated by men, such as Henry Hilton, seemed an appropriate arena for businesswomen, even if it did not cater to women directly, as the beauty and fashion industries did. After all, everyone agreed that women were the caretakers of the home, and a hotel was simply a home-away-from-home. Domesticity demanded a combination of characteristics ranging from organizational skills, efficiency, and attention to detail, to warmth, selflessness, and the ability to get along with others. These were precisely the qualities an enterprising woman needed to run a boardinghouse, a hotel, or a resort.

As entrepreneurs in the hospitality industry, Isabella Greenway and Jennie Grossinger had certain qualities in common. Both combined warmth, charm, and love of home with creative business skills to build nationally renowned resorts. But that is where the similarities ended. Greenway founded the Arizona Inn, the first luxury hotel in Tucson, Arizona; Grossinger built one of the first resorts that catered to Jewish families–Grossinger's, in the Catskill Mountains of New York. And while Isabella Greenway's roots were firmly planted in American soil, Jennie Grossinger was a poor Jewish immigrant from Austria.

Isabella Greenway (1886–1953) was born Isabella Selmes in Boone County, Kentucky. Her mother was the daughter of a Minnesota pioneer and jurist; her father was a descendent from the settlers of the Massachusetts Bay Colony.[25] As a young girl, Isabella Selmes lived a life of privilege in the West. She divided her time between her mother's family farm in Kentucky, where she learned the skills of farming, and her father's ranch in the Dakota Territory, where she became acquainted with her neighbor on a nearby ranch, the future President Theodore Roosevelt. When she was nine, the patterns of Selmes's life changed abruptly when her father suddenly died. She and her mother left their home on the Dakota ranch and moved to St. Paul, Minnesota, to be near her paternal grandfather. Six years later they made a more drastic change, moving to New York City. At the age of fifteen the young Selmes found herself in the nation's largest city, where immigrants, African Americans, rich, and poor interacted in ways unheard of on her father's ranch or her mother's farm. Selmes moved in an elite social circle: she attended the Spence School and then Miss Chapin's School, two of the most exclusive private schools for girls in the city; she was a debutante, and her social connections included author Edith Wharton and Eleanor Roosevelt.

Isabella Greenway, 1933

In 1904 Selmes and Eleanor Roosevelt began a friendly correspondence that continued for the rest of their lives. Over the years they wrote numerous letters, sharing their most intimate hopes and fears, celebrating each other's happy moments, and supporting each other in times of sickness and death. In 1905 Selmes was a bridesmaid in the wedding of Eleanor and Franklin Roosevelt. A few months later Eleanor Roosevelt rejoiced when nineteen-year-old Selmes married. It was a suitable match for a young woman of Selmes's social class. Robert Munro Ferguson was a thirty-seven-year-old man from a Scottish landowning family, a close family friend of the Roosevelt's, and a Rough Rider in Cuba with Teddy Roosevelt.

Isabella Selmes Ferguson settled into her life as a young wife in New York City. She had two children in the first two years of marriage. During this time she completely renovated her city home, unknowingly beginning her building career. Unfortunately, the happiness of these early years of her marriage was shattered when Robert was diagnosed with tuberculosis. Searching for a healthier climate, the family left New York City and settled briefly in the Adirondack Mountains. But when Robert's health did not improve, his doctor urged him to move to the Southwest. A friend, fellow Rough Rider

John C. Greenway, advised them to settle in the southwestern part of the New Mexican Territory. It was a suggestion that would ultimately lead Isabella Ferguson to her life's work.

Isabella, her two young children, and her long-time nanny accompanied her husband west. For several years, they lived in tents in relative isolation. It was a lonely period for the young wife and mother. With no school nearby, she took on the responsibility of teaching her children, and with neighbors hundreds of miles away, the Fergusons were delighted when their friend John Greenway drove two hundred miles to visit. "One grows to consider anyone within two or three hundred miles as neighbors," she recalled.[24] In 1921 the family moved again, this time to Santa Barbara, California, where the summer climate was milder. Isabella kept herself busy caring for her husband, teaching her children, and building and furnishing yet another house. But nothing could cure Robert; he died in the fall of 1922.

Isabella was not alone for long; John Greenway had fallen in love with her during his visits to his ailing friend in New Mexico. In November 1923, a year after her husband's death, the young widow married her deceased husband's close friend and joyfully embarked on her new life as Isabella Greenway. "I've basked in a happiness that I find hard to believe," she wrote to Eleanor Roosevelt. The new couple settled down in Arizona to a traditional marriage. John oversaw his mining operation while Isabella happily built a new home and had another baby. "[T]he very world seems turned to magic," she rejoiced to Eleanor.[25]

Unfortunately, Greenway's happiness was short-lived. In anticipation of a trip to Africa, her husband had agreed to his doctor's recommendation that he undergo gallbladder surgery. The preventative measure seemed reasonable given the lack of reliable medical care in Africa. Tragically, he died a week after the operation, and Greenway was once again a widow. She continued to raise her children, educating them herself at home. But she branched out in new directions as well. She immersed herself in the affairs of World War I veterans, one of John's projects. And with women recently enfranchised, she turned her attention to politics. She worked with Eleanor Roosevelt on New York governor Al Smith's presidential campaign in 1928, served as Democratic national committeewoman for Arizona from 1928 to 1932, seconded the nomination of Franklin Roosevelt at the Democratic National Convention in 1932, and in 1933 was elected Arizona's first congresswoman, serving until 1937 as the state's sole member of the House of Representatives.

Greenway also embarked on a number of entrepreneurial projects. She bought and operated a cattle ranch in Arizona, a project she and her first husband had planned together, and from 1929 to 1934 she owned Gilpin Airlines, a regional company that serviced the states of California, Arizona, and New Mexico.

It was during this period of her life that Greenway launched her most successful entrepreneurial venture, the Arizona Inn. Ironically, she never fit the model of a typical entrepreneur–her goal was neither profit nor individual gain. Instead, the idea behind the Arizona Inn sprang from Greenway's deep commitment to the welfare of others. The inn had its origins in a furniture factory, the Arizona Hut, which Greenway opened in 1937 to employ disabled veterans of World War I. The Hut was a project of the heart that combined Greenway's commitment to disabled servicemen, her lifelong passion for building projects, and her budding interest in entrepreneurial pursuits. It won quick recognition nationwide. Newspapers, among them the *New York Times*, publicized the furniture made by disabled veterans and their families, while department stores, including Marshall Field's in Chicago and Abercrombie & Fitch and Bonwit Teller in New York, sold the furniture. Greenway incorporated the business in 1929, but it never recovered from the stock market crash a few months later. Motivated by principles rather than by profit, she tried to keep the project alive by investing her own money and ultimately lost over twenty thousand dollars.

With a large surplus of furniture on her hands, Greenway came up with an ingenious solution–the Arizona Inn. Even in the midst of the Depression, the timing was right. In the first three decades of the twentieth century, Tucson had enjoyed a period of gradual growth, from a population of just over 7,500 residents in 1900 to 32,500 in 1930. By 1929 the city had at least two major downtown hotels, one resort, and a total of 1,342 rooms.[26] In this era of growth in Tucson's hospitality industry, Greenway carved out a special niche–an intimate, luxurious hotel.

Breaking the conventional rules of entrepreneurship, Greenway put the comfort of her guests and the welfare of her employees before considerations of cost and profit. She oversaw every detail of the building of her hotel, from the precise placement of the beds to maximize the best views, to the location of awnings for the pool and porches to minimize the sun's glare, to the construction of closets to accommodate her guests' steamer trunks. Greenway decorated in an eclectic but elegant style, placing the tables, chairs, and beds that were built at the Hut alongside her personal antiques, items from her African safari, and her nineteenth–century Audubon prints. She surrounded her guests with luxury. They ate off Irish linen tablemats, drank coffee poured from silver coffee pots, and penned letters at antique writing desks. Along with this unbounded luxury, Greenway offered her guests privacy and informality.

While Greenway labored tirelessly to meet the high standards of her wealthy clientele, she never forgot the welfare of her employees. Again, profit took a back seat, this time to fairness. In one case, rather than fire a worker when she learned that he had been in prison, she gave him another chance. Her decision paid off. Not only did he give Greenway important advice on hotel security, he married one of the chambermaids and became a member of her surrogate family of loyal employees. In another incident, when her architect proudly announced cost cuts on a building project, Greenway responded sharply that savings at the expense of the crew's welfare was unacceptable and that she would fire anyone responsible for paying substandard wages. Greenway expected her employees to behave with the same respect she gave them. When they complained about eating with an African American employee, Greenway demonstrated by her own example that their behavior was unacceptable to her. Placing herself next to the African American at the employee lunch table, she regaled them all with tales of her friendships with African Americans from her childhood in Kentucky. The message was clear; Greenway expected her employees to display the same fair-mindedness to each other that she extended to them.[27]

Greenway seemed to have found the formula for success, namely a blend of luxury, informality, and discretion combined with a passion for the welfare of others. The Arizona Inn, a luxurious getaway for the wealthy, inspired by the needs of wounded soldiers, became an immediate success. Guests flocked there with their maids, chauffeurs, and steamer trunks. Such celebrities as Clark Gable, Gary Cooper, John D. Rockefeller, and her long-time friend Eleanor Roosevelt came for a quiet but sumptuous rest. Even Greenway marveled at its instant popularity. "I cannot believe that I built an institution . . . to house furniture made by disabled ex-servicemen, and that it has become so popular that I cannot get my own beloved Aunt and Uncle in on short notice," she wrote in 1932, barely a year after she opened the inn.[28]

Greenway had a knack for innkeeping. Even as a congresswoman she oversaw the inn, turning it into one of the major luxury establishments in the West. In 1939 she married Harry O. King, an industrialist who worked in Roosevelt's National Recovery Administration. Though her third marriage forced her to divide her time between Washington, D.C., and Tucson, she remained the heart and sole of the Arizona Inn. Greenway died on December 18, 1953, on the twenty-third anniversary of its opening. By then, the Arizona Inn had become a national institution. Her youngest son, John, took it over, and continued its tradition as a gracious hideaway in the West. Listed on the National Register of Historic Places and ranked by Zagat as one of the best one hundred hotels in the country, the Arizona Inn remains today a testament to Greenway's unique version of entrepreneurship.

᪥ Jennie Grossinger (1892–1972), "the gentle Jewish mother" of the hospitality industry, combined the qualities of homemaker and entrepreneur and turned a modest boardinghouse into the family-run resort known as Grossinger's in the Catskill Mountains of New York.[29] In an era of anti-Semitism, when Jews were not welcome at luxury or even middle-class resorts, Grossinger provided a hotel where Jews could celebrate their religious and cultural identity. And in the years after World War II, when assimilation into the American "melting pot" seemed the route to success, she turned Grossinger's into a model of diversity; Catholic and Protestant religious figures, celebrities, politicians, African African leaders, even European royalty all flocked there, along with thousands of middle-class non-Jewish vacationers. In Grossinger's eyes, her resort symbolized the ideal of democracy. Moreover, no one could deny that Grossinger's vision of democracy, a unique blend of Jewish culture and diversity, was good business. She transformed Grossinger's into a seven-million-dollar-a-year business, the major resort complex in the Catskills, and one of the largest resort complexes in the country, if not in the world.

Jennie Grossinger's childhood was far from the opulence and luxury of the Grossinger's family resort. She was born in Austria, where her family lived very modestly.[30] When she was five, her father, an estate overseer, immigrated to New York in the hope of building a more secure life for his family. He settled in the Lower East Side, where he worked as a coat presser. Three years later he had saved enough money to bring his wife, eight-year-old Jennie, and her younger sister to New York in 1900. But the family was together only briefly. When her mother gave birth to a son who was deaf and mute, she returned with him to Europe for medical care, taking her younger daughter with her. For almost four years, until her mother and siblings returned, Jennie remained alone with her father. Determined to help him repay his debts, she dropped out of school and found a job sewing buttonholes in a local sweatshop. Although she lived in the same city at the same time as Isabella Selmes Greenway, their lives were radically different. Grossinger never came near the private schools or elite social gatherings so familiar to Greenway. Instead, her landmarks were Ellis Island and the city's Lower East Side. Like Ida Rosenthal, Hattie Carnegie, and Lane Bryant, Jennie Grossinger entered the workplace doing piecework in the garment industry.

Unable to make it in the city, Jennie Grossinger's father bought a farm in 1914 in Ferndale, New York, in the heart of the Catskill Mountains. Situated about one hundred miles northwest of New York City, the Catskills were the heart of a burgeoning Jewish leisure community, where enterprising Jewish families ran kosher inns for Jewish guests seeking a summer retreat. Initially Jennie's father intended to return to the farming he had once known in Austria, but the rock-strewn land was not good for agriculture. Instead the run-down seven-room house with an old barn and chicken coop attracted Jews looking for an inexpensive escape from the city heat. In their first summer, the Grossinger family entertained nine guests, each of whom paid nine dollars to stay a week in the beautiful, secluded spot with delicious kosher food.

Just two years before, Jennie had married a cousin, Harry Grossinger, and in 1915 they moved to the farm to be part of the new family business. Everyone had a role. Jennie worked as bookkeeper, hostess, and chambermaid; her mother cooked the meals; Harry traveled between New York City and Ferndale, promoting the inn and sending customers; and Jennie's father managed the operation. In its early days, the inn was a very modest venture at best. It had no electricity, heat, or indoor plumbing. But guests were attracted to Jennie Grossinger's warmth and friendliness as well as to her mother's delicious kosher meals. It was not long before the onetime dream of farming had been transformed and realized–the family had begun building a successful vacation enterprise.

In 1919, at Jennie Grossinger's suggestion, the family sold the original farmhouse and purchased a nearby hotel on sixty-three acres, the site of what would ultimately become the world-renowned Grossinger's resort. Situated on a lake with rolling hills, it had an authentic country ambience that was a magnet for Jews seeking a summer escape from the heat and congestion of the city. But Jennie Grossinger wanted the family

The dining room at
Grossinger's

getaway spot to be more than a modest country retreat. A visit to a posh New Jersey
resort gave her ideas about how to transform Grossinger's into a grand hotel. By the
1920s, Grossinger's had tennis courts, a bridle path, a social director to organize daytime
activities and evening entertainment, and a children's camp. Guests still ate kosher food
but they dined under crystal chandeliers in a four-hundred-person dining room where,
at Jennie Grossinger's insistence, men wore coats and ties to dinner. Well aware of the
impact of advertising, she hired a public relations man to get the word out. "Grossinger's
has everything" became the hotel's slogan. Grossinger's quickly became the vacation
spot for a rising middle class of Jews from New York.

The economic depression of the 1930s was a difficult time for Grossinger's; in fact,
the resort barely broke even. Still, Jennie Grossinger, who had become the legal owner of
the resort after her father's death in 1931, was always ready to innovate and improve the
business. Though she hated professional fighting, she recognized a good business
opportunity when she saw one. When the Orthodox Jewish boxer Barney Ross needed a
place to train where he could observe his religious traditions, Jennie invited him to
Grossinger's, providing him with excellent facilities, kosher meals, and the services of a
rabbi. It was a brilliant business move. The press covered Ross's training at his Jewish
home-away-from-home, giving Grossinger's enormous publicity, especially when he
became the world lightweight champion. Over the years, Grossinger's became a training

*Resort life with lavish
meals at Grossinger's, 1950s*

center for fighters. In the 1950s the world-famous Rocky Marciano trained there. Just as Ross had been attracted to its kosher food and Jewish environment, Marciano found that Jennie Grossinger respected his Italian customs and willingly allowed his mother, who accompanied him to the resort, to cook her son's pasta.

In the years after World War II, Grossinger's expanded even further and took its place as the premier Jewish resort in the country. It was a large complex with six hundred rooms, dining for seventeen hundred, a nightclub with two stages, an Olympic-sized pool, a golf course, tennis courts, a riding academy, an airport, a ski slope, and its own post office. Though it was originally founded for Jewish vacationers at a time when they were excluded from other hotels, Jennie Grossinger's ultimate goal was to make Grossinger's a universal resort. With this in mind, she began to take steps in the late 1940s to reach out beyond her Jewish clientele. She offered entertainment on Friday night, the Jewish Sabbath, and she provided space for Christian religious services.

Jennie's efforts paid off, and Grossinger's gradually became a national resort, attracting guests from well beyond the Jewish community. Many were public figures from all arenas of American life. Eleanor Roosevelt, Cardinal Spellman, New York governor Nelson Rockefeller, and New York senator Robert Kennedy all visited Grossinger's. In addition, Jennie welcomed baseball star Jackie Robinson and United Nations diplomat Ralph Bunche, sending a clear signal that African Americans were welcomed at Grossinger's.

While public figures flocked to Grossinger's, most non-Jewish guests were private citizens seeking the boundless vacation opportunities Grossinger's offered. By the 1960s, non-Jewish guests made up one-quarter to one-third of the resort's 150,000 annual visitors.[31] With her warm personality and shrewd business skills, Jennie struck an ideal balance at Grossinger's. She skillfully preserved the hotel's original mission as a resort for Jewish Americans, while expanding Grossinger's to become a universal resort for all Americans.

Jennie strove to balance her Jewish and American identity in her personal style as well. She spoke fluent English, which she learned in her early years in New York City, but often laced her conversation with Yiddish phrases. She balanced the grandeur of her hotel with homey warmth, greeting her guests as though they were friends. And while her hotel was opulent, she personally shied away from the "flashy" look that "often caricatured . . . life in the Catskills."[32] Instead, her clothing conveyed an understated elegance, much like the Hattie Carnegie look so popular among socialites of the day. Her philanthropic commitments embodied the same balance. She was a tireless supporter of the nation's soldiers during World War II, raising one million dollars' worth of bonds at her hotel, and opening the Grossinger Canteen-by-Mail, which sent packages of gum, cigarettes, candy, and other supplies to the men and women in the military who had been her guests or employees. Her work did not go unnoticed. To acknowledge her contributions, the United States Army named a plane "Grossinger." While she generously supported her country during the war, she later focused her efforts on the newly founded country of Israel, raising money for both a medical center and a convalescent home.

Grossinger also strove for balance in her private life as she sought to juggle the demands of work with those of wife and mother. Of the two, she found marriage the easier to balance. Work was always an integral part of her marriage to Harry, and they complemented each other well. From the beginning, their respective responsibilities reflected acceptable gender roles. In the early days, Harry was both the general handyman and promoter of the hotel, traveling regularly to New York City to attract new guests. Meanwhile Jennie managed its daily operations and greeted guests as though they were members of the family. As Grossinger's grew into a large resort, Harry handled matters behind the scenes while Jennie continued to be the public face of the business, preserving its warm family atmosphere as the hostess of the resort.

Balancing business with motherhood proved to be a far greater challenge. Despite Jennie Grossinger's public reputation as "the gentle Jewish mother" of the Catskills, guilt characterized her private relationship to her children. Her first child was born in 1915, the year that she and Harry began to work in the family business. With no time to ease gradually into her new duties as either mother or innkeeper, Jennie plunged into her work and relied on family and staff to take care of her son whenever possible. It must not have been an ideal situation, for when Jennie's second child was born in 1927 she took a different approach, hiring a governess to take care of her baby daughter. The governess became a surrogate mother, staying until Grossinger's daughter turned eighteen and entered college.

The conflicting demands of motherhood and work persisted, however, exacerbated by poor health. Throughout her adult life, Jennie suffered from physical ailments commonly associated with overwork and stress, including high blood pressure, back ailments, severe headaches, and bouts of depression. These ailments were a painful reminder of the personal price she paid for public success. Though she was publicly revered as a "real mother figure," the reality was that Jennie Grossinger never found a satisfactory balance between the enormous demands of running Grossinger's and the endless duties of motherhood.[33]

Despite the private stress she endured, Jennie Grossinger's public life was a resounding success. Under her guidance, Grossinger's became a multimillion-dollar world-renowned resort. But in Jennie's eyes, Grossinger's importance extended well beyond its business success to its social influence. In an era of assimilation, Jennie eagerly welcomed guests regardless of race, religion, or ethnicity to vacation together at Grossinger's. She hugged Jackie Robinson on the popular television show, *This Is Your Life*, making a public display of her open-hearted embrace of differences in people. At a time when the melting pot was a symbol of American democracy, Jennie proudly proclaimed that Grossinger's had become "a social laboratory" and offered it as an alternative vision of ideal democracy.[34] In the 1960s, as family vacation patterns changed, Grossinger's began to decline. Nevertheless, as the Civil Rights Movement gained momentum in this same era, Jennie Grossinger's vision of a national resort provided a model of democracy that celebrated diversity and foreshadowed the national debate that was about to explode over the nature of democracy in American society.

In the same era that Isabella Greenway built the Arizona Inn, Jennie Grossinger built Grossinger's family resort. The two hotels were studies in contrast. Grossinger's was large, with thirty-five buildings on twelve hundred acres. The Arizona Inn was small, with only eighty-six rooms on fourteen acres. Grossinger's had a full menu of recreational activities; the Arizona Inn had only a pool and two tennis courts. Grossinger's was deliberately lavish; the Arizona Inn was understated in its elegance. Jennie Grossinger put crystal chandeliers in the seventeen-hundred-person dining room; Isabella Greenway provided finger bowls and afternoon tea. Celebrities and politicians went to Grossinger's for publicity; they went to the Arizona Inn for privacy. Grossinger's boldly promised "everything" to its guests; the Arizona Inn modestly promised privacy and quiet. Grossinger's was a showcase for the new wealth of a growing Jewish middle class; the Arizona Inn frowned upon such public displays of materialism and cultivated an atmosphere of deliberately understated graciousness. While newly successful Jews proudly displayed their status at Grossinger's, the clientele at the Arizona Inn did all they could to downplay theirs.

Jennie Grossinger and Isabella Greenway created strikingly different hotels; as women, however, they shared certain traits—warmth, concern for people, and a desire to create homelike comfort for their guests and to welcome them like family. They brought these traditionally feminine qualities to the hospitality industry, targeting two distinctly different markets. Grossinger's embraced an emerging Jewish middle class, proud of its accumulation of new wealth; the Arizona Inn attracted the understated elite, secure in its generations of wealth and social prestige. Thus female culture blended with class and ethnic identities to create two very successful and unique hotels.

⟳ While Greenway and Grossinger were in the leisure business, offering relaxation to those seeking a retreat from work, African American entrepreneur Maggie Lena Walker (1867–1934) was in the banking business, encouraging African Americans to invest their hard-earned money, if they were fortunate enough to have a job.

Maggie Lena Walker shared much in common with her contemporary, Madam C. J. Walker. Both were part of the first generation of African Americans born into freedom, and they came of age believing in the possibility of the American dream. But as they built their fortunes, they redefined the dream. Community and collective support replaced individualism and independence. Their own financial successes were not simply ends in themselves; they were also powerful tools to promote the broader goal of progress for people of their race. And within the African American community, their particular concern was the uplift of women. Yet while Madam C. J. Walker made her fortune catering to women in the beauty business, Maggie Lena Walker broke the gender barriers, established a bank, and made her way in the male world of finance.[35]

Maggie Lena Walker had a goal for African American women: they would "put their mites together, put their hands and their brains together and make work and business for themselves."[36] Her own life was an ideal model. As the leader of a black insurance company, the founder of a black department store, and the first woman bank president in the United States, she worked to help the African American community, especially women in her native city of Richmond, Virginia, become economically independent.

Born during the early years of Reconstruction, Maggie spent much of her childhood in the safety and comfort of a secure nuclear family.[37] Though she never knew her Irish-born father, an abolitionist and newspaper reporter for the *New York Herald,* her mother, Elizabeth Draper, provided security and stability. In her earliest years Maggie lived with her mother, who was a cook in the home of Elizabeth Van Lew, the wealthy abolitionist and Union spy. In 1868 her mother married the butler, William Mitchell, and when he landed the coveted position of headwaiter at the St. Charles Hotel, the Mitchell family left Van Lew's household and moved into town to strike out on its own. Maggie Lena Mitchell settled down to a comfortable family life with her parents and her new baby brother.

But in 1876 the security of Maggie's girlhood was shattered instantly when her father was found dead in the nearby James River. The authorities claimed it was a suicide, but Maggie's mother, well aware of the widespread lynchings of the day, insisted that her husband had been the victim of robbery and murder. His death left an irreplaceable void. Maggie's mother was now the sole provider for her two children. She expanded her laundry business, one of the few areas of enterprise open to African American women, and put Maggie to work picking up and delivering the clothes to her white customers. Helping her mother keep the family afloat, Maggie learned the value of hard work and industry. And she never forgot the fear and pain caused by her family's sudden financial insecurity.

Maggie pursued her education in the city's newly created public school system and immersed herself in religious training and activities at the local black Baptist church. A top student, at her graduation in 1883 she led a protest against the policy of segregation that prevented the black students from holding their ceremony in the same theater where white students graduated. It was the beginning of her lifetime of activism for the black community.

After graduating, Maggie became a teacher at her school. Her teaching job catapulted her from the status of the working poor into a salaried position in the black middle class. Three years later, she married Armstead Walker, an industrious young man who worked both as a mail carrier and in a family bricklaying and construction business. His income enabled the newly married Maggie Lena Walker to give up her teaching job. Being supported by their husbands' incomes was a highly sought privilege among African American women accustomed to working hard simply to survive; the very fact that Walker did not work gave her respectability and status in an age when middle-class women devoted their lives to marriage and motherhood. And that is precisely what Walker settled down to do. While she lost one son in infancy, by 1897 she had two sons and an adopted daughter. Meanwhile, she became increasingly involved in outside activities, particularly in the Independent Order of St. Luke's.

St. Luke's was one of the many black organizations that emerged in the years after the Civil War to provide financial benefits to its members in times of sickness and death. It was a spiritual as well as a practical institution, admitting members without a doctor's examination, but not without a devotion to God. Founded in 1867 by Mary Prout, a former slave, it was open to men, women, and children. St. Luke's was the ideal organization

Banker Maggie Lena
Walker, 1900

for the religious but extremely practical Walker. With the lesson of her father's unexpected death ever before her, she understood all too well the importance of life insurance and joined St. Luke's when she was only fourteen. She devoted herself to the organization until she died.

From the beginning, there was always work for Walker to do. As a student and a teacher, she moved up the ranks of the St. Luke's volunteers: she visited the sick, attended conventions, collected and recorded weekly fees, and administered small payments. She also took classes in accounting and business management. These were important training years, providing her with valuable business experience and organizational skills. In 1895, in the midst of her childbearing years, she organized a juvenile division at St. Luke's, run by women. Under her leadership, the newly created juvenile department encouraged its young members to study the Bible, work hard, and save their pennies. Her dream was that her pupils would take her message of piety, industriousness, and enterprise into adulthood to achieve success for themselves and the black community. To help them along the way, she established an educational loan fund for college.

But by 1899 St. Luke's faced serious decline. Membership was low, the treasury had less than $40, debts were over $400, and the man who had been Grand Worthy Secretary declined reappointment to his $300 position. Walker took over, accepted an annual salary of $100, and set St. Luke's on a new course for the twentieth century. She left a stunning legacy. Over the twenty-five years of her leadership, she collected more than $3.4 million, expanded the membership to over one hundred thousand members in twenty-four states, and built up a $70,000 cash reserve.

As its new leader, Walker understood that St. Luke's had enormous potential that reached well beyond its original function as a mutual benefit society. She had a bold vision, to transform St. Luke's into a vital organization that would bring enterprise and

Home of Maggie Lena Walker and her family, from 1904 to 1922, in Richmond, Virginia

economic opportunity to the black community, particularly to women. Step by step, she accomplished her goals. She began by building an inner circle of women. Her "first work," she recalled years later, "was to draw around me women."[38] She encouraged them to run for leadership positions, and in 1901, women were elected to six of the nine executive board positions.

Surrounded by a committed group of women leaders, Walker wasted no time. In 1902 she chose Lillian Payne to be the managing editor of her next project, a weekly newspaper. The *St. Luke Herald* was a brilliant business innovation. Walker used it to advertise the Order, market its services, and promote communication with the African American community. Its success led to the creation of a profitable printing business. At the same time, the *St. Luke Herald* became a vehicle to speak out against lynching, racial discrimination, the lack of equal educational opportunities for black children, and the dearth of meaningful economic opportunities for black women.

Having established a vehicle to promote St. Luke's, Walker turned her attention to her next project, the creation of a bank. "What do we need to still further develop and prosper us, numerically and financially?" she urged. "First we need a savings bank, chartered, officered and run by the men and women of this Order."[39] It was another bold innovation. When the St. Luke Penny Savings Bank opened in 1903, Walker became the first woman bank president, black or white, in the United States.

Walker's bank was a creative business venture. It provided a place for the rapidly growing Order to house and monitor its increasing funds, and at the same time it encouraged economic empowerment in the black community. As a penny savings bank, it welcomed all deposits, no matter what size. Calling on African American men and women to patronize her bank, she declared, "Let us put our money out as usury among ourselves, and realize the benefit ourselves. Let us have a bank that will take the nickels and turn them into dollars."[40] From the very beginning, Richmond's black community, especially its washerwomen, responded to her call, depositing their small but hard-earned savings in Walker's bank.

Walker was an inspirational bank president. Under her leadership, the St. Luke Penny Savings Bank made a major contribution to the economic development of Rich-mond's black community, helping its depositors achieve greater financial self-sufficiency. Gradually, she translated its slogan, "Bring It All Back Home," into concrete results—namely, more black home ownership. By 1920, Walker could proudly point to 645 homes that were "entirely paid for through our bank's help."[41]

Walker used her bank to teach children the importance of saving money (color-plate 7). She provided cardboard boxes for them to deposit their pennies. When they had saved a dollar, she invited them to open a savings account. She was an inspiration for the many children who eagerly responded to her invitation to get an early start on achieving financial independence. "Numbers of children have bank accounts from one hundred to four hundred dollars," she announced with pride.[42]

Over the years, Walker guided the bank through several mergers. During the eco-nomic depression of the 1930s, as many banks failed around the country, she kept it afloat, merging it with two other banks. When the newly formed Consolidated Bank and Trust Company opened in 1933, Walker chaired the board of the only black bank in Richmond.

Having launched a newspaper and a bank in the first three years of her leadership of St. Luke's, Walker directed her entrepreneurial skills to her next project, a department store in Richmond owned and run by blacks for blacks. Very deliberately, Walker was building a separate sphere of black business, independent of white control, where black merchants would sell to the black community and black consumers would be treated with dignity and respect. Just as she believed that Richmond's blacks needed a bank of their own, so she was firmly convinced that they needed their own department store. Their economic independence and self-respect depended on it.

With twenty-one other women from St. Luke's, Walker opened the St. Luke Empo-rium in 1905. Founded at a time when department stores and chain stores proliferated around the country, the Emporium fit squarely within the burgeoning consumer econ-omy of the day. But as a store owned by black entrepreneurs, staffed by black employees, and geared to the black consumer, the Emporium was unique. Situated on Broad Street, Richmond's major commercial avenue, in a three-story building with an elevator, the store sent a powerful message: the black community of Richmond, Virginia, was well on its way to economic self-sufficiency. It would participate in the nation's consumer econ-omy, but on its own terms.

The Emporium was more than a beacon to race pride and economic empowerment. It offered practical advantages unavailable to African Americans from Richmond's white-run businesses: the Emporium sold quality goods at prices below those in the white-run stores, and it was an important source of black employment. At a time when most black women worked as domestics or laundresses, the Emporium opened its white-collar positions to black women only. Employing fifteen black women as salesclerks, it gave the community a taste of the advantages of black-controlled businesses.

Unfortunately, the Emporium was a short-lived venture. From the very beginning, it encountered organized opposition from the white business community and resistance from black consumers who continued to patronize white stores. Walker issued forceful pleas to the black community to support the Emporium. Claiming that "white business associations . . . in Broad Street and in every business street of Richmond" were trying to destroy "every business effort which we put forth," she called on black consumers to stop the drain of their dollars to the white merchants.[45] But despite her strong appeals, the Emporium lost money every year and finally closed in 1911.

African American architect Charles T. Russell designed this building for the St. Luke Penny Savings Bank.

As Walker established her reputation as a leader in the black business community, she used her growing influence to fight racial prejudice and to work for racial progress. Her reach extended from Richmond throughout the country. She was the founder and lifelong president of Richmond's Council of Colored Women and a founder and vice president of Virginia's Negro Organization Society. During the 1910s and 1920s, she became more involved in nationwide efforts to win the political and economic empowerment of black men and women. She joined with Margaret Murray Washington to start the International Council of Women of the Darker Races, which was committed to creating an international network of women of color; she brought her business experience to the National Association of Colored Women, chairing its business, finance, and budget committees; and she was on the national board of the National Association for the Advancement of Colored People. At every turn, she linked business with economic improvement for black people, dedicating her work to empowering the African American community, and especially its women.

As Walker built her fortune and public reputation, her private life was a source of both joy and tragedy. In the early years of her marriage, Walker recreated the stable nuclear family she had enjoyed when she was a little girl. In 1905, the year that she opened the Emporium, she moved with her entire family into a two-story brick row house. As her financial position improved, she expanded the house into a twenty-two-room home that enabled her to keep her extended family together under one roof. The house was also a public showplace, proof of her financial success and influence in the black community and a testament to her gospel of self-help and racial solidarity. African American leaders and luminaries, including W. E. B. Du Bois, Langston Hughes, and Mary McLeod Bethune, visited her there.

But the house, a source of pride and happiness, was also the site of unforeseen accidents and tragedy. A fall left her limping and in severe pain for years, eventually forcing her to use a wheelchair. Then in 1915, without warning, tragedy once again shattered Walker's domestic happiness when her eldest son shot and killed his father, believing he was a burglar. Overnight, Walker became a widow at the hands of her own son as he sought to protect her home. The incident raised eyebrows in the community, but Walker successfully defended him in court and held onto her power in St. Luke's.

In fact, Walker continued to be a powerful voice in the African American community, wielding power and influence even from her wheelchair. Richmond honored her by naming a street, a theater, and a high school after her. When she died in 1934, she was eulogized as "the greatest of all Negro leaders of Richmond . . . and one of the three or four ablest women her race ever produced in America."[44] Walker had come a long way from the poverty of her childhood. Her financial empire epitomized the dreams of opportunity and success that freedom promised African Americans after the Civil War. Yet her accomplishments reached well beyond her personal wealth. In the era of women's institution building, when Julia Morgan designed buildings for the all-women's Mills College and the YWCA, Walker established separate all-black institutions to serve the black community, particularly African American women. With black women laundresses and domestic servants at the center of her plan, she linked individual entrepreneurship with racial solidarity to create a blueprint for the empowerment of the African American community.

CⱭ While Isabella Greenway and Jennie Grossinger sold leisure to adults and families, other enterprising women capitalized on a new segment of the consumer economy: children. Just as the fashion and beauty industries had exploded in the early twentieth century with the rise of the New Woman as consumer, so the toy industry expanded significantly in the post–World War II era as young couples settled into their domestic lives, buying homes and raising families. Creative entrepreneurs flooded the market with musical toys, board games, and toy guns. Within this burgeoning toy industry, the long tradition of a gendered marketplace persisted as women entrepreneurs once again carved out their own corner of the marketplace, designing dolls for young girls. While men were also in the business of doll manufacturing, women brought a gendered perspective to doll making; they were particularly concerned about the quality of craftsmanship as well as the special relationship that developed between a young girl and her doll.[45]

The timing was right for the development of a domestic doll industry. Throughout the nineteenth and early twentieth centuries, German-made dolls dominated the market until the outbreak of World War I closed the door to German goods. Enterprising women seized the opportunity to market their own dolls and created a domestic doll market. With the birth of the "baby boom" generation in the years after World War II, women entrepreneurs continued to shape the growth of the doll industry. From the lovely Madame Alexander dolls and the adorable Ginny dolls to the landmark Barbie dolls and the historical American Girl dolls, women entrepreneurs have been a driving force behind the evolution of the doll industry.

Beatrice Alexander (1895–1990), the founder of the Alexander Doll Company, knew as a young girl that she wanted to devote her life to dolls.[46] Her father, a Russian Jewish immigrant, opened the first doll hospital in the United States. Beatrice Alexander grew up watching tearful young girls bring their broken dolls to her father for repair. The experience inspired her future. She resolved that "some day I was going to make unbreakable dolls."[47] Years later, married and the mother of a young daughter, she sat down at her kitchen table to follow her dream. With sixteen hundred dollars of start-up capital and World War I raging in Germany, she launched the Madame Alexander Doll Company.

Hearkening back to her love of reading as a young girl, Alexander devised a creative marketing idea: she modeled her dolls after characters in children's classics; these included an Alice in Wonderland doll and a series of dolls from Charles Dickens's novels. As Hollywood produced blockbuster movies throughout the years of the Great Depression, she captured the popular enthusiasm for films with her special dolls. The film *Little Women* in 1933 inspired a series of March sister dolls that became an instant success. When *Gone with the Wind* was released in 1939, Alexander captured the southern belle craze and got exclusive rights from Metro-Goldwyn-Mayer to produce and market Scarlett O'Hara dolls. And as the Dionne quintuplets captured the nation's hearts in the 1930s, Alexander negotiated exclusive rights to a series of Dionne dolls.

From the very start, Alexander set out to elevate the status of the American doll industry by producing high-quality dolls. She accomplished her goal. Beautifully designed, exquisitely outfitted, and carefully packaged in her signature blue box, Madame Alexander dolls became the symbol of the very best in the industry. Mothers and grandmothers eagerly bought the beautiful dolls, confident in the quality and status of their purchase.

But it was more than status and reputation that drew young girls to the beautiful dolls. Alexander had a unique marketing concept that captured the imagination of young girls. Rejecting ordinary dolls with their "empty smiles," she set out to "create dolls with souls."[48] With this in mind, every doll she produced came with a card bearing a special message for its new owner. "My Dear Young Friends," it began, "[y]our doll is your very own, to be with you at all times. . . . Let her be your dearest friend and companion."[49] It was an irresistible message, giving each doll a unique personality and encouraging each owner to cherish her new doll forever.

Fame and Fortune
Mary Pickford

Behind the persona of "America's Sweetheart," Mary Pickford (1892–1979) was a hard-driving, tough-minded businesswoman. Pickford turned America's love affair with her irresistible beauty into business, using her enormous popularity and box office appeal to build a major Hollywood institution.

Born Gladys Smith, she began her acting career as a child, after her father died leaving her seamstress mother to raise three children. Driven to succeed, she talked her way onto the Broadway stage at age fourteen, when she changed her name and became Mary Pickford. With her eye on the higher-paying movie industry, she caught the attention of D. W. Griffith, whom she persuaded to hire her. Starring roles in movies such as *Poor Little Rich Girl*, *Rebecca of Sunnybrook Farm*, and *The Little Princess* catapulted Pickford to Hollywood stardom. Fortune followed fame: by 1917, she commanded a staggering $350,000 per film, earning over one million dollars that year alone.

Two years later, in 1919, Pickford used her wealth and influence to launch United Artists. Her partners (shown here from right to left), included Griffith, Charlie Chaplin, and her soon-to-be husband, Douglas Fairbanks. Though she was the only woman, Pickford was one among equals within the powerful group. United Artists was an innovative venture for its day. As a studio owned and run by artists, it nurtured creative freedom and independent production. Despite what industry skeptics predicted, United Artists grew, its promise of artistic freedom luring major Hollywood stars, directors, and producers.

While the independence at the heart of United Artists contrasted with Pickford's sweetheart image onscreen, it was precisely this freedom that guided her entire career, both as a major box office star and successful businesswoman. Moreover, as the lone female founder of United Artists, Pickford blazed a path for the many women who followed her example in seeking creative and financial autonomy in the movie industry. ✐

Alexander won the hearts of young girls who adored her dolls and the adults who bought them, and the Alexander Doll Company grew quickly. Alexander moved out of her kitchen and into her own storefront and factory. Toy stores such as F. A. O. Schwarz and major department stores such as Macy's and Marshall Field's began to carry her dolls. By 1936, in the midst of the Depression, with more than fifty companies competing in the doll industry, Alexander had turned her company into one of the top three doll manufacturers in the nation. Her achievement did not go unnoticed. *Fortune* magazine reported that Alexander was referred to "by all the gallants of the business as the Queen of Dolls."[50] Over the years her company and her reputation continued to grow. In 1953 she moved the business into an old Studebaker factory in Harlem, where it remains today. Alexander sold her company in 1988 when she was ninety-three, but the Alexander Doll Company carries on her legacy as the last major manufacturer of handcrafted dolls in the country.

      Like Beatrice Alexander, Ruth Handler (1916–2002) was the daughter of Jewish immigrants.[51] And just as Alexander's girlhood experiences motivated her to create beautiful, indestructible dolls, Handler's experience as a mother inspired her to create her own line of dolls. But while Alexander created exquisite dolls that girls collected, Handler designed dolls that girls emulated. When her voluptuous Barbie doll hit the stores in 1959, it changed the doll industry forever.

Ruth Mosko was born in Denver, Colorado, in 1916, the tenth child of Polish Jewish immigrants Joseph and Ida Mosko. From an early age, she was an entrepreneur at heart. While her peers played, she loved to work at the soda fountain in her aunt and uncle's store. During her sophomore year at the University of Denver she took a vacation in Los Angeles and never looked back. Her high school boyfriend, Izzy Elliott Handler, followed her to Los Angeles; they married in 1938 and settled down to the business of work and family.

The Handlers began their business career by producing lucite items until the military demand for plastic during World War II threatened their fledgling business. Ruth Handler salvaged a large order of picture frames by redesigning them in wood, and with friend and production expert Harold Matson, Ruth and Elliott Handler launched the Mattel Toy Company, named after its two male owners. Though Ruth had been the chief marketing strategist, her name was left out. "It never occurred to me," she admitted years later. In the 1940s "a woman got her identity through her husband."[52] When Matson sold out in 1947, the company name remained the same.

The Handlers had two children, Barbara in 1941 and Ken in 1944. While other young women of her generation embarked on a life of domesticity, Handler was determined to blaze her own path as wife, mother, and businesswoman. It was not an easy road. In this period of domesticity and the Feminine Mystique, Handler's daughter wanted her working mother to be "an *ordinary* mom." Thus the same creative businesswoman who would one day make thousands of young girls happy often cried herself to sleep because she could not please her own daughter. Still Handler refused to give up her career; instead, she and Elliott took steps to balance work and family. They left the office every day at 5:30 to eat dinner at home, and they took all their vacations with their children. While she happily made these accommodations, Ruth simply could not imagine a life outside "the fast-paced business world" that she loved. "If I had to stay home," she confessed, "I would be the most dreadful, mixed-up, unhappy woman in the world." In an era when

Elliot and Ruth Handler with Walt Disney (center), ca. 1955

June Cleaver was the popular ideal of womanhood, Ruth Handler was the first to admit that she thrived on "the adrenaline rush that came with closing a tough sale and delivering a gigantic order on time."[53]

Mattel got off to a good start by creating products that catered to the popular mood. The country's fascination with television star Arthur Godfrey and his ukulele inspired the musical Uke–A–Doodle, their first toy and their first hit, eleven million of which were sold by 1957; a series of toy guns captured the Western cowboy craze. Yet even while guiding Mattel into the mainstream of American toy manufacturing, the Handlers retained a management style that was far from conventional. Most companies demanded formality and hierarchy; Ruth and Elliot asked their employees to call them by their first names. Racial tension was increasing nationally; the Handlers hired workers regardless of race and ethnicity and expected them all to work together.

In 1955 the Handlers invested a half–million dollars to become a sponsor for Walt Disney's newest project, a television show called the "Mickey Mouse Club." It was a risky move, for their investment in the show represented their entire net worth. But their gamble paid off, tripling their annual sales in just three years. Moreover, the Handlers introduced a new marketing strategy, year–round advertising, which changed the toy industry forever. While toy manufacturers had traditionally limited their advertising to the holiday season between Thanksgiving and Christmas, Mattel now bombarded consumers year round. Manufacturers that resisted the new marketing strategy, such as the Marx toy company, did not survive.[54] Mattel also took its case directly to children–it bypassed the adults, who had always bought toys; accelerated the creation of the new child consumers; and sowed the seeds for the explosion of the youth market in the 1960s.

While Elliot created toy guns and holsters for boys, Ruth cast her sights on young girls. Inspired by her daughter, who loved to play with the adult paper dolls, Ruth conceived of a new idea, a grown-up doll for girls to identify with and project their futures onto (colorplate 11). The result was an eleven-inch doll with breasts, long tapered legs, and a thin waist. Barbie, named after the Handler's daughter, swept the doll industry. While other dolls were round and childlike, Barbie was glamorous, womanly, and had a designer line of clothing. Barbie became a barometer of young girls' interests and aspirations. She changed her hair with the times, she sailed and hiked as the fitness craze took over, she went to college, and she had a multitude of careers. Under Ruth Handler's guidance, Mattel gave Barbie an entire social circle of dolls, including a boyfriend, Ken, and a best friend, Midge. Yet, Barbie's perfect body highlighted many young girls' dissatisfaction and discomfort with their own developing bodies.

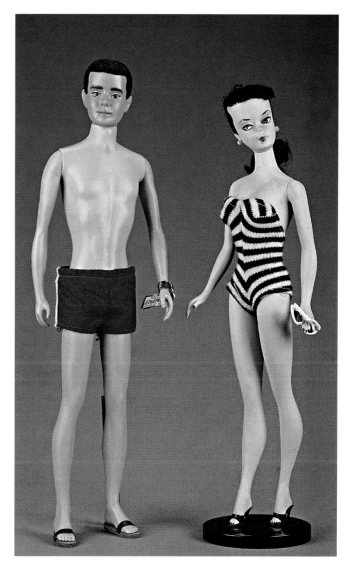

While some critics lamented the unattainable fantasy Barbie presented to impressionable young girls, from the moment she was introduced in 1959, Barbie always dominated the doll market. By the mid-1960s, Mattel was producing tens of thousands of Barbie dolls a week, and there were 8,500 chapters of the Barbie Fan Club. By 1964 Mattel, which had begun with a modest family loan of $20,000 in 1949, had net sales of $96 million. By 1993 it was not unusual for girls between the ages of three and ten to own eight or more Barbie dolls. Around the world Barbie was sold in 140 countries at the rate of two dolls per second.[55] Mattel went on to introduce other successful toys, including the talking Chatty Cathy doll and Elliot's brilliant Hot Wheels. Unlike other toy crazes that vanished quickly, Barbie not only became a permanent fixture in the doll industry; she became an American icon. In fact, there was nothing in the entire Mattel product line that ever surpassed the sales and success of Ruth Handler's brainchild, Barbie.

Over the years, Handler left her mark on Mattel in other ways. As a woman with power and autonomy in her own company, she used her influence to reshape Mattel's corporate culture and to create a workplace that was sensitive to the needs of its female employees. She pushed for salary increases and promotions for the female employees, and at their request, she

Early examples of Barbie and Ken by Mattel, Inc.

Party of Thousands
Brownie Wise

Brownie Wise (1913–1992) was a marketing genius. She took plastic kitchenware that had been languishing on department store shelves, brought it directly into women's homes, and turned it into a hallmark of the post–World War II period. When Wise transformed the selling of Tupperware into a social event, she also created an American institution–the Tupperware party. In the process, this divorced mother, who struggled to support her son, became the first woman to grace the cover of *Business Week* magazine.

Being a single mother herself, Wise (shown standing, at right) understood completely the needs of the housewives and mothers to whom she sold Tupperware door-to-door. Isolated in their postwar, suburban homes, women wanted more than plastic kitchenware–they wanted social interaction. Wise's Tupperware party was the ideal marketing innovation for its day, combining community with consumption, entertainment with entrepreneurship. Women eagerly flocked to Tupperware parties, where a hostess entertained her friends, earned money by selling Tupperware, all in the comfort of her own home, where she could still tend to her children.

Wise's marketing scheme solved the dilemma common to women who aspired to improve their lifestyle: it allowed them to earn the money and prizes they needed to elevate their standard of living without violating the then-prevailing gender ideal of wife as stay-at-home mother and homemaker. Tupperware demonstrations were not "work," they were "parties." The product perceptually enhanced the woman's role as preparer of meals and

guardian of the family's food budget and health. Wise encouraged her salespeople to involve their families and friends in their activities, since women's networks, far from being liabilities, were the ligaments of the home-party business. Parties could be held when children were at school and men were at work, which allowed women to tailor their businesses to their domestic schedules. Recruiters courted the husbands of prospective demonstrators as much as the women themselves, for it was understood that women needed their husbands' permission to work.

Her energy and charisma assisted Wise in easily recruiting women to her vision of home marketing. In emphasizing initiative and independence, she offered women an opportunity for entrepreneurship that did not threaten to disrupt their traditional domestic roles, while she turned Tupperware Home Parties Incorporated into a multimillion-dollar enterprise. ✍

changed the dress code at Mattel to permit women to wear pantsuits. Her efforts were a poignant reminder of the sexual politics of the business world.

Beyond the walls of Mattel, there were other reminders of the shifting tides of gender relations in the toy industry. Handler broke new ground when she became the first woman elected to the board of directors, and then to the vice presidency of the Toy

Manufacturers Association. But sex discrimination went hand-in-hand with progress. Businessmen often treated her with condescension or ignored her altogether. Many resented her when meetings had to be moved from men-only clubs and facilities to accommodate her. And the same Toy Manufacturers Association that had elected her its first woman vice president was unwilling to give her the presidency the following year. Ruth Handler may have made it into the inner circle of the toy manufacturing industry, but she remained isolated because of her gender. "Being the only woman was often a lonely experience," she admitted years later.[56]

Discrimination was not the only hurdle Handler encountered. In 1970 she suffered a personal hardship when she was diagnosed with breast cancer and had a mastectomy. The operation left her cancer-free but physically and emotionally scarred. Then in 1973 the Securities and Exchange Commission audited Mattel and concluded that the company had overstated its earnings and contrived to mislead its stockholders. Ruth and Elliot Handler pleaded innocent to any involvement but left the company in 1975.

For the first time in her adult life, Handler was not working—but not for long. Her fruitless search for a breast prosthesis, combined with her need to work and her passion for business, inspired her to embark on a new enterprise. Unlike Mattel, which Ruth built with Elliot, Nearly Me was completely hers. She brought her business acumen and her first hand experience as a breast cancer survivor to her new enterprise. In the midst of the women's health movement of the era, she created a work culture based on sisterhood and the shared experience of breast cancer, hiring only women who had gone through the experience of a mastectomy. At the same time, Handler marshaled her business resources and contacts to develop and market her product. She turned to former members of the old Mattel design and production teams to create artificial breasts. She marketed them to the fashionable Neiman Marcus department store by emphasizing both community service and the opportunity to develop a new group of customers. She traveled around the country promoting Nearly Me and personally fitting women who were willing to pay up to two hundred dollars for comfortable and well-fitting breast prostheses.

Nearly Me was the logical culmination of a lifetime career that began when Handler introduced Barbie, the first doll with breasts. As she explained: "When I conceived Barbie, I believed it was important to a little girl's self-esteem to play with a doll that has breasts. Now I find it even more important to return that self-esteem to women who have lost theirs."[57]

Olive Ann Beech (1903–93) was a woman in a man's industry. Unlike quilt production, the hospitality industry, or toy manufacturing, airplane production was well outside of women's usual business endeavors. Though she manufactured airplanes, Beech never even learned to fly a plane. Still, as the president of Beech Aircraft Corporation, she successfully navigated her company through World War II and the Korean War and led it into the uncharted territory of the space age.

In some ways, Beech followed a similar path to entrepreneurship as Edna Ferber's fictitious Emma McChesney. She began as a secretary, married the boss, and became a partner in her husband's firm. At the same time, her life was like that of real business-women from the century before. Like nineteenth-century entrepreneurs Rebecca Lukens and Martha Coston, widowhood catapulted Beech to the head of the family business. And just as steel production and maritime technology were well beyond the parameters of nineteenth-century women's traditional sphere, the aviation industry, in which Beech was a pioneer, symbolized the epitome of masculinity in the mid-twentieth century. Thus, Beech joins the group of businesswomen in American history for whom family crises led to entrepreneurship in male-dominated industries.

Olive and Walter Beech standing beside a Beechcraft 18, March 1947

From girlhood, Olive Ann Mellor was always interested in the details of business.[58] Both her mother and her father, a building contractor in rural Kansas, encouraged her to open her own bank account when she was seven years old. At the age of eleven, she was writing checks and overseeing the family accounts. When she was an adolescent, her family moved to Wichita. In this more urban setting, she attended the American Secretarial and Business College, one of the many schools preparing women to take their "proper place" in the burgeoning corporate world as secretaries and clerical workers. Armed with her new office skills, Olive moved to August, Kansas, in 1921 to become office manager and bookkeeper for an electrical appliance and contracting firm. Eighteen years old and single, she was one of thousands of young women who flocked to cities in search of independence, adventure, and a clerical career. In 1924, now an experienced office worker, she returned to Wichita, where Walter Beech, a former World War I pilot and engineer, hired her as a bookkeeper for his newly founded Travel Air Manufacturing Company. It was a career move that changed Olive's life.

Olive found herself the only woman in a twelve-person firm of esteemed airline pilots and aviation experts; she had never even flown in an airplane. A co-worker drew her a labeled diagram of an airplane that she relied on for years. Still, no one could deny her business capabilities, as she skillfully managed the books, conducted banking business, and took over the company correspondence. Olive quickly rose to become Walter Beech's personal secretary, and she managed the office as the company grew. By 1929, Beech had turned Travel Air into the largest commercial aircraft manufacturer in the country.

But then the stock market crashed and overnight Travel Air faced hard times. As sales plummeted, Beech merged his company with Curtiss-Wright Airplane Company, became president of the company and then vice president of sales. His new responsibilities took him to New York City and then to St. Louis, but he did not go alone. In 1930 he married his personal secretary, and he and Olive set out for New York together. Neither was satisfied with the new situation. Having worked most of her life, the new Mrs. Walter Beech did not like playing the role of the corporate wife. And Walter wanted to run his own company. In 1932, in the midst of the Great Depression, they returned to Wichita and started Beech Aircraft. Walter was president and Olive was secretary. They made an ideal team. Walter was an outgoing and bold visionary with creative ideas for new planes. Olive was a soft-spoken but astute businesswoman with a decisive management style.

With a staff of former Travel Air employees, the Beeches set out to build their business. They had no income during the first year, as they worked on the design and development of their first Beechcraft airplane. In their second year, they sold one plane and made seventeen thousand dollars. Ultimately they introduced their Model 17 Staggerwing, a single-engine aircraft with a deluxe interior, fully retractable landing gear, excellent pilot visibility, and speed capability beyond the fastest military plane. Walter's innovative design set a new standard for aircraft, but the Staggerwing made a splash in the aviation industry because of Olive's astute marketing skills. As her husband planned to enter the Staggerwing in the coast-to-coast National Air Races, she came up with a bold promotional idea: let a woman fly the Staggerwing. In September 1936, two women, a pilot and a navigator, flew the Staggerwing across country in fourteen hours and fifty-five minutes and arrived in Los Angeles more than one-half hour before the second plane. The message was clear: if two women could fly the Staggerwing faster than the best male pilots could fly any other plane, then the Staggerwing was indeed an easy and speedy aircraft. The victory was a remarkable advertisement for the Staggerwing and popularized the slogan, "It takes a Beechcraft to beat a Beechcraft!"[59]

The proud female winners of the National Air Race, 1936

With the success of the Model 17 Staggerwing, the Beeches incorporated Beech Aircraft in 1936; introduced a new aircraft, the Model 18 Twin Beech, in 1937; and reached annual sales of one million dollars in 1938. Beech Aircraft grew dramatically during World War II as it raced to adapt its planes from commercial to military use. Meanwhile, changes in the Beeches' private life accompanied the company's wartime growth. First,

Olive became a mother; her daughter was born in 1937 just as the new Model 18 was introduced, and a second daughter was born in 1940 just as their wartime expansion took off. But at that time Walter became deathly sick with encephalitis in 1940 and did not return to work for nearly a year.

The wartime management of Beech Aircraft was in Olive Beech's hands. With a three-year-old and a newborn, she took over the company. Her keen business skills and her fifteen years of experience in the aircraft industry paid off. She borrowed millions of dollars to finance the company's transition to military production. She expanded and hired on a grand scale, managing the demanding task of training people who had never worked in a factory before. Under her direction, Beech Aircraft employed 14,000 workers during the war, manufactured over 7,400 military planes, and reached a sales peak of $122 million in 1945. Ultimately, the Beechcraft Model 18 proved to be the most popular military plane during the war: 90 percent of all American pilots and navigators were trained on it.[60]

After the war, the Beeches returned to commercial production of their planes, but in 1950 Walter died suddenly of a heart attack. Olive became president and chairman of the board and officially took over the responsibilities she had been performing for years since her husband's illness. She guided the company through renewed military production during the Korean War and then a productive return to commercial production. With her keen eye, she saw an opportunity for expansion at the dawn of the space age and made Beech Aircraft a leader in the production of fuel systems for NASA rockets. Throughout it all, Beech remained the epitome of femininity. She dressed in a simple but elegant style; fresh flowers, Wedgwood trays, and bowls of candy adorned her desk and office.

In 1968, Beech stepped down as president of Beech Aircraft, but remained the board's chair. She led the company in its merger with the Raytheon Corporation in 1980 and took a seat on the board of directors until she retired in 1982. While her Beech aircraft took others around the world and into space, Olive Beech remained close to her roots, continuing to live and work in Wichita, where she was a great benefactor of the arts and education until she died in 1993, just months before her ninetieth birthday.

For more than half a century, women entrepreneurs built businesses within the boundaries of the male-dominated business world. Many succeeded in the early decades of the century—through the Progressive era, World War I, and an era of plenty—when women believed in the power of their freshly earned political and social equality. And, from the Great Depression to World War II, as their economic opportunities declined then expanded again, women continued to demonstrate their business ability alongside men. Even in the 1950s, with the decade's renewed emphasis on domesticity,

"Struggling with mysteries of breakfast, lunch, dinner..."
Adelaide Alsop Robineau

Balancing work and family has always presented a challenge for women, regardless of what type of business they ran or when they lived. While art may have been a socially acceptable arena in which women could work, it did not shield them from the problem. In the May 1913 issue of her publication, *Keramic Studio*, professional potter and educator Adelaide Alsop Robineau expressed her exasperation with the fact that the unending demands of domesticity were intruding on her business:

> And now what are we going to do about the domestic problem, those of us who have homes and children and husbands and still feel called to follow the lure of art? For four long weeks the editor has been struggling with mysteries of breakfast, lunch, dinner, sewing on buttons, darning...while a two hundred and fifty dollar order stands, needing only a few hours to finish and suspended ideas in porcelain are fading in the dim distance and others are crying to be put into execution. ✐

women continued to be successful entrepreneurs. They proved that in this century of meritocracy, women had the talent, initiative, ingenuity, ambition, and financial sense to compete as equals with men. But a sea change awaited a younger generation of women who came of age in the second half of the century in a new era of prosperity. Embracing the expanded opportunities for women in American society, they flooded the American business world with their own ventures, ultimately transforming the landscape of American enterprise.

1963 Betty Friedan publishes *The Feminine Mystique*
• Assassination of President Kennedy
• President's Commission on the Status of Women issues report

1964 Gulf of Tonkin Resolution
• Civil Rights Act
• The Beatles visit U.S.A

1973 Vietnam War ends
• Arab–oil embargo
• Roe v. Wade upheld by Supreme Court
• Billie Jean King defeats Bobby Riggs

1974 President Nixon resigns presidency over Watergate
• Equal Credit Opportunity Act
• Women's Educational Equity Act

CHAPTER FIVE

"Go ahead, go ahead, go ahead. Let's go."

KATHARINE GRAHAM

1960–2000
WOMEN TAKE CHARGE

When Linda Alvarado walks onto a construction site, those unfamiliar with the petite woman with long black hair may conclude she is a trespasser onto male terrain. But Alvarado has firmly planted her feet precisely where she wants them to be. As the founder and president of Denver-based Alvarado Construction, Inc., she has literally and symbolically made the construction business "women's business." She does what men have traditionally done–construct commercial and industrial buildings–and she does it well.

Under her ownership, Alvarado Construction has left its mark on the landscape of Denver, building the Colorado Convention Center, the ten-story administration office center at the new Denver International Airport, and Mile High Stadium, home of the Broncos, Denver's professional football

1981 Sandra Day O'Connor becomes first woman Supreme Court justice
• Physicians recognize AIDS as worldwide problem
• MTV premiers

1989 Communist regimes in eastern Europe collapse
• Berlin Wall razed

1997 Madeleine Albright becomes first woman Secretary of State

2000 Nine women serve in U. S. Senate; 58 women serve in the House of Representatives

team with over four hundred employees, an office in San Francisco, and multimillion-dollar annual revenues, Alvarado has extended the reach of her construction company throughout the western part of the country. Moreover, her pioneering ventures do not stop with construction; she is part-owner of the Colorado Rockies, making her the first woman entrepreneur ever to bid for and win ownership of a major league baseball team. From buildings to baseball, Alvarado has expanded the boundaries of women's entrepreneurial success, and is a symbol of the pioneer enterprising woman of today. Her accomplishments have not gone unnoticed. She sits on the boards of several major corporations and has received numerous awards. It is no accident that the Horatio Alger Association of Distinguished Americans honored her in 2000 for her initiative, hard work, and commitment to excellence and enterprise.

Just as Madam C. J. Walker and Hattie Carnegie incarnated the American dream for African American and Jewish immigrant women at the turn of the twentieth century, Linda Alvarado embodies the American dream for the twenty-first century, one with room for a Hispanic woman at the highest echelons of commercial construction and professional baseball. To be sure, women have run successful enterprises in traditionally male businesses for centuries, but most of them, such as Rebecca Lukens and Martha Coston, inherited their businesses. In contrast, Alvarado relied on individual initiative, not inheritance, to found her construction company. Having achieved on her own in arenas traditionally closed to both women and Hispanics, she is reanimating the American dream to be one that, as she proudly proclaims, "is not based on race or gender."[1]

While Alvarado's story reflects much of the progress in the history of women entrepreneurs—the opening of traditionally male areas of business to women and the expansion of business opportunities to new minority women—Martha Stewart epitomizes the continuity that links women entrepreneurs of the past, such as Elizabeth Murray, Ellen Demorest, and Elizabeth Arden to those of the present. Her market is women; her business is lifestyle, the modern expression of the enduring feminine role of domesticity. The roots of her business lie in her childhood home in Nutley, New Jersey, where she learned to cook and sew from her mother and to garden from her father. Like so many other women entrepreneurs, past and present, Stewart has built a business based on that with which she is familiar: women's traditional roles.[2]

But Stewart has taken domesticity to new heights. While Murray sold dry goods to colonial women, Demorest sold dress designs in the Victorian era, and Arden sold cosmetics in the age of the New Woman, Stewart sells a lifestyle—tips, products, and creative ideas that help the homemaker with every facet of domestic life today. No area of home life is omitted, from cooking and sewing to gardening and entertaining. Nor is anyone at home left out, from babies to wedding couples to grandparents at family gatherings. As founder and CEO of Martha Stewart Living Omnimedia, Inc., Martha has turned domesticity into very big business.

Together, Linda Alvarado and Martha Stewart—one competing successfully with men and the other an icon in the world of women's business—personify the limitless possibili-

(page 148)

Katharine Graham, publisher of the Washington Post newspaper and owner of the Washington Post Company

ties for women entrepreneurs in the twenty-first century. Though exceptional in power and prestige, both are part of a group of millions of women entrepreneurs who own businesses throughout the country. The last quarter of the twentieth century witnessed a sharp expansion of entrepreneurial business ventures instigated by women. In 1977 women owned just 7 percent of all businesses in the United States; by 1987, 4.1 million women owned businesses, accounting for 30 percent of all American businesses, an increase of more than 400 percent and twice the growth rate of businesses started by men.

The growth of entrepreneurship by women continued through the close of the century. In 1990 there were 5.4 million women-owned businesses. These firms employed close to 11 million people, about 10 percent of all U.S. workers and about the same percent as the *Fortune* 500 companies combined.[3] The tally of women-owned businesses almost doubled by 1999 to 9.1 million women-owned businesses throughout the country. Representing 38 percent of all businesses, employing 27.5 million workers, and generating over $3.6 trillion in annual sales, women entrepreneurs at the dawn of the twenty-first century have taken a prominent place in the business world.[4]

But numbers tell only part of the story. While most women entrepreneurs are still in services and retail trade, and sell primarily to women, many have transcended past patterns and moved into fields formerly defined as the business of men. Linda Alvarado is just one exemplar of women in the construction industry; in the years between 1987 and 1996, while she turned Alvarado Construction into a major building company, women-owned construction companies increased 171 percent. At the same time, women-owned manufacturing companies grew by 112 percent and those involved in the transportation and communications industries jumped 140 percent.[5]

Race and ethnicity have also changed the face of women entrepreneurs. Oprah Winfrey, whose Harpo Entertainment Group has left an indelible mark on the entertainment and communications industries, defines the pinnacle of success for African American women—indeed, for all women entrepreneurs. Many other minority women, as well, have been successful entrepreneurs. Asian-born Joyce Chen popularized authentic Chinese cooking through her Cambridge, Massachusetts, restaurant as well as through her cookbooks and unique line of Chinese cookware. Mexican-born Maria de Lourdes Sobrino founded Lulu's Desserts, the first company in the United States to sell prepared gelatin products. African American Cathy Hughes owns Radio One, which is among the major radio broadcast companies in the country.

Behind these individual stories of success are hundreds of thousands of minority women entrepreneurs. The number of firms owned by women of color grew exponentially in the last years of the twentieth century. The brief period between 1987 and 1992 saw an increase in their numbers of 85 percent—from 388,000 to 717,000.[6] The greatest expansion in the proportion of businesswomen of color has been in nontraditional businesses. Between 1987 and 1996, minority women-owned businesses increased 319 percent in construction, 276 percent in wholesale trade, and 253 percent in transportation, communications, and public utilities.[7]

This growing community of minority women entrepreneurs is itself increasingly diverse. A century ago, when African American women and Jewish immigrant women first became entrepreneurs, both groups were considered to be new racial and ethnic minorities in the world of business. Today, African American women entrepreneurs retain their minority status among women entrepreneurs. In contrast, Jewish women are no longer considered minority women entrepreneurs by virtue of ethnicity; they have been replaced by other minorities, particularly Latinas and Asian Americans. Today no one can deny the obvious fact: women entrepreneurs–of all races and ethnicities–have become part of the business landscape. Whether competing with men or working by their side, they have made America's business women's business.

This dramatic growth in the number of women entrepreneurs has its roots in the of 1960s and 1970s. Following the conformity and conservatism of the 1950s, women of the 1960s and 1970s, like their predecessors a century before, began to examine the restrictions of their conventional roles as wives and mothers and launched a modern women's movement to redefine and expand the parameters of their lives. A number of landmark events coincided in the early 1960s to reinforce their efforts. Betty Friedan's *Feminine Mystique* arrived in the bookstores in 1963, shattering the image of the happy house-wife. That same year, the report of the President's Commission on the Status of Women documented women's second–class status in all areas of society, from the workplace to the family and destroyed yet another myth–that women had "made it" in American society. The reports of fifty state commissions revealed how widespread and ingrained were women's legal and cultural handicaps, thus reinforcing the expectation of reform.

The passage of Title VII of the 1964 Civil Rights Act promised concrete reform. Though the category of "sex" was not included in the original bill, it was introduced as a maneuver to defeat the legislation. The strategy backfired and Title VII passed, outlawing discrimination by unions, private employers, and employment agencies on the basis of gender as well as race, color, religion, and national origin. The creation of the Equal Employment Opportunity Commission (EEOC) to monitor compliance with the new law was yet another signal that the climate was changing. When the EEOC failed to pursue sanctions against sex discrimination in the workplace, women joined together in 1966 and created the National Organization of Women. At the same time, a younger genera-tion of predominantly white, middle–class women began to join together, because of shared frustration with their second–class treatment in the antiwar, civil rights, and stu-dent movements of the day. In the 1970s, an increasingly diverse population of women pursued higher education. Many went on to professional schools, entering the fields of medicine, law, and business. Meanwhile, Congress passed the Equal Credit Opportunity Act in 1974, which prohibits creditors, banks, finance companies, credit card companies, and the like from discriminating against applicants on the basis of sex as well as those of race, color, religion, national origin, marital status, and age.

The movement toward women's equality provided fertile ground for a new genera-tion of women entrepreneurs. Nurtured by the legal and social reforms of the 1960s and

1970s, women entrepreneurs blossomed in the 1980s and 1990s, changing the landscape of American business. Yet, in the midst of this period of reform and progress, familiar patterns persisted. Most women entrepreneurs continued to cluster in service and retail businesses; they still thrived in a women's market, selling goods and services to the female consumer.

Mary Kay Ash, for one, made her fortune in the beauty business, following in the footsteps of Madam C. J. Walker, Matilda Harper, and Elizabeth Arden.[8] Like Harper she grew up white and working–class; like Walker she created a door–to–door operation that provides affordable beauty products to female consumers and inspiration, opportunity, and upward mobility to her "consultants," women who sell her cosmetics; and like Arden, she built a multimillion–dollar company in the cosmetics industry.

In 1963, Mary Kay broke free of the domestic restrictions Betty Friedan exposed in *The Feminine Mystique*. With her life–savings of five thousand dollars, she launched her own business. Mary Kay Cosmetics offers entrepreneurship with a twist. Its unique priorities–"God first, family second, career third"–send the message that the company values piety, domesticity, and the dollar. Moreover, its message, "At Mary Kay, you're in business for yourself, but never by yourself," emphasizes community over competition.[9] In the hard-driving, competitive business world, this reinterpretation of entrepreneurship reflects the style and sensibilities of many women. As Ash explained, "Men don't usually understand our system, but it works! Everyone helps everyone else."[10]

From the beginning it was clear that Mary Kay's unique business model was a formula for success. In its first year her company realized $198,000 in wholesale sales and the figure quadrupled to $800,000 after the second year. By 1992 her company was on *Fortune*'s list of the five hundred largest corporations in the country. By the end of the century, her onetime storefront operation with nine consultants had mushroomed into a multibillion-dollar enterprise with over a half-million consultants selling Mary Kay Cosmetics worldwide.

Fashion also attracted women entrepreneurs. Like nineteenth–century pattern-maker Ellen Demorest and early–twentieth–century fashion designer Hattie Carnegie, women have continued the tradition of turning fashion into business. Just as fashion pioneer Lane Bryant understood the fashion needs of the early–twentieth–century New Woman, Liz Claiborne and Donna Karan turned their understanding of the contemporary woman into thriving fashion companies.

Like cosmetics and fashion, the food industry has attracted women entrepreneurs. Minority women have built businesses by bringing their ethnic traditions to women's universal role as family cook. In 1958, Peking-born Joyce Chen opened a Chinese restaurant in Cambridge, Massachusetts. At a time when Chinese restaurants typically offered two menus, one for Chinese customers and the other for Americans, and when American customers expected to find French bread at their tables, Chen had a different vision. She wanted a restaurant that served authentic northern Chinese cuisine to her Chinese and American customers alike, one that "would make American customers happy and Chinese customers proud."[11] Aware of the novelty of her food, Chen cleverly encouraged her clientele to take a risk and expand the experience of their palates. She coined terms like "Peking ravioli" to encourage her customers to try new foods. Her buffet table introduced the adventurous diner to authentic Chinese cuisine, such as moo-shu pork and hot-and-sour soup, while offering Western foods to those less daring. Her restaurant was a success and she opened additional restaurants in Boston and on Cape Cod.

As an ambitious entrepreneur, Chen looked for ways to broaden her business beyond its regional base. In 1962 she published the *Joyce Chen Cook Book* to make the recipes for her northern Chinese cuisine accessible to the broader public. In 1966 her public station television show, "Joyce Chen Cooks," brought her into America's homes each week. Having enticed the public with her recipes, she launched Joyce Chen Products, selling a line of Chinese cookware featuring specially shaped woks; she then expanded into supermarkets with Joyce Chen Specialty Foods, a line of prepared sauces and seasonings. Known as the "Godmother of Chinese cooking," Joyce Chen introduced the foods of her childhood to the United States. She brought diversity to dining as she built a business dedicated, as she explained, to "a cultural exchange."[12]

Similarly, Mexican-born Maria de Lourdes Sobrino turned her mother's gelatin recipe into a thriving business in southern California.[13] To her parents in Mexico, it seemed like a foolhardy venture, and they wanted her to come home. Two prior ventures had already failed, first a flower shop and then, in 1982, a travel company. But motivated by her self-described entrepreneurial spirit, Sobrino was unafraid of the risk and decided to stay, even when her husband returned to Mexico and the couple divorced. Driven by her passion "to start something and be [her] own boss," she turned to what she knew best, the Mexican foods of her childhood.[14] Her roasted peanuts and jalapeño-spiced carrots did not sell, but then she hit on another idea: ready-to-eat gelatin, a popular dessert in Mexico that was unavailable in southern California.

Sobrino began small, preparing three hundred cups of gelatin a day in 1983 for local stores. But soon, a decade before Kraft's Jell-O offered prepared gelatin products, a growing Mexican population in southern California clamored for what she called "Lulu's Dessert." By the 1990s, Sobrino had turned the Mexican infatuation with prepared gelatin into big business: Lulu's Dessert and Fancy Fruit Corp. had become a multimillion-dollar enterprise that sold over forty food products, most notably more than seventy million gelatin cups a year.

While the majority of women entrepreneurs are still found in traditionally female enterprises, the growing numbers that are gravitating toward areas such as construction, manufacturing, and transportation reveal how women entrepreneurs are establishing themselves in the business mainstream. Following in the footsteps of Hetty Green, Muriel Siebert blazed a new path in the world of finance, becoming the first woman to buy a seat on the New York Stock Exchange and the first to own a New York Stock Exchange brokerage firm.

The rise of computer technology opened up previously unimagined opportunities in the communication industry and women entrepreneurs are flooding the gates. But this is not a new phenomenon. New technologies often expand economic opportunities for women. In the early twentieth century, for example, the typewriter created new office jobs for thousands of women who left home for economic independence and adventure in the city; by the end of the century, the computer had expanded women's economic opportunities in new ways, enabling them to run businesses without even leaving their homes. "[A]ll talent is welcome, regardless of gender," explained Donna Dubinsky, developer of handheld computers.[15] The time was certainly right for Meg Whitman, who, as CEO of eBay, turned a startup auction venture into a major company in on-line commerce.

Other women have moved into nongendered fields the old-fashioned way, through inheritance. Ellen Gordon inherited her family's candy company, Tootsie Roll Industries.[16] As a young girl, Gordon spent hours in the factory, taste-testing candies and sharpening her arithmetic skills by adding telephone numbers. But, despite her early interest in the business, Gordon was not raised to carry it on. Instead, her parents attempted to redirect her into typically female activities. "I grew up learning how to pour tea," she admits. Although she set her eyes on the accounting department of the candy company, she was assigned to the advertising department, where she ended up as the poster girl for a Tootsie Roll ad in *Life* magazine. When she majored in math at Vassar, her parents warned her, "Don't be too smart or you'll never catch a husband."[17]

But Gordon's parents need not have worried. Their daughter married when she was eighteen and, with her husband Melvin Gordon, she raised four daughters and took over the family candy company. With the familiar Tootsie Roll always at the heart of the enterprise, she expanded the company over the years to include other favorites such as Junior Mints, Sugar Daddy, and Charleston Chew. Under her careful watch, Tootsie Roll Industries became one of the largest candy companies in the country.

While Ellen Gordon's early passion for business prepared her to take over the family candy business, Katharine Graham's adherence to traditional gender roles left her ill-equipped to run her family's publishing concern. In fact, Graham's story explodes the myth that a woman becomes an entrepreneur overnight simply by inheriting a business.[18] For Graham this was no overnight event; while inheritance enabled her to own a company, that was but the first step in her long process of becoming an entrepreneur.

Graham began her adult life as a traditional wife and mother, but the suicide of her husband, Phil, turned her world upside down. Overnight she was a widow with four children and the owner of a family business, The Washington Post Company, that she was unprepared to run. Gradually, she metamorphosed from wife and mother into a powerful publisher and influential businesswoman as well.

But her journey was not smooth. Born into a family of comfort and privilege, she had been shielded from the world of business while she absorbed the notions of traditional femininity. She received an unambiguous message: "Women [are] intellectually inferior to men . . . [incapable] of governing, leading, managing anything but our homes and our children."[19] When she married Phil Graham, her father gave him more stock in the company than he gave his daughter because, as he explained, "[N]o man should be in the position of working for his wife." Not surprisingly, she defined herself as "the tail to his kite."[20] For years she remained in the background, the quiet, supportive wife, until her husband's sudden suicide catapulted her into a new role—owner of the *Washington Post.*

Graham took over the *Washington Post* in 1963 and transformed it from a local newspaper with a modest circulation into one of the top-ranked newspapers in the country. From a business perspective, she was, in the words of her longtime editor, Ben Bradlee, "a great owner."[21] By 1993, when she turned the Washington Post Company over to her son, it was included in the *Fortune* 500 list. But she did not do it alone. Like Martha Coston a century before, she was fortunate to have influential friends and associates, including columnists Walter Lippmann and James Reston as well as author Truman Capote, to help her as she came out of the shadows and found her stride. An early boost came from Luvie Pearson, wife of columnist Drew Pearson, whose straightforward advice encouraged the reticent new owner of the *Post* to run the paper herself: "Don't be silly, dear. You can do it. . . . You've just been pushed down so far you don't recognize what you can do."[22] Meanwhile her loyal team, including Bradlee and business adviser Warren Buffett, helped her rise to the top. By the time she finally handed over the reins of power to her son, the onetime supportive wife had turned the Washington Post Company into a two-billion-dollar media empire with newspaper, broadcast, cable, and magazine properties, including *Newsweek* magazine. Along the way she stood up for freedom of the press, brought down a president, and became one of the most powerful and admired businesswomen of the twentieth century.

Women like Graham, Stewart, and Winfrey are icons in the business world, the women entrepreneurs whose achievements at the highest reaches of business have become national symbols of the possibilities of success for women. Others, like Alvarado, Siebert, and Gordon, are part of an exceptional elite among women entrepreneurs who have competed as equals with men and often surpassed them. Millions of less well-known women have flooded the business world in the last decades of the twentieth century. But even as they have planted themselves firmly in the soil of American business, there is much in the business landscape that appears not to have changed. Women entrepreneurs continue to confront challenges and perpetuate patterns that would have been familiar to Hazel Bishop fifty years ago, Madam C. J. Walker at the dawn of the twentieth century, Martha Coston during the Civil War, and even Elizabeth Murray in colonial New England.

In this new century, a major concern continues to be access to capital.[23] Women entrepreneurs identified this as their biggest challenge in the 1970s but were optimistic about improvement, particularly due to the passage of the Equal Credit Opportunity Act in 1974.[24] Unfortunately, such optimism was misplaced. Acquiring capital continued to be the major obstacle confronting women entrepreneurs throughout the last quarter of the twentieth century, as it does even into the twenty-first century. The Equal Credit Opportunity Act benefits women consumers more than entrepreneurs and many banks continue to deny commercial loans to women without the signature of a husband or male family member. Today, even as women's businesses grow in number, size, and revenue, women entrepreneurs receive a remarkably small 4 percent of available venture capital funds.[25] Access to capital continues to be even more difficult for minority women.[26]

Of course, not all women entrepreneurs have been left out. Those with proven track records, particularly in the high-tech industry, have been welcomed by the venture capital community. The success of Palm Computing guaranteed Donna Dubinsky easy access to capital with which to start her new company, Handspring.[27] Most women entrepreneurs, however, have been unable to break into the network of venture capital. As a result, they have continued a familiar pattern: reliance on personal savings or funds from family and friends. Liz Claiborne started her business with money raised from family and friends; Linda Alvarado went to six banks, all of which rejected her business plan, before she turned to her parents, who mortgaged their home to help her get started.[28]

To many women business owners, the root of the problem has been skepticism among the financial community about women's experience and long-term commitment to entrepreneurship.[29] At the same time, many women entrepreneurs have shied away from venture capital. Cautious about asking for help that might be construed as weakness or concerned about giving up equity ownership to outside investors, they rely on personal credit cards over commercial bank loans. The impact is significant; the lack of venture capital has stunted the growth of women's start-ups. Their companies begin small and grow slowly.

Women entrepreneurs continue to face other familiar challenges as well. Despite the legal, institutional, and social reforms that have advanced a woman's position or role in American society, conventional attitudes toward a woman's "proper place" persist when women entrepreneurs try to venture beyond the service and retail trade industries of fashion, food, and cosmetics. Ellen Gordon's parents worried about her interest in candy manufacturing. Neither Katharine Graham's father nor the men in charge of the *Post* initially believed that she had any business in—not to mention any ability for—running the family publishing company. While Alvarado's parents supported her efforts to launch a construction company, she encountered hostility, including graffiti on walls, lewd pictures, and a general distrust from men who believed that she did not belong in the male-dominated construction industry.[30]

At the same time that women entrepreneurs are still required to break down old barriers in the business community, they continue to face personal challenges as well, namely the task of juggling the demands of their public and private lives. Many women see business ownership as the answer to this problem. In contrast to the corporate workplace, entrepreneurship offers women the autonomy and freedom to set their schedules and control their work pace.[31] Moreover, an at-home business provides an additional advantage, particularly appealing to mothers of young children—the ability to incorporate work and family into a single space. By the mid–1990s, women had founded an estimated 3.5 million home–based businesses.[32] Turning their backs on the separation of work and family, they use computers and new technology to recreate a new version of the old pre–industrial model, where work and family were integrated into the household.

But the freedom implied by entrepreneurship, even at home and with the latest technology, does not always enable women to transcend the continuing struggle to balance work and family. In the 1970s, as the women's movement embarked on its ambitious goals of challenging women's domestic role and expanding their opportunities beyond the home, many women entrepreneurs were wary of the pitfalls of marriage and motherhood. Aware of the demands of business and family, some sacrificed marriage while others looked for spouses who would support their business commitments.[33] But by the 1990s, in spite of the accomplishments of the women's movement, women entrepreneurs still faced the dual demands of home and work. Mothers continued to assume primary responsibility for child rearing, while the care of older relatives fell on the shoulders of all women entrepreneurs, regardless of marriage and motherhood.[34]

At the dawn of the twenty–first century, therefore, the key to balancing family responsibilities with business remains the same as it was over a century ago: finding the right partner, who is supportive and willing to share the responsibilities of both work and home. The task is not always an easy one. Katharine Graham's marriage totally silenced her business potential; Martha Stewart's marriage fell apart as her business grew. But other relationships are testimony to the advantage of marriage when business and personal life are entwined: Linda Alvarado and Ellen Gordon are among the many women entrepreneurs who have successfully integrated public and private, business and family, helped by their marriages. Like Myra Bradwell's, Ellen Demorest's, Ida Rosenthal's, and those of other of their predecessors, contemporary marriages thrive on a division of labor between husband and wife that fuels the business and sustains the family. Their marriages reveal the constancy of an historical pattern: for a woman with a supportive husband, marriage enriches rather than detracts from business.

While the growing numbers of women entrepreneurs have changed the face of America's business owners, they are changing the heart and soul of American business as well. Of course, women entrepreneurs embrace the same goals as their male counterparts, namely independence, financial opportunity, and the chance to create and build. However, women bring their own goals to business ownership as well. The desire to break through the glass ceiling of the corporate workplace, and balance work and family are just two. Like male business owners, women entrepreneurs share a body of business knowledge, take risks, and invest capital as they strive to earn profits and build their businesses. Yet, at various points along the way, women entrepreneurs make decisions that distinguish them from their male counterparts. In both the wholesale and retail trades, women hire women employees at a rate 20 percent greater than do men business

158   ENTERPRISING WOMEN

owners.[35] Employee benefits offered also reflect the female composition of their work-force as well as women's sensitivity to family issues. In addition to the basic benefits of health insurance, paid vacation, and personal leave, which they offer at the same rate as male entrepreneurs, women are more likely to provide their employees with flex-time options and tuition-reimbursement programs. With an eye to future security, women entrepreneurs are less likely than men to put their employees' retirement plan invest-ments at risk and more likely to offer profit-sharing opportunities.[36]

Women entrepreneurs have their own business style as well. Having had fewer mentors and less experience than men, they place a high value on relationships and advice from others. As they prepare to launch a business, women more often consult than men with family members, accountants, and other business owners.[37] Men often launch a business with a flashy business plan, an expensive marketing campaign, and a list of venture capital investors. In contrast, women, with less access to capital markets, tend to start small, often work from home, then expand their businesses to meet demand. The result is a cautious business style that has paid off. Women-owned busi-nesses are more stable and last longer than men's: while only two-thirds of all firms founded in 1991 were still in operation three years later, nearly three-fourths of women-owned businesses were still viable enterprises in 1994.[38] Moreover, like women entrepre-neurs of generations gone by, contemporary women business owners, particularly those of high net worth, ardently carry on the tradition of philanthropy. In fact, they con-tribute more money and are more likely to take on leadership responsibilities in philan-thropic organizations than their male counterparts.[39]

Finally, women entrepreneurs have joined together to advance and support their business endeavors. Women-owned consulting firms advise women-owned businesses; successful women entrepreneurs pool their resources to invest in other women's start-up ideas. Meanwhile, such organizations as the National Foundation for Women Business Owners, the National Association of Women Business Owners, the National Women's Business Council, the Small Business Administration's Office of Women Business Ownership, the Commonwealth Institute, and the Committee of 200 all institutionalize and formalize women entrepreneurs' efforts to support and mentor each other.[40] These separate all-women's organizations provide their constituencies with a valuable network of support by women for women. In doing so, they reach back to the historical tradition of a separate arena of women's business. In this era of increasing gender equality, the all-women's organizations reconstruct the separate world of women's business, reinterpreting it for a new age.

⟋⟍ The story of enterprising women in the twenty-first century is just beginning to unfold. As women forge new paths in business for the new century, they build on the legacy of the past, providing a road map that connects the past to the present and ulti-mately reaches into the future. Let us not forget that when President Calvin Coolidge declared in the 1920s that the "chief business of the American people is business," he was not thinking about women. But two hundred and fifty years of American business reveal an incontrovertible fact–women have always thought about business. Indeed, despite changing, yet persistent, discrimination–economic, legal, and cultural–that enterprising women faced, there has never been a time when they were not a part of the growth and development of American enterprise.

Beginning in early America, Eliza Pinckney, Katherine Goddard, and Elizabeth Murray left little doubt that women played an important role in the economic development of colonial America and the new nation. Pinckney's cultivation of indigo, Goddard's printing enterprise, and Murray's dry goods shop spanned the broad range of women's participation in business. Moreover, their work foreshadowed themes for the future. Goddard and Pinckney revealed that women could succeed in enterprises more commonly associated with men and Murray helped lay the foundation for the rise of a gendered market and a consumer economy. While their ventures were diverse, they shared a belief in the prevailing ideology that linked political freedom to the free market, and they built businesses that were critical to the growth of the new nation. Their enterprises left little doubt that women were an integral part of the early struggle to define the contours of free enterprise in the nascent years of American democracy.

In the nineteenth century, a new generation of women entrepreneurs once again took their place at the center of the economic and social movements of the era. They participated in the building of the industrial nation and they championed the spirit of reform that shaped the prevailing cultural climate of the country. Rebecca Lukens, a pioneer industrialist, Hetty Green, a prominent financier, and Martha Coston, an enterprising inventor, were important contributors to the emerging industrial economy. Lukens manufactured the iron needed to build railroads and ships; Coston built new maritime technology; and Green used her enormous wealth to help finance industrial growth. At the same time, other women entrepreneurs elaborated a gender identity in their ventures and self-consciously linked their "women's" businesses with reform, particularly for women. Lydia Pinkham produced home remedies that met women's demands for painless, noninvasive therapeutics in the midst of the popular health movement; Ellen Demorest sold fashions that combined style with comfort, then founded a tea company that offered dependent women a respectable route to economic independence. Meanwhile, Myra Bradwell proved that women could bridge the two sides of nineteenth-century entrepreneurship. Her *Chicago Legal News* was at once central to the communications revolution and the reform movements of the day. It played a vital role in the shift from the local practitioner to the corporate lawyer, and it propelled Bradwell's agenda for reform, particularly as it affected the legal rights of women.

The dawn of the twentieth century promised greater opportunities for enterprising women. As the possibilities of the American dream permeated the nation's consciousness, Hattie Carnegie, Maggie Lena Walker, and other minority women revealed that the ideal of the "self-made man" could be a reality for women, regardless of race or ethnicity.

While many eighteenth- and nineteenth-century women successfully tied their businesses to women's interests, gender-identification reached a new height during the first half of the twentieth century. As Madam C. J. Walker, Elizabeth Arden, Ida Rosenthal, and others built businesses around hair products, lipstick, and lingerie, the fashion and beauty industries became quintessential expressions of a woman's market for which women entrepreneurs produced goods specifically for women consumers. Other entrepreneurs, including Julia Morgan, Jennie Grossinger, and Ruth Handler, exemplify the ways women continued to penetrate into a range of business arenas beyond the boundaries of fashion and beauty, bringing their female imprints to ventures from architecture to the leisure industry and toy manufacturing. In an era when the New Woman coincided with the new female consumer, enterprising women capitalized on the demands for meritocracy while marketing to the contemporary female consumer. In doing so, they revealed that women entrepreneurs could, like their male counterparts, participate in the creation of the new consumer economy for the twentieth century.

In the century's last decades, the promise of free enterprise first offered in the new nation was well on its way to being fulfilled for women. New government regulations legislated greater opportunity for women in the economy; business schools opened doors to women wider than ever before; and corporations, once the sanctuary of male enterprise, admitted women. These advances paved the way for enterprising women who are forging new paths in business for the twenty-first century. While many will continue to build businesses the principal clientele for which are women, others will strike out in new directions, going wherever they recognize opportunity, regardless of the lure of a gendered marketplace. And enterprising women will penetrate the highest echelons of corporate America, transferring their entrepreneurial skills into the arena of management. While a few–like Carleton S. Fiorina, chief executive of Hewlett-Packard– have already reached the top, other women will surely follow, bringing change to the corporation, from ground floor to boardroom.

Yet, with all the promise of change, enterprising women in the twenty-first century will share many of the trials of their predecessors: gender discrimination, access to capital markets, and the balance between work and family.

Moreover, the challenge for each individual woman entrepreneur remains the same as it has been for every entrepreneur, woman or man, past or present: she must stand on her own, take a risk, confront her competition, build a business, and make it grow. Perhaps Katharine Graham embodied the sprit of entrepreneurship best. As she considered whether to publish the Pentagon Papers, she was well aware of the magnitude of the risk. She understood only too well that not only was the "soul" of the *Washington Post* at stake; a decision "to publish [the Pentagon Papers] could destroy the [news] paper." She knew she could not escape the hard truth that the responsibility for that decision was hers alone. It was a risk that demanded courage and a bold, swift move. "Go ahead, go ahead, go ahead. Let's go."[41] Her words are an inspiration, indeed an anthem, for all women entrepreneurs, past, present, and future.

NOTES

CHAPTER 1
SEEKING INDEPENDENCE, 1750–1830

1. Joyce Appleby, *Inheriting the Revolution: The First Generation of Americans* (Cambridge: Harvard Univ. Press, 2000), esp. pp. 56–89; Gary Walton and James F. Shepherd, *The Economic Rise of Early America* (New York: Cambridge Univ. Press, 1979); Douglass C. North, *Growth and Welfare in the American Past: A New Economic History* (Englewood Cliffs, N.J.: Prentice-Hall, 1966); Richard Hofstadter, *America at 1750: A Social Portrait* (New York: Vintage, 1973); Margaret Ellen Newell, "The Birth of New England in the Atlantic Economy: From Its Beginning to 1770," in Peter Temin, ed., *Engines of Enterprise: An Economic History of New England* (Cambridge: Harvard Univ. Press, 2000), pp. 11–68; and Winifred Barr Rothenberg, "The Invention of American Capitalism: The Economy of New England in the Federal Period," in Temin, *Engines of Enterprise*, pp. 69–108.

2. John Demos, *A Little Commonwealth: Family Life in Plymouth Colony* (New York: Oxford Univ. Press, 1970); Douglas Lamar Jones, *Village and Seaport: Migration and Society in Eighteenth-Century Massachusetts* (Hanover, N.H.: Univ. Press of New England, 1981). On women in early American society, see Carol Berkin, *First Generations: Women in Colonial America* (New York: Hill and Wang, 1996); Elisabeth Anthony Dexter, *Colonial Women of Affairs: A Study of Women in Business and the Professions in America before 1776* (New York: Houghton Mifflin, 1924); Nancy Cott, *The Bonds of Womanhood: "Woman's Sphere" in New England, 1780–1835* (New Haven: Yale Univ. Press, 1977); Lisa Norling, *Captain*

Ahab Had a Wife: New England Women and the Whalefishery, 1750–1870 (Chapel Hill: Univ. of North Carolina Press, 2000); Mary Beth Norton, *Liberty's Daughters: The Revolutionary Experience of American Women, 1750–1800* (Boston: Little, Brown, 1980); Julia Cherry Spruill, *Women's Life and Work in the Southern Colonies* (New York: Norton, 1972); and Laurel Thatcher Ulrich, *Good Wives: Image and Reality in the Lives of Women in Northern New England, 1650–1750* (New York: Oxford Univ. Press, 1983).

3. On women's legal status, see Joan Hoff, *Law, Gender, and Injustice: A Legal History of U.S. Women* (New York: New York Univ. Press, 1991); and Linda K. Kerber, *Women of the Republic: Intellect and Ideology in Revolutionary America* (New York: Norton, 1980). On marriage in particular, see Nancy F. Cott, *Public Vows: A History of Marriage and the Nation* (Cambridge: Harvard Univ. Press, 2000). For the nineteenth century, see Hendrick Hartog, *Man and Wife in America: A History* (Cambridge: Harvard Univ. Press, 2000); and Michael Grossberg, *Governing the Hearth: Law and the Family in Nineteenth-Century America* (Chapel Hill: Univ. of North Carolina Press, 1985).

4. Appleby, *Inheriting the Revolution*, pp. 56–89.

5. For Eliza Lucas Pinckney's correspondence, see Elise Pinckney, ed., *The Letterbook of Eliza Lucas Pinckney, 1739–1762* (Columbia, S.C.: Univ. of South Carolina Press, 1997); and Harriott Horry Ravenel, *Eliza Pinckney* (New York: Scribner's, 1896). On Pinckney, see Berkin, *First Generations*; Constance B. Schulz, "Eliza Lucas Pinckney," in G. J. Barker Benfield and Catherine Clinton, eds., *Portraits of American Women: From Settlement to the Present* (New York:

Oxford, 1998), pp. 65–81; Darcy Fryer, "The Mind of Eliza Pinckney: An Eighteenth-Century Woman's Construction of Herself," *South Carolina Historical Magazine*, vol. 99 (1998), pp. 215–37; Edward T. James et al., eds., *Notable American Women, 1607–1950: A Biographical Dictionary*, vol. 3 (Cambridge, Mass.: Harvard Univ. Press, 1973), pp. 69–71 (hereafter cited as *NAW*); Dexter, *Colonial Women of Affairs*; and Elise Pinckney, "Elizabeth Lucas Pinckney," in *NAW*, pp. 69–71.

6. Pinckney, *Letterbook of Eliza Lucas Pinckney*, p. 7.

7. Ibid., p. 7.

8. Ibid., p. 35.

9. Ravenel, *Eliza Pinckney*, p. 38.

10. Pinckney, *Letterbook of Eliza Lucas Pinckney*, p. 16.

11. Ibid., p. 6.

12. Ravenel, *Eliza Pinckney*, p. 117.

13. Pinckney, *Letterbook of Eliza Lucas Pinckney*, p. 144.

14. Ravenel, *Eliza Pinckney*, p. 105.

15. On Mary Katherine Goddard, see Ward L. Miner, *William Goddard, Newspaperman* (Durham, N.C.: Duke Univ. Press, 1962); Clarence S. Brigham, *Journals and Journeymen: A Contribution to the History of Early American Newspapers* (Philadelphia: Univ. of Pennsylvania Press, 1950); Christopher J. Young, "Mary K. Goddard: A Classical Republican in a Revolutionary Age," *Maryland Historical Magazine*, vol. 96, no. 1 (spring 2001), pp. 5–27; a biographical essay is in *NAW*, pp. 55–56, and one of her mother, Sarah, is in *NAW*, pp. 56–57. See also Lawrence C. Wroth, *The Colonial Printer* (Portland, Maine: Southworth-Anthoensen, 1938. The *Maryland Journal* and the *Baltimore Advertiser* are available at the Houghton Library, Harvard University, Cambridge, Mass.

16. Brigham, *Journals and Journeymen*, pp. 72–73.

17. David A. Copeland, *Colonial American Newspapers: Character and Content* (Newark, N.J.: Univ. of Delaware Press, 1997), p. 279.

18. Miner, *William Goddard*, p. 166.

19. Ibid., p. 167.

20. Ibid., pp. 166–67.

21. Brigham, *Journals and Journeymen*, p. 101.

22. Miner, *William Goddard*, p. 149.

23. Ibid., p. 178.

24. Ibid., p. 183.

25. On she-merchants in eighteenth-century urban America, see Patricia Cleary, " 'She Will Be in the Shop': Women's Sphere of Trade in Eighteenth-Century Philadelphia and New York," *Pennsylvania Magazine of History & Biography* 119 (July 1995): 181–200; and Jean P. Jordan, "Women Merchants in Colonial New York," *New York History* (October 1977): 412–39.

26. See T. H. Breen, " 'Baubles of Britain': The American and Consumer Revolutions of the Eighteenth Century," *Past and Present* 119 (1998): 73–104.

27. The best source on Elizabeth Murray is Patricia Cleary, *Elizabeth Murray: A Woman's Pursuit of Independence in Eighteenth-Century America* (Amherst: Univ. of Massachusetts Press, 2000). See also Mary Beth Norton, "A Cherished Spirit of Independence: The Life of an Eighteenth-Century Boston Businesswoman," in Carol Ruth Berkin and Mary Beth Norton, eds., *Women of America: A History* (Boston: Houghton Mifflin, 1979), pp. 48–67; and Mary Beth Norton, *Liberty's Daughters: The Revolutionary Experience of American Women, 1750–1800* (Boston: Little, Brown, 1980). An invaluable source of Murray family correspondence is Nina Moore Tiffany, ed., *Letters of James Murray: Loyalist* (Boston: n.p., 1901).

28. Cleary, *Elizabeth Murray*, pp. 56, 57; see also *Boston Evening-Post*, August 20, 1750. For other examples, see Cleary, " 'She Will Be in the Shop' " p. 187.

29. Cleary, *Elizabeth Murray*, p. 62.

30. Ibid., p. 68.

31. Norton, *Liberty's Daughters*, p. 149.

32. Ibid.

33. Cleary, *Elizabeth Murray*, p. 133.

34. Norton, *Liberty's Daughters*, p. 217.

35. Norton, "A Cherished Spirit of Independence," p. 52.

36. Norton, *Liberty's Daughters*, p. 151.

CHAPTER 2

PROFIT IN THE SERVICE OF WOMEN, 1850–1890

1. Alfred D. Chandler, Jr., *The Visible Hand: The Managerial Revolution in American Business* (Cambridge: Harvard Univ. Press, 1977), pp. 50–51, 61.

2. Ibid., p. 60.

3. Ibid., pp. 82–88.

4. Catharine Beecher, *A Treatise on Domestic Economy* (Boston: T. H. Webb, 1841), and *The Domestic Receipt Book* (New York: Harper, 1846); T. S. Arthur, "Sweethearts and Wives," in *Godey's Lady's Book* 23 (December 1841): 264–69, reprinted in Nancy F. Cott, ed., *Root of Bitterness: Documents of the Social History of American Women* (New York: Dutton, 1972), pp. 157–70; Madeleine B. Stern, *We the Women: Career Firsts of Nineteenth-Century America* (Lincoln: Univ. of Nebraska

Press, 1940), p. 239. On widows, see Judith Scheffler, " ' . . . there was difficulty and danger on every side': The Family and Business Leadership of Rebecca Lukens," *Pennsylvania History* 66 (summer 1999): 276–310.

5. On Rebecca Lukens, see Scheffler, " ' . . . there was difficulty and danger on every side' "; Stern, *We the Women*, pp. 237–50; Robert Wilson Wolcott, *A Woman in Steel– Rebecca Lukens (1794–1854)* (Princeton, N.J.: Princeton Univ. Press, 1940); Edward T. James et al., eds., *Notable American Women, 1607–1950: A Biographical Dictionary* Vol. 2 (Cambridge: Harvard Univ. Press, 1973), p. 442 (hereafter cited as *NAW*). Lukens Steel Company Papers, Eleutherian Mills Historical Library, Wilmington, Del.; additional papers are in the Lukens Collection, Hagley Museum and Library, Greenville, Del.; Chester County Archives, West Chester, Penn.; and Chester County Historical Society, West Chester, Penn.

6. Rebecca Lukens, memoir for her children, Lukens Collection, Hagley Museum (photocopy), n.d., p. 5; original in possession of Huston Family, Coatesville, Penn.

7. Ibid.

8. Anna M. P. Stern, "Rebecca Pennock Lukens," Chester County Archives, n.d., p. 1.

9. Stern, *We the Women*, p. 240. On the impact of Quaker values on the Lukens family, see Scheffler, " ' . . . there was difficulty and danger on every side.' "

10. Stern, *We the Women*, p. 243.

11. Stern, "Rebecca Pennock Lukens," p. 3.

12. Stern, *We the Women*, 246. On Quaker support of women's business, see Scheffler, " ' . . . there was difficulty and danger on every side' "; and Andrea Constantine Hawkes, " 'Feeling a Strong Desire to Tread a Broader Road to Fortune': The Antebellum Evolution of Elizabeth Wilson McClintock's Entrepreneurial Consciousness" (master's thesis, Univ. of Maine, 1991).

13. Chandler, *The Visible Hand*, p. 6; Stern, *We the Women*, p. 250.

14. Letter of Rebecca Lukens to Hannah Steel, May 22, 1837, Lukens Collection, Hagley Museum.

15. Stern, *We the Women*, p. 247. On the participation of women in the Whig campaign of 1840, see Elizabetha R. Varon, *We Mean To Be Counted: White Women and Politics in Antebellum Virginia* (Chapel Hill: Univ. of North Carolina Press, 1998), pp. 71–102.

16. Ibid., p. 247.

17. The Lukens Company, which has been through innumerable changes, mergers, and restructurings, stayed in the hands of Rebecca's descendants through Charles

Huston until, in 1974, Charles Lukens Huston, Jr., retired, marking the end of over 180 years of Lukens family dominance. See Christopher T. Baer, "A Guide to the History and Records of the Lukens Steel Company" (unpublished), Hagley Museum and Library, Wilmington, Del., March 8, 1994. On protecting her daughters' inheritance in her will, see Scheffler, " ' . . . there was difficulty and danger on every side.' "

18. Stern, *We the Women*, p. 250.

19. Rebecca Lukens, "Statement of Rebecca W. Lukens in connection with adjustment of her interest in her Father's estate, and a history of her labors in conducting her business affairs," Brandywine, Penn., September 10, 1850, Chester County Historical Society, as cited in Scheffler, " ' . . . there was difficulty and danger on every side,' " p. 293; also cited in Stern, *We the Women*, p. 249.

20. The best historical analysis of Lydia Pinkham remains Sarah Stage, *Female Complaints: Lydia Pinkham and the Business of Women's Medicine* (New York: Norton, 1979). See also *NAW*, vol. 3, pp. 71–72; Linda Zierdt-Warshaw, Alan Winkler, and Leonard Bernstein, eds., *American Women in Technology: An Encyclopedia* (Santa Barbara, Calif.: ABC-CLIO, 2000), pp. 249–51; and Ethlie Ann Vare and Greg Ptacek, *Mothers of Invention: From the Bra to the Bomb–Forgotten Women and Their Unforgettable Ideas* (New York: Morrow, 1988), pp. 50–3. See Papers of Lydia Pinkham and the Lydia E. Pinkham Medicine Company, Arthur and Elizabeth Schlesinger Library on the History of Women in America, Harvard University, Cambridge, Mass.

21. *Lynn Daily Item*, January 23, 1893, as cited in Stage, *Female Complaints*. 31.

22. Mrs. Mott, *Ladies' Medical Oracle; or Mrs. Mott's Advice to Young Females, Wives, and Mothers* (Boston, n.p. 1834). The author would like to thank Susan Porter for information on Mrs. Mott, Otis House Files, History and Background, folder 1, Society for the Preservation of New England Antiquities, Boston, Mass.

23. As quoted in Stage, *Female Complaints*, p. 106.

24. Ibid., p. 42.

25. On Ellen Demorest, see Claudia B. Kidwell, *Cutting a Fashionable Fit: Dressmakers' Drafting Systems in the United States* (Washington, D.C.: Smithsonian Institution, 1979), pp. 74–91; Joy Sanabel Emery, "Dreams on Paper," in Barbara Burman, ed., *The Culture of Sewing: Gender Consumption and Home Dressmaking* (Oxford, Eng.: Bay Publishers, 1999); *NAW*, pp. 459–60; John A. Garraty and Mark C. Carnes, eds., *American National Biography* (New York: Oxford Univ. Press, 1999), pp. 419–20; Caroline Bird, *Enterprising Women* (New York: Norton, 1976); Vare and Ptacek, *Mothers of*

Invention, pp. 71–73; Frank Luther Mott, *A History of American Magazines, 1865–1885*, vol. 3 (Cambridge: Harvard Univ. Press, 1938); Anne L. Macdonald, *Feminine Ingenuity: How Women Inventors Changed America* (New York: Ballantine Press, 1992); and Anne Commire, ed., *Women in World History: A Biographical Encyclopedia* (Waterford, Conn.: Yorkin, 1999), pp. 500–504. See also Wendy Gamber, *The Female Economy: The Millinery and Dressmaking Trades, 1860–1930* (Chicago: Univ. of Illinois Press, 1997). An obituary appears in the *New York Times*, August 11, 1898. See also Papers of Anna May Curtis Morris, Schlesinger Library, Harvard Univ., Cambridge, Mass. The only full-length biography is Ishbel Ross, *Crusades and Crinolines: The Life and Times of Ellen Curtis Demorest and William Jennings Demorest* (New York: Harper and Row, 1963); however, the accuracy of some of its information has been questioned.

26. Kidwell, *Cutting a Fashionable Fit*, esp. pp. 74, 81–83. On paper patterns and dressmaking, see generally Burman, *The Culture of Sewing*.

27. Gamber, *Female Economy*, p. 137.

28. Ibid., p. 135.

29. Ibid.

30. Ross, *Crusades and Crinolines*, pp. 23, 46–47. Wendy Gamber suggested to me the idea of a woman's "information revolution."

31. Kidwell, *Cutting a Fashionable Fit*, pp. 81, 83.

32. Garraty and Carnes, *American National Biography*, p. 419.

33. Bird, *Enterprising Women*, pp. 85–87.

34. Ross, *Crusades and Crinolines*, p. 129. Elizabeth McClintock, one of the participants in the 1848 women's rights meeting in Seneca Falls, learned the hard way about the difficulties of becoming a merchant. She had long wanted to become a silk merchant, but despite her contacts with influential merchants in Philadelphia, who were sympathetic with her goal, neither she nor her friends, Lucy Stone or Elizabeth Cady Stanton, were able to persuade these men to take them on. Ultimately, McClintock gave up her dream and settled for a retail shop. See Hawkes, " 'Feeling a Stong Desire to Tread a Broader Road to Fortune.' "

35. Ross, *Crusades and Crinolines*, p. 60.

36. On Martha Coston, see Lisa A. Marovich, " 'Let Her Have Brains Too': Commercial Networks, Public Relations, and the Business of Invention," *Business and Economic History* 27 (fall 1998): 140–61; Vare and Ptacek, *Mothers of Invention*, pp. 209–12; Anne L. Macdonald, *Feminine Invention: Women and Invention in America* (New York: Ballantine, 1992). See

also Zierdt-Warshaw, Winkler, and Bernstein, *American Women in Technology*, p. 66; and *Women Inventors to Whom Patents Have Been Granted by the United States Government, 1790 to July 1, 1888* (Washington, D.C.: Government Printing Office, 1888). See also Coston's autobiography, *Signal Success: The Work and Travels of Mrs. Martha J. Coston* (Philadelphia: J. B. Lippincott, 1886), and Martha J. Coston, *Coston's Telegraphic Night Signals. Patented in the United States and Europe, and Adopted by the Government of the United States, France, Italy, Denmark Holland, Hayti, and the New-York, Brooklyn, and Eastern Yacht Clubs* (New York: [n.p.], 1873).

37. Coston, *Signal Success*, pp. 23, 33.

38. Marovich makes this point about the relation between inventiveness, entrepreneurship, and women's familial position in " 'Let Her Have Brains Too,' " p. 143.

39. Coston, *Signal Success*, p. 37.

40. Ibid., pp. 271–72.

41. Ibid.

42. Ibid., p. 45.

43. *Women Inventors*, pp. 3–4.

44. Coston, *Signal Success*, p. 76.

45. Ibid., p. 48.

46. Ibid., p. 50.

47. Ibid., p. 54.

48. Ibid., p. 84.

49. Ibid., p. 89.

50. On the *Monitor*, see Marovich, " 'Let Her Have Brains Too,' " p. 148.

51. *Women Inventors*, pp. 9–11.

52. "The Coston Light," in Bernard C. Nalty, Dennis L. Noble, and Truman R. Strobridge, eds., *Wrecks, Rescues & Investigations: Selected Documents of the U.S. Coast Guard and its Predecessors* (Wilmington, Del.: Scholarly Resources, 1978), pp. 1–2.

53. Letter from Martha Coston, in *New Century for Women*, vol. 1 (1876), p. 5.

54. Macdonald, *Feminine Ingenuity*, p. 81.

55. Jeanne Madeline Weimann, *The Fair Women* (Chicago: Academy Chicago, 1981), p. 432.

56. *Demorest's Illustrated Monthly Magazine and Mme. Demorest's Mirror of Fashions* (September 1876): 456, cited in Macdonald, *Women and Invention in America*, p. 92.

57. On Myra Bradwell, see Jane M. Friedman, *America's First Woman Lawyer: The Biography of Myra Bradwell* (Buffalo, N.Y.: Prometheus, 1993); *NAW*, pp. 413–16; Virginia G. Drachman, *Sisters in Law: Woman Lawyers in Modern American History* (Cambridge: Harvard Univ. Press, 1998), pp. 6–36;

Virginia G. Drachman, *Women Lawyers and the Origins of Professional Identity in America: The Letters of the Equity Club, 1887 to 1890* (Ann Arbor: Univ. of Michigan Press, 1993); Bradwell v. State of Illinois, 83 U.S. (16 Wall.) 442 (1873); *In re Bradwell*, 55 Ill. 535 (1869).

58. Garraty and Carnes, *American National Biography*, p. 390.

59. Interview with Myra Bradwell, *Chicago Tribune*, May 12, 1889, as cited in Friedman, *America's First Woman Lawyer*, p. 18.

60. *In the Matter of the Application of Myra Bradwell to Obtain a License to Practice as an Attorney at Law*, Supreme Court of Illinois, September Term, 1869; as cited in Drachman, *Sisters in Law*, p. 17.

61. *In re Bradwell*, 55 Ill. 537, as cited in Drachman, *Sisters in Law*, p. 18.

62. Drachman, *Sisters in Law*, p. 119, and table 2, p. 253.

63. Friedman, *America's First Woman Lawyer*, p. 79.

64. *Chicago Legal News* 7 (Oct. 5, 1874): 21, as cited in Friedman, *America's First Woman Lawyer*, p. 85.

65. Drachman, *Sisters in Law*, p. 255.

66. Boyden Sparkes and Samuel Taylor Moore, *The Witch of Wall Street: Hetty Green* (New York Doubleday, Doran & Co., 1935), p. 41.

67. Joanna Massey, "Admirers Promote Hetty Green," *The New Bedford (Mass.) Standard Times*, November 22, 1999; and Louis Menand, "She Had to Have It," *The New Yorker* (April 23–30, 2001): 70.

68. On Hetty Green, see Sparkes and Moore, *The Witch of Wall Street*; Menand, "She Had to Have It"; and Louis Menand, *The Metaphysical Club: A Story of Ideas in America* (New York: Farrar, Straus and Giroux, 2001), pp. 164–75; *NAW*, vol. 2, pp. 81–83. An obituary is in the *New York Times*, July 4, 1916.

69. Sparkes and Moore, *The Witch of Wall Street*, p. 15.

70. Ibid.

71. Menand, "She Had to Have It," p. 64.

72. *NAW*, vol. 2, p. 81.

73. Ibid., p. 82.

74. Sparkes and Moore, *The Witch of Wall Street*, pp. 138–39.

75. "Hetty Green's Son and Heir Trained by Her," *New York Times Magazine*, July 9, 1916.

76. Ibid., p. 4.

77. Hetty Green, "Words of Wisdom from the Wealthiest Woman in America: The Benefits of a Business Training to Women," *Woman's Home Companion* in Roy Brousseau, comp., *Looking Forward: Life in the Twentieth Century as Pre-*

dicted in the Pages of American Magazines from 1895 to 1905 (New York: American Heritage, 1970), p. 123.

78. Sparkes and Moore perpetuate Hetty's reputation as the Witch of Wall Street. See also Menand, *Metaphysical Club*, p. 175. For a more positive perspective on Hetty, see Hetty Green, "Words of Wisdom" and "Hetty Green's Son and Heir Trained by Her."

CHAPTER 3

FASHIONING THE BUSINESS OF BEAUTY, 1830–1890

1. Edna Ferber's Emma McChesny novels include: *Roast Beef Medium: The Business Adventures of Emma McChesney* (New York: Frederick A. Stokes, 1913); *Personality Plus: Some Experiences of Emma McChesney and Her Son, Jock* (New York: Frederick A. Stokes, 1914); and *Emma McChesney & Co.* (New York: Grosset & Dunlap, 1915).

2. Ferber, *Emma McChesney & Co.*, p. 25.

3. On the rise of a consciousness of the businesswoman in American society, see Candace A. Kanes, "American Business Women, 1890–1930: Creating an Identity" (Ph.D. diss., Univ. of New Hampshire, 1997).

4. There is an exciting historiography emerging on women entrepreneurs in the beauty industry. See, for example, A'Lelia Bundles, *On Her Own Ground: The Life and Times of Madam C. J. Walker* (New York: Scribner, 2001); Kathy Peiss, *Hope in a Jar: The Making of America's Beauty Culture* (New York: Henry Holt, 1998); Kathy Peiss, " 'Vital Industry' and Women's Ventures: Conceptualizing Gender in Twentieth-Century Business History," *Business History Review* 72 (summer 1998): 219–41; Jane R. Plitt, *Martha Matilda Harper and the American Dream: How One Woman Changed the Face of Modern Business* (Syracuse, N.Y.: Syracuse Univ. Press, 2000); and Julie A. Willett, *Permanent Waves: The Making of the American Beauty Shop* (New York: New York Univ. Press, 2000). See also Lois Banner, *American Beauty* (New York: Knopf, 1983).

5. Leon Harris, *Merchant Princes: An Intimate History of Jewish Families Who Built Great Department Stores* (New York: Kodansha International, 1994).

6. On Mary Ann Magnin, see Harris, *Merchant Princes*, esp. pp. 247–48, 250; Ava F. Kahn, "Mary Ann Cohen Magnin," in Paula E. Hyman and Deborah Dash Moore, eds., *Jewish Women in America: An Historical Encyclopedia*, vol. 1 (New York: Routledge, 1998), pp. 881–82 (hereafter cited as *Jewish Women in America*). An obituary is in the *San Francisco Chronicle*, December 16, 1943. See also Magnin Family

Papers, Archives of the Western Jewish History Center, Berkeley, Calif.

7. On Carrie Marcus Neiman, see Harris, *Merchant Princes*, esp. pp. 169–80; "Mrs. Neiman Dead; store Co-Founder," *New York Times*, March 8, 1953.

8. Stanley Marcus, *Minding the Store: A Memoir* (Denton: Univ. of North Texas Press, 1974), p. 79.

9. On the rise of a consumer culture, see Ellen Gruber Garvey, *The Adman in the Parlor: Magazines and the Gendering of Consumer Culture, 1880s to 1910s* (New York: Oxford, 1996); Jennifer Scanlon, *Inarticulate Longings: The Ladies' Home Journal, Gender, and the Promises of Consumer Culture* (New York: Routledge, 1995); Jennifer Scanlon, ed. *The Gender and Consumer Culture Reader* (New York: New York Univ. Press, 2000); William Leach, *Land of Desire: Merchants, Power and the Rise of a New American Culture* (New York: Pantheon, 1993); Stuart Ewen, *Captains of Consciousness: Advertising and the Social Roots of the Consumer Culture* (New York: McGraw Hill, 1976); and Stuart Ewen and Elizabeth Ewen, *Channels of Desire: Mass Images and the Shaping of American Consciousness* (New York: McGraw Hill, 1982).

10. Nancy F. Koehn, *Brand New: How Entrepreneurs Earned Consumers' Trust, from Wedgwood to Dell* (Boston: Harvard Business School Press, 2001), p. 147.

11. Ibid., p. 148.

12. Peiss, *Hope in a Jar*, p. 105.

13. Koehn, *Brand New*, pp. 147–48.

14. Helena Rubinstein, "Manufacturing–Cosmetics," in Doris E. Fleischman, ed. *An Outline of Careers for Women: A Practical Guide to Achievement* (New York: Doubleday, Doran, 1934), pp. 327–31; quote at 331. On the gendered construction of the cosmetics industry during this era, see Kathy Peiss, "Making Faces: The Cosmetics Industry and Cultural Constructions of Gender, 1890–1930," *Genders* (spring 1990): 143–69.

15. See Peiss, *Hope in a Jar*, esp. pp. 61–96, 203–38.

16. Walter Fisher, "Sarah Breedlove Walker," in Edward T. James et al., eds., *Notable American Women, 1607–1950: A Biographical Dictionary*, vol. 3 (Cambridge, Mass.: Harvard Univ. Press, 1973), pp. 533–35; quote at 534 (hereafter cited as *NAW*).

17. Bundles, *On Her Own Ground*, p. 248.

18. The best history of Sarah Breedlove Walker is Bundles, *On Her Own Ground*. See also Peiss, *Hope in a Jar*, and Willett, *Permanent Waves*.

19. Bundles, *On Her Own Ground*, p. 48.

20. On Annie Minerva Turnbo Malone, see Bettye Collier-Thomas, "Annie Turnbo Malone," in Jessie Carney Smith, ed., *Notable Black American Women* (Detroit: Gale Research, 1992), pp. 724–7 (hereinafter *NBAW*); Jeanne Conway Mongold, "Annie Minerva Turnbo-Malone," in Barbara Sicherman and Carol Hurd Green, eds., *Notable American Women: The Modern Period* (Cambridge: Harvard Univ. Press, 1980), pp. 700–702 (hereafter cited as *NAWM*). Bundles, *On Her Own Ground*; and Peiss, *Hope in a Jar*.

21. Bundles, *On Her Own Ground*, p. 60.

22. Ibid., p. 83. On the advantages of business ownership, see Tiffany Melissa Gill, " 'I had my own business–so I didn't have to worry': Beauty Salons, Beauty Culturists, and the Politics of African-American Female Entrepreneurship," in Philip Scranton, ed., *Beauty and Business: Commerce, Gender, and Culture in Modern America* (New York: Routledge, 2000).

23. Bundles, *On Her Own Ground*, p. 138.

24. Ibid., p. 92. For an analysis of the intersection of gender and economics in the direct selling industry, see Katina L. Manko, " 'Now You Are in Business for Yourself': The Independent Contractors of the California Perfume Company, 1886–1939," *Business and Economic History* 26 (fall 1997):5–16.

25. Bundles, *On Her Own Ground*, p. 96.

26. Ibid.

27. Ibid., p. 145.

28. Ibid., p. 198.

29. *The New York Times Magazine*, November 2, 1917, as cited in Bundles, *On Her Own Ground*, p. 216.

30. Ibid., p. 235.

31. Ibid., p. 236.

32. Ibid., p. 153.

33. On women as pioneers in the franchise method of business, see Peiss, " 'Vital Industry' and Women's Ventures." See also Nicole Woodsy Biggart, *Charismatic Capitalism: Direct-Selling Organizations in America* (Chicago: Univ. of Chicago Press, 1989). Thomas S. Dicke looks at the post–World War II period, but without the innovations of women entrepreneurs, in *Franchising in America: The Development of a Business Method* (Chapel Hill: Univ. of North Carolina Press, 1992).

34. Bundles, *On Her Own Ground*, pp. 178, 179.

35. Ibid., p. 153.

36. Ibid.

37. Ibid., p. 275.

38. Ibid., p. 277.

39. Ibid., p. 124.

40. Ibid., p. 276.

41. Nancy Shuker, *Elizabeth Arden: Cosmetics Entrepreneur* (Englewood Cliffs, N.J.: Silver Burdett Press, 1989), p. 14.

42. "Lady's Day in Louisville," *Time* (May 6, 1946): 57, 58, 60, 63; see p. 60 for Arden's estimated income.

43. There is no definitive biography of Elizabeth Arden. In addition to Shuker, *Elizabeth Arden*, and "Lady's Day in Louisville," cited above, one may gather information from a range of sources. See Alfred Allan Lewis and Constance Woodworth, *Miss Elizabeth Arden* (New York: Coward, McCann & Geoghegan, 1972); Peiss, *Hope in a Jar*; Albro Martin, "Elizabeth Arden," *NAWM*, pp. 32–33; Carol P. Harvey, "Elizabeth Arden," in Frank Magill, ed., *Great Lives from History: American Woman Series* (Pasadena, Calif.: Salem Press, 1995), pp. 78–82; " 'I Am a Famous Woman in This Industry,' " *Fortune* (October 1938): 58, 60–65, 142, 145–46, 148, 152, 154; Margaret Case Harriman, "Profiles of Glamour, Inc.," *The New Yorker* (April 6, 1935): 24–30. Obituary in the *New York Times*, October 19, 1966.

44. " 'I Am a Famous Woman in This Industry,' " p. 62.

45. Shuker, *Elizabeth Arden*, see ch. 8, esp. pp. 77–79.

46. " 'I Am a Famous Woman in This Industry,' " p. 63.

47. Harriman, "Profiles of Glamour, Inc.," p. 26.

48. " 'I Am a Famous Woman in This Industry,' " p. 61.

49. Ibid., p. 142.

50. Ibid., pp. 63–64.

51. Ibid., p. 145.

52. Harvey, "Elizabeth Arden," p. 80.

53. Harriman, "Profiles of Glamour, Inc.," pp. 26, 27.

54. "Lady's Day in Louisville," p. 60.

55. " 'I Am a Famous Woman in This Industry,' " p. 63.

56. Obituary, *New York Times*.

57. "Lady's Day in Louisville," p. 60.

58. " 'I Am a Famous Woman in This Industry,' " p. 60.

59. Obituary, *New York Times*.

60. Ibid.

61. There is no biography of Hazel Bishop. For biographical sketches, see Anne Commire, ed., *Women in World History* (Westport, Conn.: Yorkin, 1999), pp. 562–63, and *Current Biography Yearbook* (New York: H. W. Wilson, 1957), pp. 11–12. Selected news articles on Bishop include "Business and Finance Leaders: Hazel Bishop," *New York Herald Tribune*, August 8, 1951; and "Woman Chemist Hits Lipstick Jackpot," *Business Week* (March 17, 1951): 42, 44–45. For an obituary, see Mary Tannen, "Hazel Bishop, 92, an Innovator Who Made Lipstick Kissproof," *New York Times*, December 10, 1998, Section B, p. 16. The Hazel Bishop Papers are in the Arthur and Elizabeth Schlesinger Library on the History of Women in America, Harvard University, Cambridge, Mass.

62. "Hazel Bishop: The Woman and the Firm," *Sunday Star Ledger*, September 6, 1987.

63. "Woman Chemist," p. 42.

64. *Current Biography Yearbook*, p. 12.

65. James H. Winchester, "A Lift for Milady's Spirits," *Petroleum Today* 4, no. 3 (1963): 3:11.

66. "Beauty Carries On," *Business Week* (May 1, 1943): 77–80, quote at 77. See also Ruth Bayard Smith, "The Girls of Summer," *Boston Globe Magazine* (August 7, 1988): 50–51; and Peiss, *Hope in a Jar*, pp. 239–45.

67. "Toiletries and Cosmetics," *Modern Packaging* (October 1954): 68.

68. Leila V. Hager, "Consumer Speaks Project on Teen-Agers' Preferences," *Journal of Home Economics* (May 1959): 370.

69. Ibid. Hazel Rawson Cades, "Is Your Makeup a Hit or a Miss?" *Women's Home Companion* 77 (1950): 129.

70. "Career Background Presented at the Cosmetic Executive Luncheon," New York, Hotel Pierre, May 14, 1981, carton 4, Bishop Papers.

71. Hazel Bishop autobiography, carton 4, folder "1940s and 1950s kept for literature," Bishop Papers.

72. "Woman Chemist," p. 45.

73. The advertisement first appeared in the *Washington Daily News*, February 1, 1950, p. 52.

74. "Woman Chemist," p. 45.

75. See, for example, "Hazel Bishop Lasting Lipstick" brochure, carton 3, Bishop Papers.

76. Cynthia Lowry, "All Rules Broken with Lasting Lipstick," *Austin (Texas) Statesman*, May 27, 1951, in Bishop Papers; and "Business and Finance Leaders," *New York Herald Tribune*.

77. "Lipsticks," *Consumer Reports* (August, 1951): 350–52.

78. *Current Biography Yearbook*, p. 12.

79. "Hazel Bishop," *New York Times*.

80. Ibid.; and *Current Biography Yearbook*, p. 12.

81. Harold A. Clement, "The Smear Behind That No-Smear Lipstick," *Top Secret Magazine* (October, 1954): 11. See also Lawrence Bernard, "Specter of Wealth Haunts Adman Spector," *Advertising Age*, February 7, 1955, in Bishop Papers.

82. *Current Biography Yearbook*, p. 12.

83. Joyce Antler, *The Journey Home: Jewish Women and the American Century* (New York: Free Press, 1997).

84. On Hattie Carnegie, see: L. H., "Profiles: Luxury, Inc." *The New Yorker* (March 31, 1934): 23–7; Russell Maloney, "Hattie

Carnegie," *Life* (November 12, 1945): 62–70; Hambla Bauer, "Hot Fashions by Hattie," *Collier's* (April 16, 1949): 26–27 ff. For an obituary, see "Hattie Carnegie Dies Here at 69," *New York Times*, February 23, 1956. For biographical essays, see Dennita Sewell, "Hattie Carnegie," in Hyman and Moore, eds., *Jewish Women in America*, vol. 1, pp. 207–208; and Alma A. Kenney, "Hattie Carnegie," in *NAWM*, pp. 135–36. Variations on the spelling of Köningeiser include Konengeiser and Koeningeiser.

85. On the gendered construction of the millinery business, see Wendy Gamber, "Gendered Concerns: Thoughts on the History of Business and the History of Women," *Business and Economic History* (fall 1994): 129–40. See also Edith Sparks, "Married women and economic choice; Explaining why women started in businesses in San Francisco between 1890 and 1930," *Business and Economic History* (winter 1999). On the difficulties women faced as they sought to strike out on their own as entrepreneurs in Boston, see Sarah Deutsch, *Women and the City: Gender, Space and Power in Boston, 1870–1940* (New York: Oxford, 2000), pp. 115–35.

86. L. H., "Profiles: Luxury, Inc.," p. 27.

87. Ibid., p. 26.

88. "Hattie Carnegie," *Life*, p. 64.

89. Ibid.

90. L. H., "Profiles: Luxury, Inc.," p. 26.

91. Kenney, "Hattie Carnegie," in *NAWM*, p. 136.

92. L. H., "Profiles: Luxury, Inc.," p. 23.

93. "Hattie Carnegie," *Life*, p. 70.

94. On Lane Bryant, see Rebecca Bailey, "Fashions in Pregnancy: An Analysis of Selected Cultural Influences, 1850–1980" (Ph.D. diss., Michigan State Univ., 1981); Louise Klaber, "Lane Bryant Malsin," in *Jewish Women in America*, vol. 1, pp. 886–87; "Lane Bryant Dies; Founder of Chain," obituary in *New York Times*, September 27, 1951, and "Mrs. Malsin's Estate," *New York Times*, June 6, 1954. See also "The First Lane Bryant Garment Was Cut by My Own Hands Twenty-Six Years Ago," introduction, *Lane Bryant Style Book* (New York: Lane Bryant, 1927), p. 3.

95. Bailey, "Fashions in Pregnancy," p. 23.

96. Ibid., p. 260.

97. *Lane Bryant Style Book*, p. 3.

98. Klaber, "Lane Bryant Malsin," p. 886.

99. "Lane Bryant Dies," *New York Times*.

100. "Mrs. Malsin's Estate," *New York Times*, and Klaber, "Lane Bryant Malsin," p. 886.

101. "Lane Bryant Dies," *New York Times*.

102. On Ida Rosenthal, see Joy A. Kingsolver, "Ida Cohen Rosenthal," *Jewish Women in America*, vol. 2, pp. 1181–82; Caroline Bird, *Enterprising Women* (New York: Norton, 1976), pp. 191–95; Irene D. Neu, "Ida Cohen Rosenthal," in *NAWM*, pp. 604–605; Catherine Coleman Brawer, "Ida Rosenthal," in Magill, *Great Lives from History*, vol. 4 (Pasadena, Calif.: Salem Press, 1995), pp. 1547–50. Articles on Rosenthal in popular magazines include Michele Morris, "The Mother Figure of Maidenform," *Working Woman* (April 1987): 82–83, 86–88; "I Dreamed I Was a Tycoon . . . ." *Time* (October 24, 1960): 92; and "Maidenform's Mrs. R.," *Fortune* (July 1950): 75–6, 130–32. See also Rosenthal's obituary, "Ida Rosenthal, Co-Founder of Maidenform, Dies," *New York Times*, March 30, 1973. For William Rosenthal's obituary, see "William Rosenthal Dead, a Manufacturer," *New York Times*, April 14, 1958.

103. "Ida Rosenthal, Co-Founder of Maidenform, Dies."

104. See generally, Janet Zandy, " 'Women Have Always Sewed': The Production of Clothing and the Work of Women," *Women's Studies Quarterly* 1 and 2 (1995): 162–80; and Bernard Smith, "Market Development, Industrial Development: The Case of the American Corset Trade, 1860–1920," *Business History Review* 65 (spring 1991): 91–129.

105. "Ida Rosenthal, Co-Founder of Maidenform, Dies," *New York Times*.

106. The Maidenform "Dream" campaign has attracted much analysis. See, for example, Barbara J. Coleman, "Maidenform(ed): Images of American Women in the 1950s," *Genders* (1995): 3–29; James N. Stull, "The Maidenform Campaigns: Reaffirming the Feminine Ideal," *Connecticut Review* (spring 1992): 1–7; and "Uplifting," *The New Yorker* (September 27, 1993).

107. Peiss, " 'Vital Industry,' " p. 81.

CHAPTER 4
BREAKING NEW GROUND, 1890–1960

1. Jeannette Phillips Gibbs, *Portia Marries* (Boston: Little, Brown, 1926).

2. On the new meritocracy, see Edward A. Purcell, Jr., *The Crisis of Democratic Theory: Scientific Naturalism and the Problem of Value* (Lexington: Univ. of Kentucky Press, 1973). On women, meritocracy, and the public sphere, see, for example, Nancy F. Cott, *The Grounding of Modern Feminism* (New Haven: Yale Univ. Press, 1987); Rosalind Rosenberg, *Beyond Separate Spheres: Intellectual Roots of Feminism* (New Haven: Yale Univ. Press, 1982); Ellen Fitzpatrick, *Endless Crusade: Women Social Scientists and Progressive Reform* (New

York: Oxford Univ. Press, 1990). On women in male-dominated professions, see, for example, Virginia G. Drachman, *Sisters in Law: Women Lawyers in Modern American History* (Cambridge: Harvard Univ. Press, 1998); Ellen S. More, *Restoring the Balance: Women Physicians and the Profession of Medicine, 1850–1955* (Cambridge: Harvard Univ. Press, 1999); and Patricia M. Hummer, *The Decade of Elusive Promise: Professional Women in the United States, 1920–1930* (Ann Arbor: Univ. of Michigan Research Press, 1979).

3. Ethlie Ann Vare and Greg Ptacek, *Mothers of Invention: From the Bra to the Bomb: Forgotten Women and Their Unforgettable Ideas* (New York: Morrow, 1988), pp. 241–43.

4. See Sarah Deutsch, *Women and the City: Gender, Space, and Power in Boston, 1870–1940* (New York: Oxford Univ. Press, 2000), p. 117; and Candace A. Kanes, "American Business Women, 1890–1930: Creating an Identity" (Ph.D. diss., Univ. of New Hampshire, 1997), esp. pp. 1–10.

5. See, for example, Angel Kwolek-Folland, *Engendering Business: Men and Women in the Corporate Office, 1870–1930* (Baltimore, Md.: Johns Hopkins Univ. Press, 1994); and Margery W. Davies, *Woman's Place is at the Typewriter: Office Work and Office Workers, 1870–1930* (Philadelphia: Temple Univ. Press, 1982). On Seymour, see Kanes, "American Business Women," esp. pp. 47–84.

6. On business schools, see Willis Jay Winn, *Business Education in the United States: A Historical Perspective* (New York: American Newcomen Society, 1964). On the rise of the corporation, see Alfred D. Chandler, Jr., *The Visible Hand: The Managerial Revolution in American Business* (Cambridge: Harvard Univ. Press, 1977).

7. See, for example, Jean Strouse, *Morgan: American Financier* (New York: Perennial, 2000).

8. See Richard Hofstadter, *Social Darwinism in American Thought* (Boston: Beacon, 1955).

9. On women's inability to achieve equality with men in the professions, see Hummer, *Elusive Promise*; Drachman, *Sisters in Law*; and More, *Restoring the Balance*. See also Karen Ward, "From Executive to Feminist: The Business Women's Legislative Council of Los Angeles, 1927–1932," in Mary A. Yeager, ed., *Women in Business*, vol. 3 (Northampton, Mass.: Elgar Reference Collection, 1999), pp. 633–48.

10. *Marion* (Indiana) *Daily Chronicle*, November 8, 1922, quoted in Marie D. Webster, *Quilts: Their Story, and How to Make Them* (Santa Barbara, Calif.: Practical Patchwork, 1990), p. 217.

11. Nancy E. Owen discusses this gendered dichotomy in *Rookwood and the Industry of Art: Women, Culture, and Com-*

merce, 1880–1913 (Athens: Ohio Univ. Press, 2001), esp. pp. 26–27. On women in the Arts and Crafts Movement, see Erika E. Hirshler, *A Studio of Her Own: Women Artists in Boston, 1870–1940* (Boston: Museum of Fine Arts, 2001), pp. 45–53.

12. The best source on Webster is Rosalind Webster Perry, "Marie Webster: Her Story," in Webster, *Quilts*. See also Cuesta Benberry, "Marie Webster: Indiana's Gift to American Quilts," in *Quilts of Indiana: Crossroads of Memories*, Marilyn Goldman and Marguerite Niebusch (Bloomington: Indiana Univ. Press, 1990), pp. 88–93; Thomas K. Woodard and Blanche Greenstein, *Twentieth Century Quilts, 1900–1950* (New York: E. P. Dutton, 1988), pp. 11, 20; Elizabeth V. Warren and Sharon L. Eisenstat, *Glorious American Quilts: The Quilt Collection of the Museum of American Folk Art* (New York: Penguin Studio, 1996), pp. 93–96; and E. Duane Elbert and Rachel Kamm Elbert, *History from the Heart: Quilt Paths Across Illinois* (Nashville, Tenn.: Rutledge Hill Press, 1995), pp. 147–49.

13. Perry, "Marie Webster," p. 214.

14. Benberry, "Marie Webster," p. 92. See also Perry, "Marie Webster," p. 219.

15. On Julia Morgan, see Sara Holmes Boutelle, *Julia Morgan, Architect* (New York: Abbeville Press, 1988); for biographical essays, see Elinor Richey, "Julia Morgan," in Barbara Sicherman and Carol Hurd Green, eds., *Notable American Women: The Modern Period* (Cambridge: Harvard Univ. Press, 1980), pp. 499–501 (hereafter cited as *NAWM*); and Pamela Kett-O'Connor, "Julia Morgan," in Frank N. Magill, ed., *Great Lives from History: American Women Series*, vol. 5 (Pasadena, Calif.: Salem Press, 1995), pp. 1294–99. On the Hearst Castle, see Victoria Kastner, *Hearst Castle: The Biography of a Country House* (New York: Abrams, 2000).

16. Estelle B. Freedman first coined this term in "Separatism as Strategy: Female Institution Building and American Feminism, 1870–1930," *Feminist Studies*, vol. 5 (1979): 512–19.

17. Boutelle, *Julia Morgan, Architect*, pp. 116–18.

18. Ibid., p. 44.

19. Ibid., p. 45.

20. Ibid., p. 20.

21. Ibid., p. 214.

22. Kett-O'Connor, "Julia Morgan," p. 1298.

23. On Isabella Greenway, see Blake Brophy, "Tucson's Arizona Inn: The Continuum of Style," *Journal of Arizona History* 24 (autumn 1983): 1–28; Kristie Miller, "A Volume of Friendship: The Correspondence of Isabella Greenway and Eleanor Roosevelt, 1904–1953," *Journal of Arizona*

History 40 (summer 1999): 121–56; and Hope Chamberlain, *A Minority of Members: Women in the U.S. Congress* (New York: Praeger, 1973).

24. Miller, "A Volume of Friendship," p. 125.

25. Ibid.

26. Brophy, "Tucson's Arizona Inn," p. 5.

27. Ibid., pp. 18–19, 25.

28. Ibid., p. 9.

29. Richard F. Shepard, "Jennie Grossinger Dies at Resort Home," *New York Times*, November 21, 1972.

30. On Jennie Grossinger, see Joel Pomerantz, *Jennie and the Story of Grossinger's* (New York: Grosset and Dunlop, 1970); Tania Grossinger, *Growing up at Grossinger's* (New York: David McKay Co., 1975); Harold Irving Taub, *Waldorf-in-the-Catskills: The Grossinger Legend* (New York: Sterling Co., 1952). Biographical essays include Paula E. Hyman, "Jennie Grossinger," in *NAWM*, pp. 294–95; Andra Medie, "Jennie Grossinger," Paula E. Hyman and Deborah Dash Moore, eds., *Jewish Women in America: An Historical Encyclopedia* (New York: Routledge, 1998), pp. 556–58 (hereafter cited as *Jewish Women in America*); and Shepard, "Jennie Grossinger Dies at Resort Home." On Grossinger's in the context of the Catskill Mountains' leisure culture, see, for example, Myrna Katz Frommer and Harvey Frommer, *It Happened in the Catskills* (San Diego, Calif.: Harcourt Brace Jovanovich, 1991); Phil Brown, *Catskill Culture* (Philadelphia: Temple Univ. Press, 1998); Jenna Weissman Joselit, "Leisure and Recreation," in *Jewish Women in America*, pp. 818–27; and Andrew R. Heinze, "Advertising and Consumer Culture," in *Jewish Women in America*, pp. 23–32.

31. Shepard, "Jennie Grossinger Dies at Resort Home," p. 46; and Hyman, "Jennie Grossinger," p. 295.

32. Shepard, "Jennie Grossinger Dies at Resort Home," p. 46; and generally, Joselit, "Leisure and Recreation," esp. pp. 818–23.

33. Shepard, "Jennie Grossinger Dies at Resort Home," p. 46.

34. Ibid.

35. On African American women's activism in this era, see, for example, Evelyn Brooks Higginbotham, *Righteous Discontent: The Women's Movement in the Black Baptist Church, 1880–1920* (Cambridge: Harvard Univ. Press, 1993); Dorothy C. Salem, *To Better Our World: Black Women in Organized Reform, 1890–1920* (Brooklyn, N.Y.: Carlson, 1990); and Rosalyn Terborg-Penn, *African-American Women in the Struggle for the Vote, 1850–1920* (Bloomington: Indiana Univ. Press, 1998). Juliet E. K. Walker refers to this era as the "golden age of black business" in *The History of Black Business in America: Capitalism, Race, Entrepreneurship* (New York: Macmillan, 1998), pp. 182–224.

36. As cited in Elsa Barkley Brown, "Womanist Consciousness: Maggie Lena Walker and the Independent Order of Saint Luke," *Signs: Journal of Women in Culture and Society* 14 (spring 1989): 610–32, quote at p. 618.

37. On Maggie Lena Walker, see Brown, "Womanist Consciousness"; Celia Jackson Suggs "Maggie L. Walker," Maggie Walker National Historic Site, Richmond, Virginia; and biographical essays including Margaret Duckworth, "Maggie L. Walker," in Jessie Carney Smith, ed., *Notable Black American Women*, vol. 1 (Detroit: Gale Research, 1992–96), pp. 1188–93; Gertrude W. Marlowe, "Maggie Lena Walker, *NAW*, vol. 3, pp. 1214–19; and Dorothy C. Salem, "Maggie Lena Walker," in Magill, *Great Lives from History*, pp. 1835–39. Walker's papers, including addresses, diaries, and photographs, are at the Maggie Walker National Historic Site, Richmond, Virginia.

38. Brown, "Womanist Consciousness," p. 617.

39. Suggs, "Maggie L. Walker," p. 4.

40. Ibid.

41. Duckworth, "Maggie L. Walker," p. 1191.

42. Ibid.

43. Brown, "Womanist Consciousness," p. 626–27.

44. Duckworth, "Maggie L. Walker," p. 1188.

45. Miriam Formanek-Brunell, *Made to Play House: Dolls and the Commercialization of American Girlhood, 1830–1930* (New Haven, Conn.: Yale Univ. Press, 1993).

46. On Beatrice Alexander, see Jere Van Dyk, "The Magic of Madame Alexander Dolls," *Smithsonian* 13 (March 2001): 105–9; Carolyn Cook, Michilinda Kinsey, and Scott Wood, *I Had That Doll!* (New York: Park Lane, 1996); see also biographical sketches such as *Current Biography Yearbook* (New York: H. N. Wilson, 1957), pp. 13–15; and Julie Altman, "Ruth Mosko Handler," in *Jewish Women in America*, pp. 591–93.

47. Van Dyk, "The Magic of Madame Alexander Dolls," p. 106.

48. Ibid.

49. Cook, Kinsey, and Wood, *I Had That Doll!*, p. 38.

50. Van Dyk, "The Magic of Madame Alexander Dolls," p. 107.

51. On Ruth Handler, see Ruth Handler, *Dream Doll: The Ruth Handler Story* (Stamford, Conn.: Longmeadow Press, 1994); and M. G. Lord, *Forever Barbie: The Unauthorized Biography of a Real Doll* (New York: William Morrow, 1994).

52. Handler, *Dream Doll*, p. 47.

53. Ibid., p. 47.

54. Lord, *Forever Barbie*, p. 21.

55. Handler, *Dream Doll*, pp. 57, 106.

56. Ibid., p. 112.

57. Altman, "Ruth Mosko Handler," p. 593.

58. On Olive Beech, see the Walter H. and Olive Ann Beech Collection, at the Wichita State University Special Collections and University Archives, in Wichita, Kans., on-line at <www.wichita.edu/public/scwww/public html/exhibita.html>. See also National Aviation Hall of Fame, <www.nationalaviation.org/enshrinee/beech-olive.html>; and Frank Hedrick, *Pageantry of Flight: The Story of the Beech Aircraft Corporation* (New York: Newcomen Society, 1967).

59. "Olive Ann Beech," National Aviation Hall of Fame.

60. "Biographical Sketch," Walter H. and Olive Ann Beech Collection.

CHAPTER 5

WOMEN TAKE CHARGE, 1960–2000

1. Horatio Alger Association of Distinguished Americans, <www.horatioalger.com/member/alv01.htm>. Numerous newspaper and magazine articles are available on Linda Alvarado. See, for example, Marice Richter, "Business Owner Laughs at Her Detractors," *Tampa Tribune*, December 14, 1994; sec. Baylife; and Mike Klis, "Minority Owner, Major Accomplishment," *Denver Post*, November 16, 1999.

2. See Martha Stewart's website, <www.marthastewart. com>. On Stewart, see Christopher M. Byron, *Martha Inc.: The Incredible Story of Martha Stewart Living Omnimedia* (New York: Wiley, 2002). There are many articles on Stewart in newspaper and magazines; see for example Jura Koncius, "Heeeeerrrre's Martha," *Washington Post*, November 28, 1991, sec. Home; the Arts & Entertainment network broadcast a biography of Stewart, May 4, 2001. See also the biographical essay in *Current Biography Yearbook* (New York: H. W. Wilson, 1993), pp. 555–59.

3. *Women-Owned Businesses, the New Economic Force* (Washington, D.C.: National Foundation for Women Business Owners [NFWBO], 1992), esp. pp. 1, 3.

4. "Facts on Women-Owned Businesses: Trends in the U.S. and the 50 States" and "Facts on Women-Owned Businesses: Trends in the Top 50 Metropolitan Areas," both from Facts of the Week, NFWBO, January–June 1999, available at <www.nfwbo.org/jan-jun99.html>.

5. "Women Business Owners' Economic Impact Re-Affirmed," NFWBO Research Summary, March 27, 1996, available at <www.nfwbo.org/LocLink/BIZC/Research/LinkTo/3-27-1996/3-37-1996.htm>.

6. "Number of Minority-Owned Businesses and Revenues Increase Substantially Between 1987 and 1992," U.S. Bureau of the Census, NFWBO, Facts of the Week, June–December 1996, at <www.nfwbo.org/jun-dec96.html>.

7. "1996 Facts on Women-Owned Businesses: Trends Among Minority Women-Owned Firms," Facts of the Week, NFWBO, July–December 1997, available at <www.nfwbo.org/jul-dec97.html>. For a comparison of Latina and white women entrepreneurs in San Diego, see Sally Ann Davies-Netzley, *Gendered Capital: Entrepreneurial Women in American Society* (New York: Garland, 2000).

8. On Ash, see Russell R. Taylor, *Exceptional Entrepreneurial Women: Strategies for Success* (New York: Quorum, 1988), pp. 66–71; *Current Biography Yearbook* (New York: H. W. Wilson, 1993), pp. 27–31; Robert L. Shook, *The Entrepreneurs: Twelve Who Took Risks and Succeeded* (New York: Harper & Row, 1980), pp. 102–14; Mary Kay Ash, *Mary Kay* (New York: Harper & Row, 1981); Mary Kay Ash, *Mary Kay on People Management* (New York: Warner, 1984). Kathy Peiss includes Ash in *Hope in a Jar: The Making of America's Beauty Culture* (New York: Owl, 1999), pp. 262, 268.

9. *Current Biography Yearbook*, 1993, p. 30.

10. Shook, *The Entrepreneurs*, p. 112.

11. Jeanne Weiland, "Joyce Chen, Godmother of Authentic Chinese Cuisine," in *Nation's Restaurant News*, special issue, February 1996, p. 56. On Joyce Chen, see Joyce Chen, *Joyce Chen Cook Book* (Cambridge, Mass.: Joyce Chen Associates, 1962), pp. 1–3; Kenneth T. Jackson, ed., *Scribner Encyclopedia of American Lives* (New York: Scribner's, 1996), pp. 85–86; Bo Burlingham, "Joyce Chen & the Szechuan-Cambridge Connection," *The [Boston] Real Paper*, June or July 1974; Diane Stoneback, "Joyce Chen: She Reigns as Julia Child of Chinese Cooking," *Fort Lauderdale News/Sun-Sentinel* April 28–29, 1982. For obituaries, see *Boston Globe*, August 25, 1994; and *New York Times*, August 26, 1994. See also <www.joycechen.com>.

12. Jackson, *Scribner Encyclopedia of American Lives*, p. 85.

13. On Sobrino, see Jim Hopkins, "Childhood Treat Helps Sobrino Savor Sweet Success," *USA Today*, May 16, 2001; Lee Romney, "Latinas Get Down to Business," *Los Angeles Times*, November 13, 1998; Rosalva Hernandez, "Just Desserts," *Orange County Register*, May 12, 1998; and Michelle Prather, "Gettin' Jiggly with It," *Entrepreneur* (January 2000). See also the company's website, <www.lulusdessert.com>.

14. Hopkins, "Childhood Treat."

15. "Q&A, Donna Dubinsky: The Whole Word in Her Handheld," *Harvard Business School Bulletin* (June 2001): 1.

16. On Ellen Gordon, see, for example, Katy Kelly, "Chewy Sweets Can't Be Beat After a Century," *USA Today*, March

28, 1996; Susan Tiffany, "Tootsie Roll Keeps Rolling in the Riches," *Candy Industry* (June 1993); Stephan Wilkinson, "The Practical Genius of Penny Candy," *Working Woman* (April 1989); Patricia L. Magee, "Ellen Gordon Reaches 'Top of the Mountain,' " *Candy Industry* (September 1985); and Jonathan Eig, "Ellen Gordon: Success Is So Sweet," *Priorities* 1, issue 3.

17. Kelly, "Chewy Sweets."

18. See Katharine Graham, *Personal History* (New York: Vintage Books, 1998).

19. Ellen Goodman, "A Death in the Family of Newspapers," *Boston Globe*, July 19, 2001.

20. Graham, *Personal History*, pp. 181, 231.

21. Francis X. Clines, "At Katharine Graham Funeral, Parade of Boldface Names," *New York Times*, July 24, 2001.

22. Graham, *Personal History*, p. 319.

23. From "Entrepreneurial Vision in Action: Exploring Growth Among Women- and Men-Owned Firms," Facts of the Week, NFWBO, June 11, 2001, available at <www.nfwbo.org/jan-jun01.html>.

24. Eleanor Brantley Schwartz, "Entrepreneurship: A New Female Frontier," *Journal of Contemporary Business* 1 (winter 1976): 47–76, see esp. 60–62.

25. Teri Cavanagh, "A New Ceiling for Women," *Boston Globe*, October 22, 2000; and Teri Cavanagh, "Women Business Owners, Debt Isn't an Enemy," *Boston Globe*, July 7, 2001.

26. "Women Business Owners of Color: Challenges and Accomplishments," Facts of the Week, NFWBO, January–June 1998, available at <www.nfwbo.org/jan-jun98.html>.

27. Kevin Maney, "Tech Duo's Game Plan: Palm Pilot for Kids," *USA Today*, December 9, 1998.

28. "Hispanic Leader a Woman of Many Firsts," *Arizona Republic*, September 18, 2000.

29. "Credibility, Creativity and Independence: The Greatest Challenges and Biggest Rewards of Business Ownership among Women," Facts of the Week, NFWBO, June–December 1996. See also Linda Pinson and Jerry Jinnett, *The Woman Entrepreneur* (Tustin, Calif.: Out of your mind . . . and into the marketplace, 1992), pp. 8–9.

30. "Constructing a Better America," from American Dreams: <www.usdreams.com/alvarado6869.html>.

31. "Credibility, Creativity and Independence," Facts of the Week.

32. "Characteristics and Contributions of Home-Based Women-Owned Businesses in the U.S.," Facts of the Week, NFWBO, June–December 1996.

33. Schwartz, "Entrepreneurship," p. 64.

34. *Women-Owned Businesses*, p. 6; "Credibility, Creativity and Independence," Facts of the Week.

35. "Business Owners and Gender Equity in the Workplace," Facts of the Week, NFWBO, July–December 2000, available at <www.nfwbo.org/jul-dec00.html>.

36. "Employee Benefits Offered by Women-Owned Businesses: A Framework for Compassion," Facts of the Week, NFWBO, June–December 1996; and "Retirement Plan Trends in the Small Business Market: A Survey of Women- and Men-Owned Firms," Facts of the Week, NFWBO, January–June 1998, available at <www.nfwbo.org/jan-june98.html>.

37. "Styles of Success: The Thinking and Management Style of Women and Men Entrepreneurs," Facts of the Week, NFWBO, June–December 1996.

38. Priscilla Y. Huff, "Women's E-Businesses Are Alive and Thriving," *Women's Enews*, December 26, 2000, available at <www.womensenews.org>.

39. "Leaders in Business and Community: The Philanthropic Contributions of Women and Men Business Owners," Facts of the Week, NFWBO, July–December 2000.

40. Naomi Aoki, "Women Helping Women on Rise," *Boston Globe*, May 10, 2001.

41. Graham, *Personal History*, pp. 449, 450.

FURTHER READING

This book accompanies an exhibition that combines two areas of historical inquiry: women's history and business history. It contributes to women's history by adding women entrepreneurs to the historiography on women in careers, professions, and work. Historians have examined women in a broad range of fields including law, medicine, and the social sciences. See, for example, Rosalind Rosenberg, *Beyond Separate Spheres: Intellectual Roots of Feminism* (New Haven: Yale Univ. Press, 1982); Ellen Fitzpatrick, *Endless Crusade: Women Social Scientists and Progressive Reform* (New York: Oxford Univ. Press, 1990); Virginia G. Drachman, *Sisters in Law: Women Lawyers in Modern American History* (Cambridge: Harvard Univ. Press, 1998); Ellen S. More, *Restoring the Balance: Women Physicians and the Profession of Medicine, 1850–1955* (Cambridge: Harvard Univ. Press, 1999); and Patricia M. Hummer, *The Decade of Elusive Promise: Professional Women in the United States, 1920–1930* (Ann Arbor: UMI Research Press, 1979). The exhibition contributes to business history by moving beyond the dominant narrative of American business, which focuses on the development of the modern corporation, to bring a gender analysis to an examination of smaller businesses and independent entrepreneurs. The classic history of the corporation and big business is Alfred D. Chandler, Jr., *The Visible Hand: The Managerial Revolution in American Business* (Cambridge: Harvard Univ. Press, 1977). Sarah Stage's biography of Lydia Pinkham, *Female Complaints: Lydia Pinkham and the Business of Women's Medicine* (New York: W. W. Norton, 1979), moved beyond the corporation to examine the role of a woman in a small, family enterprise. Since then, women's historians have increasingly examined the importance of women and gender in the history of American business. See, for example, Wendy Gamber, *The Female Economy: The Millinery and Dressmaking Trades, 1860–1930* (Chicago: Univ. of Illinois Press, 1997); Kathy Peiss, *Hope in a Jar: The Making of America's Beauty Culture* (New York: Henry Holt, 1998); and Angel Kwolek-Folland, *Incorporating Women: A History of Women and Business in the United States* (New York: Twayne, 1998). Recent biographies of women entrepreneurs include

A'Lelia Bundles, *On Her Own Ground: The Life and Times of Madam C. J. Walker* (New York: Scribner, 2001); and Patricia Cleary, *Elizabeth Murray: A Woman's Pursuit of Independence in Eighteenth-Century America* (Amherst: Univ. of Massachusetts Press, 2000). Katharine Graham's memoir, *Personal History* (New York: Vintage, 1998) offers a fascinating look at the making of a businesswoman in modern America. For a recent collection of essays on gender in business history, see Philip Scranton, ed., *Beauty and Business: Commerce, Gender, and Culture in Modern America* (New York: Routledge, 2001). On the relationship between business history and women's history, see Mary A. Yeager, "Will There Ever Be a Feminist Business History?" in Mary A. Yeager, ed., *Women in Business* (Northampton, Mass.: Elgar Reference Collection, 1999), vol. 1, pp. 3–43. The essays in this three-volume collection present analyses of women's place as entrepreneurs, laborers, and consumers in the history of American business. On gender in business history, see Joan W. Scott, "Comment: Conceptualizing Gender in American Business History," *Business History Review* 72 (summer 1998): 242–49; Wendy Gamber, "Gendered Concerns: Thoughts on the History of Business and the History of Women," *Business and Economic History* 23 (fall 1994): 129–40; Alice Kessler-Harris, "Ideologies and Innovation: Gender Dimensions of Business History," *Business and Economic History* 20 (2nd series 1991): 45–51; and Kathy Peiss, " 'Vital Industry' and Women's Ventures: Conceptualizing Gender in Twentieth-Century Business History," *Business History Review* 72 (summer 1998): 219–41. On gender in the history of the corporation in its early decades, see Angel Kwolek-Folland, *Engendering Business: Men and Women in the Corporate Office, 1870–1930* (Baltimore, Md.: Johns Hopkins Univ. Press, 1994). On the intersection of race and gender in business history, see Juliet E. K. Walker, *The History of Black Business in America: Capitalism, Race, Entrepreneurship* (New York: Macmillan, 1998). Claudia Goldin analyzes woman's role in the history of the economy in *Understanding the Gender Gap: An Economic History of American Women* (New York: Oxford Univ. Press, 1990).

PICTURE CREDITS

Abbrev.

Schlesinger Library: The Arthur and Elizabeth Schlesinger Library on the History of Women in America, Radcliffe Institute for Advanced Study, Harvard University.

page ii (left to right): Coston–see page 57 credit, below; Bemis–71–185.29. Idaho State Historical Society; Neiman–page 77 credit; Walker–page 132 credit.

page iii (left to right): Keckley–see page 54 credit, below; Carnegie–page 97 credit; Handler–page 140 credit; Graham–see page 148 credit.

page 6: Declaration of Independence. Maryland State Archives.

page 13: Pinckney dress. National Museum of American History, Smithsonian Institution, on loan from Mr. Edward Rutledge Pinckney.

page 16: Goddard postmaster's appointment. Courtesy of the Rhode Island Historical Society.

page 17: Baltimore post office. Maryland State Archives.

page 19: Murray portrait; detail of colorplate 1, see below.

page 21: Murray trade bill. Courtesy of the Massachusetts Historical Society.

page 23: *Treatise of Feme Coverts*. Harvard Law School Library.

page 26: Inman House, Cambridge, Mass. Hannah Winthrop Chapter, Daughters of the American Revolution, *An Historic Guide to Cambridge* (Cambridge, Mass., 1907), facing p. 172. Courtesy of the Cambridge Historical Commission.

page 28: Demorest advertisement, "The Ever-blooming." *Demorest's Monthly Magazine*, September 1875. *Schlesinger Library*.

Page 31: Bemis in wedding gown. 75.228.43/H, Idaho State Historical Society; Bemis with horses, 1910. 62.44.7, Idaho State Historical Society.

Page 34: Lukens portrait; detail of colorplate 3, see below.

Page 36: Chester Valley Bank banknote. The Graystone Society.

Page 37: Lukens's Rolling Mill, Coatesville, Penn., 1870s. Courtesy of the Hagley Museum and Library.

Page 38: Plan of Briones's rancho. Bancroft Library, University of California, Berkeley. Briones portrait, from Florence M. Fava, *Los Altos Hills: the Colorful Story*. Woodside, Calif.: Gilbert Richards Publications, 1976.

Page 41: Pinkham's notes on clients. *Schlesinger Library*

Page 42: Pinkham and family, 1879. *Schlesinger Library*.

Page 43: Pinkham ledgers and box. *Schlesinger Library*.

Page 44: "A woman best understands a woman's ills." *Schlesinger Library*.

Page 47: Margarett Adams photograph; Adams sisters' daybook. Jo Anne Preston.

Page 48: Exterior of Mme Demorest's Emporium. *Schlesinger Library*.

Page 49: Interior of Mme Demorest's Emporium. *Schlesinger Library*.

Page 50: Skirt suspenders advertisement, *Demorest's Monthly Magazine*, April 1874. *Schlesinger Library*.

Page 51: Demorest Paris Exposition display. *Demorest's Monthly Magazine*, June 1878. National Heritage Museum; clipper ship, ca. 1872. *Schlesinger Library*.

Page 54: Keckley portrait. Anacostia Museum and Center for African American History and Culture, Smithsonian Institution. Courtesy of Catherine Gray Hurley; title page of *Behind the Scenes*, 1868. Harvard University Library.

Page 57: Martha Coston, from *Signal Success*, 1886. Miriam Y. Holden Collection, Princeton University Library.

Page 59: Coston patent. U.S. Patent Office.

Page 60: "The Loss of the *U.S.S. Monitor*." *Frank Leslie's Illustrated Newspaper*, January 24, 1863. U.S. Naval Historical Center.

Page 63: Bradwell portrait, from the *Green Bag*, 1889. Harvard Law School Library

Page 64: *Chicago Legal News*. Harvard Law School Library.

Page 65: "Rainbow" fliers. *Schlesinger Library*.

Page 71: Green on street. Getty/Hulton Archives.

Page 72: "If I Were as Rich as Hetty Green," sheet music. Edith Nichols, Hetty Green: A Frugal Woman's Museum.

Page 74: Walker in Model-A Ford. A'Lelia Bundles/Walker Family Collection.

Page 77: Neiman portrait. Dallas Historical Society.

Page 78: Neiman–Marcus advertisement, *The Dallas Morning News*, 1907. Dallas Historical Society.

Page 83: Walker agent at work. A'Lelia Bundles/Walker Family Collection.

Page 85: Walker's first home, in Delta, Louisiana. A'Lelia Bundles/Walker Family Collection; Villa Lewaro, A'Lelia Bundles/Walker Family Collection.

Page 86: Walker beauty parlor, Harlem, New York City. Museum of the City of New York, The Byron Collection. 93.1.1.10840

Page 89: Maine Chance spa. Elizabeth Arden Corporation.

Page 90: Rubinstein among workers. Image courtesy of the Helena Rubinstein Foundation.

Page 91: Arden with race horse. Elizabeth Arden Corporation.

Page 93: Harper Method advertisement. Courtesy of Jane R. Plitt.

Page 95: Bishop portrait. *Schlesinger Library*.

Page 96: Bishop lipstick advertisement. *Schlesinger Library*.

Page 97: Carnegie at desk. Alfred Eisenstaedt/Time Pix.

Page 99: Carnegie receiving Neiman Marcus award. Alfred Eisenstaedt/Time Pix.

Page 102: "Sunshine or Shadows" advertisement. From Tom Mahoney, *50 Years of Lane Bryant* [n.p.], ca. 1950. Lane Bryant Company.

Page 105: Ida and William Rosenthal. Maidenform Company.

Page 108: Beech portrait. Wichita State University Libraries. Department of Special Collections.

Page 111: Martinez giving pottery–making demonstration, Palace of the Governors, Santa Fe, New Mexico, ca. 1911. Courtesy Museum of New Mexico neg. no. 4237.

Page 116: Morgan portrait. Julia Morgan Collection, Special Collections and University Archives, California Polytechnic State University.

Page 117: Stratton with tiles. Courtesy of the Cranbrook Archives, POL-2-114-2, Nehry Scripps Booth.

Page 119: Hearst Castle; detail of colorplate 9(a), see below.

Page 121: Greenway portrait. Courtesy of the Arizona Historical Society. AHS # 66353.

Page 126: Dining room at Grossinger's. YIVO Institute for Jewish Research, Photo Archives.

Page 127: Resort life at Grossinger's, 1950s (4 photographs). YIVO Institute for Jewish Research, Photo Archives.

Page 128: Grossinger with Anderson. YIVO Institute for Jewish Research, Photo Archives.

Page 132: Walker portrait. Wms. Burg Photo Company. Courtesy National Park Service, Maggie L. Walker National Historic Site.

Page 133: Walker home, Richmond, Virginia. Courtesy National Park Service, Maggie L. Walker National Historic Site.

Page 135: St. Luke Penny Savings Bank. Courtesy National Park Service, Maggie L. Walker National Historic Site.

Page 138: Pickford with camera; Pickford with Griffiths, Chaplin, and Fairbanks. Academy of Motion Picture Arts and Sciences.

Page 140: Handlers with Walt Disney. Ruth and Elliot Handler.

Page 141: Early Barbie and Ken. The Children's Museum of Indianapolis.

Page 142: Wise hosting Tupperware party. Archives Center, National Museum of American History, Smithsonian Institution.

Page 144: Olive and Walter Beech beside Beechcraft 18. Wichita State University Libraries, Department of Special Collections.

Page 145: 1936 National Air Race winners. Wichita State University Libraries, Department of Special Collections.

Page 148: Graham portrait. ©Wally McNamee/CORBIS.

COLORPLATES

1. *Portrait of Mrs. James Smith (Elizabeth Murray)*, 1769; John Singleton Copley, American (1738–1815). Oil on canvas. Gift of Joseph W.R. Rogers and Mary C. Rogers. 42.463. Museum of Fine Arts, Boston. Reproduced with permission. © Museum of Fine Arts, Boston. All Rights Reserved.

2. Indigo production. Illustration from Henry Mouzon, Jr., *Map of the Parish of St. Stephen's in Craven County* (1775). South Carolina Historical Society.

3. Lukens portrait. The Graystone Society.

4. *Hannah Thurston Adams (1809–72) and Mary Agnes Adams (1812–90)*. Unknown artist, Manchester, New Hampshire, ca. 1845. Jo Anne Preston.

5. *Demorest Monthly Magazine, Schlesinger Library*. Trade cards for Madame Demorest and Lippincott Flower Seeds Company. Baker Library, Harvard Business School.

6. Pinkham trade cards. *Schlesinger Library*.

7. Walker and boys. Courtesy National Park Service, Maggie L. Walker National Historic Site.

8. Marie Daugherty Webster, American (1859–1956), "Grapes and Vines," 1914. Quilt. Indianapolis Museum of Art. Gift of Mrs. Gerrish Thurber.

9. (A) Hearst Castle. Photograph by Victoria Garigliano. ©Hearst Castle ® California State Park Service. (B) Asilomar Auditorium. Patrick Sheridan, Asilomar Conference Center.

10. Arden's red door. Elizabeth Arden Corporation.

11. Handlers with Barbie. Photograph ©Allan Grant. Ruth and Elliot Handler.

12. Maidenform advertisement. Maidenform Company.

INDEX

Boldface numbers refer to substantive discussions of subjects; *italicized* numbers refer to pages with pictures; colorplates are identified with the prefix *cp*.

abolition. *See* antislavery reform
Adair, Eleanor, 87–88
Adams, Hannah, 47
Adams, John Quincy, 57
Adams, Margarett, 47; *cp4*
Adams, Mary, 47
advertising: Arden and, 88–89; Bishop and, 94–
    95; *96*; Bryant and, 102; consumerism and, 78;
    Demorest and, 30; *28, 50, cp5*; department
    stores and, 78; Handler and, 140–41; Harper
    and, *93*; Murray and, 20; *21*; Pinkham and,
    44–46; *44, cp6*; Rosenthal and, 106–107; *cp12*
African Americans, 1–2, 5, 110: banking and, 130,
    133–34; beauty industry and, 79–84, 87; *83*;
    entrepreneurial ventures and, 84; Greenway
    and, 123–24; at Grossinger's, 124, 127–28, 129;
    Malone, 5, 79–81; marketing to, 81–82, 130,
    133–34; 20th-century business ownership
    among, 151–52; Winfrey, 5, 151–52. *See also*
    Civil Rights Era; Keckley, Elizabeth; Walker,
    Madam C. J.; Walker, Maggie Lena
agriculture and farming: Bemis, 31; Briones, 38;
    economy based on, 7–10; Pinckney. *See*
    Pinckney, Eliza Lucas
airplane production, 144–46
Alexander, Beatrice, **137–39**
Alvarado, Linda, 149–50, 151, 156, 157, 158
American Philosophical Society, 15
American Revolution, 15–16; Murray and, 24–25
American Secretarial & Business College, 144
Anderson, Marian, *128*
Anthony, Susan B., 64, 93
antislavery reform, 131; Bradwell and, 62;
    Pinkham and, 40–41
Arden, Elizabeth, 76, 78, 79, **87–92**, 95, 107, 150,
    153, 161; *90, 91, cp10*
Arizona Hut, 123
Arizona Inn, 120, 122–24, 130

Army, U.S., 61, 99, 128
Arts and Crafts Movement, 100; Morgan and,
    115–20; Webster and, 113–15
Ash, Mary Kay, 153
Asian Americans, 152. *See also* Bemis, Polly;
    Chen, Joyce
Asilomar Conference Center, 117; *cp9(B)*
Associated Press, 87
"At the Million Dollar Tango Ball," 72
aviation industry, 144–46

Bache, Richard, *16*
Baltimore, post office at, *17*
banks and banking industry. *See* finance and
    financial services industry
Barbie doll, 139, 141–43; *141, cp11*
beauty industry, 5, 75–107: for African Ameri-
    cans, 79–84, 87; *83*; Arden and, 87–92; Bishop
    and, 92–96; Harper and, 93; in late 20th
    century, 153; Malone and, 80–81; science in,
    89, 92–96; Walker (Madam C. J.) and, 79–87.
    See also cosmetics; hair care industry
Beech, Olive Ann, 108, 110, **143–46**; *108, 144*
Beech, Walter, 144–46; *144*
Beech Aircraft Corporation, 110, 143–46; *108,
    144, 145*
Beecher, Catharine, 32
Behind the Scenes (Keckley), 54
Bemis, Charles, 31
Bemis, Polly, 31; *ii, 31*
Bethune, Mary McLeod, 136
Bishop, Hazel, 1, 92–96, 156; *95, 96*
Bissett, Enid, 104–106
Bok, Edward, 114
Bonwit Teller, 123
Boston Herald, 45
Boston Massacre, 24–25
Bradlee, Ben, 156

Bradwell, James Bolesworth, 62, 64
Bradwell, Myra, **61–64, 66–69,** 104, 158, 160;
    63, 64
Bradwell v. State of Illinois, 61–64
Brandywine Iron Works and Nail Factory, 34–40;
    36, 37
breast prostheses, 143
Breedlove, Sarah. *See* Walker, Madam C. J.
Briones, Juana, 38
Bryant, Lane, 1, 97, **101–103,** 125, 153; *102*
Buffett, Warren, 156
Business Week, 92, 94, 95, 142
Business Woman's Journal, 111
Butterick, Ebenezer, 49, 51, 55

Californios, 38. *See also* Hispanics
Campbell, Thomas, 22, 24
capital, access to, 112; Green and, 70–71; in
    late 20th century, 156–57; Murray and, 20;
    venture, 157
Capote, Truman, 156
Carnegie, Andrew, 98, 101, 112, 113
Carnegie, Hattie, 78, **97–101,** 107, 125, 128, 150,
    153, 160; *98, 99*
Catt, Carrie Chapman, 65
Centennial Exhibition, Philadelphia (1876), 52, 61
ceramics, 111, 116, 147; *117*
Chaplin, Charlie, *138*
Chen, Joyce, 5, 151, 153–54
Chicago Legal News, 62–64, 66–69, 160
Civil Rights Act (1964), 152
Civil Rights Era, 129–30
Civil War era, 29–73; Bradwell and, 62–63;
    Coston signal flares and, 55, 58, 61; *60, 61*;
    women's lives during, 30, 33
Claiborne, Liz, 153, 157
Colby, Myra. *See* Bradwell, Myra
Committee of 200, 159

Commonwealth Institute, 159
computer(s), 155, 157
Consolidated Bank and Trust Company, Richmond, Va., 134
Constitution, U.S., 64; 19th Amendment, 110
construction industry, 149–50, 151, 157–58
Consumer Reports, 95
consumerism, 5, 160.; children and, 136–37; New Woman and, 79, 88, 136; women and, 32, 76, 77. *See also* advertising; marketing
Contraband Relief Association, 54
Coolidge, Calvin, 5, 159–60
corporations, 112
cosmetics, 78–79, 153; Bishop and, 92–96; rise in use of, 78–79, 93–94; Rubinstein and, 76, 79, 88, 92; *90. See also* Arden, Elizabeth; beauty industry; hair care industry
Coston, Benjamin Franklin, 55–56
Coston, Martha, 4, **55–61,** 144, 150, 156, 160; 57
Coston Supply Company, 58, 61
Coston's Night Signals, 56–61; 59, 60
Coston's Telegraphic Night Signals, 60
Crittenton, Charles N., 45
Croly, Jennie June, 52
Cuming, Anne and Elizabeth, 25
Curtis, Ellen. *See* Demorest, Ellen
Curtiss-Wright Airplane Company, 145

Darwin, Charles, 112
Daugherty, Marie. *See* Webster, Marie
Declaration of Independence, 8, 17; 6
Declaration of Sentiments (Seneca Falls), 33
Demorest, Ellen, 5, 46, **48–55,** 61, 91, 104, 114, 150, 153, 158, 160; *cp5*
Demorest, William Jennings, 48–50, 53, 55
Demorest's Illustrated Monthly Magazine and Mme. Demorest's Mirror of Fashions. See Illustrated Monthly
department stores, 77–78, 123; African American operated, 134–35; Arden and, 90–91; Carnegie and, 98; dolls in, 138; Walker (Maggie L.) and, 134–35
Depression (1930s). *See* Great Depression
direct sales, 84, 90, 142, 153
discrimination, gender-based. *See* sex discrimination
Disney, Walt, *140*
dolls. *See* toy industry
Domestic Receipt Book, The (Beecher), 32
Doubleday, Frank, 114
Doubleday, Page and Company, 114, 115
Draper, Elizabeth, 131
dressmaking, 48–49. Adams sisters and, 47; Demorest and, 46, 48–55; Keckley and, 54; Rosenthal and, 104–105; *See also* fashion industry; paper patterns
dry goods stores, 9. Murray and, 19–26; *See also* department stores
Dubinsky, Donna, 155, 157
DuBois, W. E. B., 87, 136

eBay, 155
Ecole des Beaux-Arts, Paris, 116, 117
economic conditions: in colonial America, 7–8; Panic of 1837, 39, 41; railroads and. *See* railroads; *See also* Great Depression
education, women's, 117, 118, 136; architecture, 115–16; business, 112; in 1970s, 152; law, 63–64; in 19th-century, 32; sciences, 92–93
employee benefits/welfare, 4; Bradwell and, 66–67; Bryant and, 103; Greenway and, 123–24; Handler and, 140, 141–42, 143; in late 20th century, 158–59; Morgan and, 118
Enid Frocks, 104–106
Equal Credit Opportunity Act (1974), 152, 156–57
Equal Employment Opportunity Commission (EEOC), 152
Estes, Lydia. *See* Pinkham, Lydia
Eustis, Jane, 25

Fairbanks, Douglas, *138*
Fairmont Hotel, San Francisco, 117
family life, 3, 100; Adams sisters and, 47; Arden and, 89–90; business and, 45; entrepreneurship and, 158; Grossinger and, 129; Handler and, 139; home-based businesses and, 157–58; in late 20th century, 158; Lukens and, 36, 39–40; Pinckney and, 12–13; Robineau on, 147; as training for entrepreneurship, 32–33; Walker (Maggie L.) and, 135–36; Wise and, 142; *See also* marriage
fashion industry, 5, 75–107, 160; Bryant and, 101–103; democratization of, 50–51; in late 20th century, 153; maternity wear and, 102–103; paper patterns and, 50–55; in post-World War II era, 100–101; Rosenthal and, 103–107; *See also* Carnegie, Hattie; Demorest, Ellen
Fashion Institute of Technology, New York, 96
feme covert, 8, 22–24; *23*
Feminine Mystique (Friedan), 152, 153
Ferber, Edna, McChesney novels by, 75–76, 144
Ferguson, Isabella Selmes, *See* Greenway, Isabella
Ferguson, Robert Munro, 121–22
finance and financial services industry: African Americans and, 130, 132–34; Bishop and, 96; Equal Credit Opportunity Act and, 152, 156–57; *See also* Green, Hetty; Walker, Maggie Lena
Fiorina, Carleton S., 161
food industry, 153–54
Fortune, 139, 151, 153, 156
Fox Films, 100
franchise, 93
Freeman's Institute, 41
Friedan, Betty, 152, 153

Gibbons, Abraham, 40
Gibbs, Jeannette Phillips, 109–10
Gilpin Airlines, 122
Goddard, Mary Katherine, 1, 8, 9, **14–19,** 26–27, 160

Goddard, Sarah Updike, 14
Goddard, William, 14–19
Godey's Lady's Book, 32–33
Gordon, Ellen, 155, 156, 157, 158
Gordon, Melvin, 155
Graham, Florence Nightingale. *See* Arden, Elizabeth
Graham, Gladys, 90
Graham, Katharine, 1, 155–56, 157, 158, 161; *148*
Graham, Phil, 155, 156
Great Depression, 120, 137; Beech and, 144–45; Carnegie and, 99; dolls during, 137, 138–39; Greenway and, 123; Grossinger and, 126–27; Walker (Maggie L.) and, 134
Green, Edward, 73
Green, Edward Henry, 71
Green, Hetty, **69–73,** 154, 160; *71, 72*
Greenway, Isabella, **120–24,** 125, 130; *121*
Greenway, John, 124
Greenway, John C., 121–22
Griffith, D. W., *138*
Grossinger, Harry, 125, 129
Grossinger, Jennie, 110, 120–21, **124–30,** 161; *128*

hair care industry, 93; for African Americans, 79–84, 87; *83;* Harper and, 79, 93; Malone and, 5, 79, 80–81; Walker (Madam C. J.) and, 80–87; *See also* beauty industry; cosmetics
Hale, Sarah Josepha, 32–33
Handler, Izzy Elliott, 139–44; *cp11*
Handler, Ruth, 110, **139–44,** 161; *cp11*
Handspring, 157
Harper, Martha Matilda, 79, 93
Harrison, Benjamin, 39
Harvard-Radcliffe Program in Business Management, 112
health care industry: Beech and, 143–44; Pinkham and, 40–46
Hearst, Phoebe, 118–19
Hearst, William Randolph, 118–20
Hearst Castle, San Simeon, Calif., 116, 118–20; *119, cp9(A)*
Hewlett-Packard, 161
Himmelstein, Lena. *See* Bryant, Lane
Hispanics, 58, 149–50; *See also* Alvarado, Linda; Briones, Juana; Sobrino, Maria de Lourdes
Hollywood: Alexander and, *138;* Carnegie and, 98, 99, 100; Pickford and, *138*
Home for Destitute Women and Children, 54
Horatio Alger Association of Distinguished Americans, 150
hospitality industry: Greenway and, 120–24, 130; Grossinger's and, 120, 124–30; *126, 127*
House Beautiful, 115
How the Other Half Lives (Riis), 97
Howe, Elias, 50
Howland family, 69–70. *See also* Green, Hetty
Hubbard, Elizabeth, 87–88
Hughes, Cathy, 151
Hughes, Langston, 136

Hunt, Martha. *See* Coston, Martha
Huston, Charles, 40

I. Magnin and Company, 77, 98, 100
"If I Were as Rich as Hetty Green," 72
Illinois Supreme Court, 63, 64, 68
Illustrated Monthly, 30, 51, 55, 61; 28, cp5
Independent Order of St. Luke's, Richmond, Va.,
   132–34
indigo industry, 8–9, 10–14; 13, cp2
Inman, Ralph, 24, 25; 26
International Council of Women of the Darker
   Races, 135
Intolerable Acts (1774), 25
iron manufacturing, 33–40

Jews, 1–2; assimilation of, 100–101, 102, 124, 152;
   in beauty industry, 79; department stores
   and, 77; discrimination against, 124; in fashion industry, 97, 101, 105–107; at Grossinger's,
   126–27, 130; in hospitality industry, 124–28;
   See also Arden, Elizabeth; Carnegie, Hattie;
   Grossinger, Jennie; Rosenthal, Ida
journalism: Bradwell and, 61–64, 66–69;
   Graham and, 155–56; Leslie and, 65; Walker
   (Maggie L.) and, 153; *See also* publishing

Kaganovich, Ida. *See* Rosenthal, Ida
Karan, Donna, 153
Keckley, Elizabeth, 54
Keramic Studio, 147
King, Harry O., 124
King, Susan A., 52–54
Knox, Rose, 4
Köningeiser, Henrietta. *See* Carnegie, Hattie
Korean War, 143, 146

Ladies' Home Journal, 78, 114
Lauder, Estee, 76, 92
law and legal issues, 2, 3; feme covert, 8, 22–24;
   in late 20th century, 152–53, 160; married
   women's property acts, 32; protective labor
   legislation, 112–13; *See also* women's rights
legal profession, 61–64, 66–69
Lelia College, 82, 84
Leslie, (Mrs.) Frank, 65
Lewis, Thomas Jenkins, 90–92
Life (magazine), 101, 155
Lincoln, Mary Todd, 54, 68
Lincoln, Robert Todd, 68
Lippincott, C. S., cp5
Lippmann, Walter, 156
lipstick, 92–96
Loyalists (Revolutionary War era), 24–25
Lucas, Eliza. *See* Pinckney, Eliza Lucas
Lucas, George, 9, 11, 13
Lukens, Charles, 34–35
Lukens, Rebecca, 4, 29, **33–40,** 56, 144, 150, 160;
   34, 37, cp3
Lukens, Solomon, 35

Lulu's Dessert and Fancy Fruit Corp., 151, 154
Lydia E. Pinkham Medicine Company. *See*
   Pinkham, Lydia

McChesney, Emma (fictional char.), 75–76, 144
MacLeish, Archibald, 107
McWilliams, Lelia, 80, 82
McWilliams, Moses, 80
Macy's, 114, 123, 138
Madam Demorest (ship), 55; 53
Madame Alexander Doll Company, 137–39
Madame Demorest's Emporium: New York, 48,
   51, 55; 48, 49; Paris, 53
Mme. Demorest's Quarterly Mirror of Fashions, 48–50.
   See also Illustrated Monthly
magazines, women's, 51, 75, 78, 111; paper
   patterns in, 49–50, 51. *See also* publishing;
   entries for specific magazine titles
Magnin, Mary Ann Cohen, 77
Maidenform, Inc., 103–106; cp12
mail-order, 78; Bryant and, 102–103; Walker
   (Madam C. J.) and, 82
Maine Chance spa, 91; 89
makeup. *See* cosmetics
Malone, Annie Minerva Turnbo, 5, 79, 80–81
Malsin, Albert, 102–103
manufacturing companies, 151; for aircraft,
   144–46; corporations and, 112; iron milling,
   34–37; production methods of, in garment
   industry, 105–106; railroads and, 37–38
Marciano, Rocky, 127
Marcus, Stanley, 99
marketing: Arden and, 88–89; Beech and, 145;
   Coston and, 58, 60–61; Demorest and, 49–51;
   Grossinger's use of, 126–27; of "kissable"
   lipstick, 94–96; Maidenform, 106–107; cp12;
   multilevel. *See* direct sales; Pinkham and,
   43–45; 44, cp6; in toy industry, 140–41; Walker
   (Madam C. J.) and, 81–82, 84; Webster and,
   113, 115; Wise and, 142; *See also* advertising;
   public relations
marriage, 11, 147; business partnership within,
   46, 104–105, 129, 139, 145, 158; and career, in
   late 20th century, 158; as help to women
   entrepreneurs, 22, 24, 31, 46, 81, 90, 100, 158;
   as hindrance to women entrepreneurs, 81; in
   post–World War II period, 142; women's
   rights altered by, 22, 32; 23; *See also* family life
married women's property acts, 32
Marshall Field, 114, 123, 138
Martha Stewart Omnimedia, Inc., 150. *See also*
   Stewart, Martha
Martinez, Julian, 111
Martinez, Maria, 111
Marx (toy company), 140
Mary Kay Cosmetics, 153
Maryland Gazette, 15
Maryland Journal, 10–19
Matson, Harold, 139
Mattel Toy Company, 139–44; 141, cp11

Maybeck, Bernard, 116
Mellor, Olive Ann. *See* Beech, Olive Ann
"Mickey Mouse Club" (television show), 140
millinery, 46, 48. *See also* fashion industry
Mills College, 117, 118, 136
Mitchell, Maggie Lena. *See* Walker, Maggie Lena
Mitchell, William, 131
Morgan, Julia, 110, 113, **115–20,** 136, 161; 116, cp9
Morse, Samuel F. B., 57
Mosko, Ruth. *See* Handler, Ruth
motherhood. *See* family life
Mott, Elizabeth, 43
Murray, Elizabeth, 8, 9, **19–26,** 32, 39, 150, 156,
   160; 19, cp1
Murray, James, 20, 22

Nathoy, Lalu. *See* Bemis, Polly
NASA, 146
National Air Races, 145
National Association for the Advancement of
   Colored People (NAACP), 85, 135
National Association of Colored Women, 79, 135
National Association of Women Business
   Owners, 159
National Federation of Business and
   Professional Women's Clubs, 74, 111
National Foundation for Women Business
   Owners, 159
National Negro Business League (NNBL), 85, 86
National Organization of Women, 152
National Woman's Suffrage Company, 65
Navy, U.S., 55–58; 60
Nearly Me, 143
Neiman, Carrie Marcus, **77–78,** 99; 77
Neiman Marcus, 77–78, 90; 78
New Century for Women, 61
New York Herald, 102, 131
New York Illustrated News, 51
New York Medical College, 52
New York Post, 87
New York Stock Exchange, 154
New York Times, 83, 92, 114, 123
newspapers. *See* journalism; publishing
Newsweek, 156
Northwestern Sanitary Commission, 62–63

Palm Computing, 157
Panic of 1837, 39, 41
paper patterns: Demorest and, 49–55, 114;
   Webster and, 114; *See also* dressmaking
Paris Exposition (1878), 51; 53
patent(s), 55, 110; Custon and, 57–58, 60; 59
Payne, Lillian, 133
Pearson, Luvie, 156
Pennock, Isaac, 33
Pennock, Martha, 33
Pennsylvania Chronicle, 14–15
Pentagon Papers, 161
Pewabic Pottery, 116

philanthropy, 159; Bryant and, 103; Grossinger and, 128–29; Murray and, 25–26; Walker (Madam C. J.) and, 85, 87

Pickford, Mary, 138

Pinckney, Charles, 10–14

Pinkham, Dan, 43, 45

Pinckney, Eliza Lucas, 8–14, 19, 26–27, 160

Pinkham, Isaac, 41–42

Pinkham, Lydia, 5, 29–30, 40–46, 160; 44, cp6

Pinkham, Will, 45

Pinkham's Vegetable Compound, 43–46; 43, cp6

politics: Bradwell and, 67; Greenway and, 122; Lukens in, 39; Walker (Maggie L.) and, 135

Polly Place, 31

Portia Marries (Gibbs), 109–10

Post, Marjorie Merriweather, 4

Postal Service, U.S., 16, 17

pottery, 111, 116, 147; 111, 117

Practical Patchwork Company, 114–15

pregnancy, clothing for, 101–103

President's Commission on Status of Women, 152

press. See journalism; publishing industry

prostheses, breast, 143

Prout, Mary, 132

Providence Gazette, 14

public relations: Grossinger and, 126–27; Pinkham and, 43. See also marketing

publishing industry, 9; Bradwell and, 62–64, 66–69; Demorests and, 48–51; Goddard and, 8, 9, 14–19; Graham and, 150, 155–56; 148; Leslie and, 65; during Revolutionary War period, 15–16; Walker (Maggie L.) and, 133; women's magazines in, 49–50, 51, 75, 78, 111

Purisma Concepcion, La, 38

pyramid organization. See direct sales

Quakers, attitudes of, 69–70, 72; concerning business, 33, 35, 37, 71; on slavery, 40–41

quilt making, 113–15; cp8

Quilts: Their Story and How to Make Them (Webster), 114

Radio One, 151

railroads, 31–32; impact of, 37–38

"rainbow" flyers, 65

ranching. See agriculture and farming

Ransom, F. B., 82

Raytheon Corporation, 146

reform movements, 160–60; Bradwell and, 62, 67–69; Demorest and, 46, 52–55; in late 20th century, 152–53; Walker (Madam C. J.) and, 84–85; Walker (Maggie L.) and, 132–36

Reston, James, 156

restrictions on women, 2, 110–11; in financing, 156–57; in large industries, 4–5

Revlon, 95–96

Revolutionary War: indigo industry and, 13; publishing and, 15; merchants and, 24–25

Riis, Jacob, 97

Robineau, Adelaide Alsop, 147

Robinson, Edward Mott, 69

Robinson, Henrietta Howland. See Green, Hetty

Robinson, Jackie, 127, 129

Roosevelt, Eleanor, 121, 122, 124, 127

Roosevelt, Theodore, 121

Rosenthal, Beatrice, 104, 106–107

Rosenthal, Ida, 97, **103–107**, 125, 158, 161; 105

Rosenthal, Lewis, 104, 106

Rosenthal, William, 104–105; 105

Ross, Barney, 126

Roth, Rose, 97–98

Rubinstein, Helena, 76, 79, 88, 92; 90

Russell, Charles T., 135

St. Luke Emporium, Richmond, Va., 134–35

St. Luke Herald, 133

St. Luke Penny Savings Bank, Richmond, Va., 133–34; 135

Sanitary Fair, Chicago (1865), 63

Saturday Evening Post, 78

Securities and Exchange Commission, U.S., 143

Selmes, Isabella. See Greenway, Isabella

Seneca Falls conference, 33

sewing machine, 50

sex discrimination, 3, 54, 110–11, 60; among African Americans, 86; in education, 112; in financing, 156–57; Goddard and, 18; Graham and, 155–56; Handler and, 143; Social Darwinism and, 112–13; Title VII and, 152

Seymour, Mary Foote, 111

she-merchants, 19–26

shopkeepers, 19–26. See also dry goods stores

Siebert, Muriel, 154, 156

signal flares, 55–61; 59, 60

Signal Success (Coston), 60; 57

slave(s) and slavery, 18, 20; Bradwell and, 62; Demorest and, 52; Keckley as, 54; Pinkham and, 40–41; See also antislavery reform

Small Business Administration (SBA), U.S., 159

Smith, James, 24

Sobrino, Maria de Lourdes, 151, 154

Social Darwinism, 112–13

social reform(s): Bradwell and, 62, 66–68; Walker (Madam C. J.) and, 84–85; Walker (Maggie L.) and, 130–36; See also antislavery reform; suffrage; temperance

Soldier's Aid Society, 63

Spectator Sports, 99

Spector, Raymond, 94–96

Squier, Ephraim George, 65

Stanton, Elizabeth Cady, 52, 64, 68

Stearns and Foster, 115

Stewart, Martha, 5, 150–51, 156, 158

Stratton, Mary Chase Perry, 116–17; 117

suffrage, 53, 65, 110; beauty industry and, 88–89; Bradwell and, 68; Leslie and, 65; See also women's rights

Supreme Court, U.S., 61, 63, 64, 66, 68

tea trade, 52–55; 53

television, 156; Chen and, 154; Handler and, 140

temperance, 43, 52

Thorndike, Jane (fictional char.), 109–10

Title VII, Civil Rights Act (1964), 152

Tootsie Roll Industries, 155

toy industry, 136–37; Alexander and, 137–39; Handler and, 140–43

Toy Manufacturers Association, 142–43

transportation: Civil War development of, 31–32; industry of, 151; railroads, 31–32, 37–38

Travel Air Manufacturing Company, 144, 145

Treatise on Domestic Economy (Beecher), 32

Tupperware, 142

United Artists, 138

United States Lifesaving Service, 60

U.S.S. Monitor, 58, 60

University of California (Berkeley), 116

Van Lew, Elizabeth, 131

venture capital, 156–57

Villa Lewaro, Irvington-on-Hudson, N.Y., 84; 85

Vogue, 78, 79

Walker, Armstead, 131–32, 136

Walker, Charles Joseph, 81–82

Walker, Madam C. J., 1, 76, 79–87, 107, 130, 150, 153, 156, 161; 74, 83, 85, 86

Walker, Maggie Lena, 110, 113, **130–36**, 160; 132, 133, cp7

Walker, Sarah Breedlove. See Walker, Madam C. J.

Walker agents, 82, 84–85; 83

Washington, Booker T., 86

Washington, Margaret Murray, 135

Washington Post, 150, 156, 161; 148

Washington Post Company, 155, 156

Webster, Marie, **113–15**, 116; cp8

Welcome Lodging House for Women and Children, 52

Whig party, 39

White, James, 72

Whitman, Meg, 155

Winfrey, Oprah, 5, 151, 156

Wise, Brownie, 142

Woman Suffrage Association, 68

Woman's Home Companion, 73, 94

Woman's Tea Company, 52–55; 53

Women's Army Corps (WAC), 99

women's rights: Arden and, 88–89; Bradwell and, 67–69; Demorest and, 52–55; 19th Amendment and, 110; Seneca Falls conference on, 33; See also law and legal issues; suffrage

World's Columbian Exposition, Chicago (1893), 61

World's Fair, Chicago (1934), 111

World War I, 110, 122, 123, 137

World War II, 110, 120, 139; Beech and, 143, 145–46; Bishop and, 92; Carnegie and, 99; Grossinger and, 128–29; Maiden Form and, 106; makeup and, 92–96

Young Woman's Christian Association (YWCA), 117–18, 136; cp9(B)

Zaft, John, 100

ACKNOWLEDGMENTS

In 1868, in Baltimore, Maryland, my grandmother's brothers founded a stationery store that ultimately became the well-known Goldsmith Brothers on Nassau Street in Manhattan. Though the family sold the business, "the store," as it was fondly referred to by my grandmother, my mother, and others within the family, remains a tremendous source of pride. Back in the early 1960s, before the emergence of modern feminism, my grandmother took me, a budding adolescent, to the floor of the New York Stock Exchange. Since I was so adept at arithmetic, she hoped that I would be inspired to carry on the family tradition and enter business. I chose a scholarly route instead. But, when I was invited to write this book, I jumped at the opportunity to explore the history of women entrepreneurs and along the way to examine my family tradition in historical context. I dedicate this book to the memory of Helen Goldsmith Rudolph and Charles Brand, whose entrepreneurial spirit I well remember.

This book accompanies the museum exhibit "Enterprising Women." As the author of *Enterprising Women*, I have been privileged to be part of the wonderful team that has brought this entire project to fruition. First, I would like to thank Jane Knowles, Acting Director of the Schlesinger Library and mastermind of the entire "Enterprising Women" endeavor, for inviting me to be the historian for the exhibit. I am deeply grateful for her faith in me, her unyielding encouragement and support of my work, and her warmth and steady guidance, even during the most challenging of times.

At the Radcliffe Institute for Advanced Study, I would like to thank three historians whom I greatly admire, Mary Dunn, Drew Faust, and Nancy Cott, for their support. I thank the dedicated staff at the Schlesinger Library whose expertise and friendly assistance created a unique working environment that no scholar would ever want to leave. And I thank Whitney Espich, Tamara Elliott Rogers, and Diane Sherlock for helping me to put my best foot forward.

I am deeply grateful to the Radcliffe Institute for awarding me a Radcliffe Institute Fellowship, which gave me the time and space I needed to work on this book. I would also like to thank Mabel Cabot and Sherrye Henry, who were early champions of "Enterprising Women." I am deeply grateful to the Cabot Family Charitable Trust for helping to get the project off the ground and to the Ford Motor Company and AT&T for their generous support that made the entire "Enterprising Women" project possible. I appreciate Tufts University's support during my sabbatical leave.

As part of the "Enterprising Women" exhibit, I was fortunate to work with a team of talented people: John H. Ott, Hilary Anderson, and the staff at the National

Heritage Museum; Alison Cornyn and Brenda MacCarthy at Picture-Projects.com; Brian Hotchkiss, Peter Blaiwas, Susan McNally, and Jean Hammond at Vernon Press; and Charles Grench at University of North Carolina Press. Barbara Charles, of Staples and Charles, creatively translated my historical ideas into captivating sets. I was delighted to reunite with Edie Mayo, curator for "Enterprising Women," with whom I worked years ago at the Smithsonian Institution. I was honored to bring Eric Rothschild on board as educational consultant. Having first introduced me to the excitement of history when I was a high school student, he once again inspired me with his unique creativity and unbounded energy.

A number of scholars gave generously of their time to advise me or to read drafts of *Enterprising Women*. They include Regina Blaszczyk, Wendy Gamber, Gerald Gill, Helen Horowitz, Angel Kwolek-Folland, Regina Kunzel, Laura Linard, Ellen Moore, Mary Yeager, and Susan Yohn. I received invaluable assistance from several Radcliffe Research Partners, including Catherine Burch, Katheryn Hayes, Charlotte Houghteling, and Iva Tsekova, Radcliffe summer intern Jeffrey Burke, Kim Frederick of Brandeis University, and Kim Fox of Tufts University.

My family has been a rock of support. My daughters Abigail and Eliza never stopped encouraging me in my work, even when it meant I was less available to them. And finally, like so many enterprising women past and present, I have benefited from the love and support of my husband, Douglas L. Jones. He demonstrates daily, in ways both large and small, his devotion to me and to my work.

Virginia G. Drachman, Ph.D.
Waban, Massachusetts

This project has been made possible by the generous sponsorship of AT&T and Ford Motor Company and I am very appreciative of their sustained and enthusiastic commitment to our endeavor. I am also grateful for funding from the Cabot Family Charitable Trust initial research and in-kind support from the U.S. Small Business Administration. Without Muffie Cabot and Sherrye Henry there would have been no exhibition. They planted the idea: Muffie found our sponsors and shared her experience of managing *Remember the Ladies*, and Sherrye shaped the Honorary Committee. I want to express my deepest gratitude to the Radcliffe Institute for Advanced Study for moral and financial support, especially to Dean Drew Gilpin Faust, Associate Dean Tamara Elliott Rogers, Communications Director Whitney Espich, and the Fay House administration. At the Schlesinger Library, I am grateful to former Director Mary Maples Dunn, incoming Director Nancy Cott, and all my colleagues who worked to bring this exhibition to fruition.

I wish to thank my partners on the exhibition team, who, bonded by e-mail, teleconferencing, FedEx, and shared databases worked hard, through thick and thin, to produce the show. This exhibition is the result of the combined talents and insightful professionalism of guest curator Edith P. Mayo, designer Barbara Charles, interactive producer Alison Cornyn, and historian and comrade-at-arms Virginia G. Drachman. It was constantly improved by the thoughtful advice of the staff of the National Heritage Museum: Executive Director John H. Ott, Director of Collections and Exhibitions Hilary Anderson, Registrar Jill Aszling, Collections Manager Maureen Harper, Michael Rizzo, designer, and Linda Patch, Alice Promisel, and Katherine Rhuda.

I am particularly grateful to, Matt Duffy, Lori Hamilton, and Matt Kuhnert at Staples & Charles Ltd.; to Liana Brazil, Jessica Ling Findley, John Keefe, and Brenda McCarthy of Picture Projects; and to independent consultant Cheryl Robertson, historian Eric Rothschild, and attorney Douglas L. Jones. I want to thank Vernon Press and Susan McNally, who worked so hard and so well to create this book, and Jean Hammond, for her wonderful design and layout. Susan Ware was a supportive friend, who generously helped with the National Endowment for the Humanities–grant proposal. Elizabeth Kaltofen was a special heroine throughout. I am grateful to my former assistant Lisa Hurlbut; to Diane Hamer, who paid the bills; our intern Jeffrey Burke; and Radcliffe research partners Katie Burch, Katheryn Hayes, Charlotte Houghteling, and Iva Tsekova. We could not have completed the project without the wise advice of Josh Basseches.

I wish to extend special thanks to institutions that have been in-kind sponsors to the project: A&E Television Networks, Anacostia Museum and Center for African American History and Culture at the Smithsonian Institution, Special Collections and University Archives at California Polytechnic State University, The Children's Museum of Indianapolis, Hearst Castle, Lane Bryant Company, Maryland State Archives, Massachusetts Historical Society, National Park Service, Maggie L. Walker National Historic Site, Peabody Museum of Archaeology and Ethnology at Harvard University, and Pewabic Pottery Museum.

At the Academy of Motion Picture Arts and Sciences, I am grateful to Kristine Krueger and Libby Wertin; at the Addison Gallery of American Art, Susan Faxon; at the American Antiquarian Society, Georgia Barnhill, Nancy Burkett, and Philip Lampe; at the American Textile History Museum, Karen Herbaugh; at the Anacostia Museum and Center for African American History and Culture, Smithsonian Institution, Jennifer Morris; at the Elizabeth Arden Corporation, James Cantela, Carol Mannino, and Barbara Panetta; at Arizona Historical Society, Susan Sheehan; at the Arizona Inn, Bill Dillon and Patty Doar; at Asilomar State Historic Park, Roxann Jacobus; at the Bancroft Library, University of California, Berkeley, Susan Snyder; at California Polytechnic State University, Special Collections and University Archives, Michael Line and

Catherine Trujillo; at the Cambridge Historical Commission, Kathleen Rawlins; at the Chester County Archives and Records Services, Diane Rofini and Lori Rofini; at the Children's Museum of Indianapolis, Andrea Hughes, Randy Johnson, and Sheila Riley; at the Connecticut Historical Society, Nancy Milner and Susan Schoelwer; at the Corcoran Gallery of Art, Rebekah Sobel; at Cranbrook Archives, Mark Coir; and at the Currier Gallery of Art, Marilyn Hoffman.

I extend thanks to Rachel Roberts at the Dallas Historical Society; at the Daughters of the American Revolution Museum, Alden O'Brien; at the Fashion Institute of Design and Merchandising, Louise Coffey-Webb; at the Fashion Institute of Technology, Costume Collection, Fred Dennis, and Valerie Steele, and in Special Collections, John Corins; at the Graystone Society, Eugene DiOrio and Scott Huston; at Hetty Green: A Frugal Woman's Museum, Edith Nichols; and at the Hagley Museum and Library, Michael Nash and Jon Williams.

I am grateful for the enthusiasm and guidance of colleagues at many Harvard University libraries: at Baker Library, Harvard Business School, Nicole Hayes and Laura Linard; at the Botany Libraries, Professor Donald Pfeiffer and Judy Warnement; at the Gray Herbarium, Emily Wood; at Harvard Law School, Special Collections, David Ferris; and at Peabody Museum of Archaeology and Ethnography, Diana Loren and Rubie Watson.

At the Heard Museum, I want to thank Diana Pardue; at Hearst Castle, Jana Seely; at the Idaho State Historical Society, Carolyn Bowler; at the Indiana Historical Society, Faith Revell; at the Indianapolis Museum of Art, Vanessa Burkhart, Niloo Imami-Paydar, and Ruth Roberts; at the Kent State University Museum, Jean Druesedow; at the Library Company of Philadelphia, James Green; at the Library of Congress, Mark Dimunation and Tambra Johnson.

I am grateful to Norah Alberto and Manette Scheiniger at the Maidenform Company,; at the Maryland Historical Society, Louise Brownell and Stanard Klinefelter; at the Maryland State Archives, Nancy

Bramucci and Rob Schoeberlein; at the Massachusetts Historical Society, Anne Bentley, Peter Drummey, and Nicholas Graham; at the Massachusetts State Archives, John Warner, Jr.; at the Monterey State Historic Park, Kris Quist; at the Museum of Fine Arts, Boston, Erica Hirshler and Pamela Parmal; at the Museum of Modern Art, New York, John Elderfield.

Many individuals at the National Museum of American History, Smithsonian Institution, were of assistance, notably Jeanne Benas, Dwight Bowers, Ron Brashear, David Burgevin, Kathy Dirks, John Fleckner, Shelly Foote, Jim Gardner, Karen Garlick, Lisa Kathleen Graddy, Margaret Grandine, Kate Henderson, Barbara Janssen, Harold Langley, David Miller, Mimi Minnick, Martha Morris, Stan Nelson, Marc Pachter, Sunae Park-Evans, Harry Rubinstein, Susan Strange, Priscilla Wood, Helena Wright, Bill Yeingst, and Joan Young.

Thanks to Rust Russell at the National Museum of Natural History, Smithsonian Institution; at the National Museum of Women in the Arts, Susan Fisher Sterling; at the National Park Service, Division of Archaeology and Ethnography, Barbara Little; at the Natural History Museum of Los Angeles County, Beth Werling; at the Naval Historical Center, Mark Wertheimer; at the New Bedford (Massachusetts) Public Library, Tina Furtado; at the New York Historical Society, Valerie Komor; at the New York Public Library, George Fletcher; at Nightingale Productions, Gail Pietrzyk; at the Oakland (California) Public Library, Carmen Martinez; at the Palace of the Governors, New Mexico, Arthur Olivas; at Pewabic Pottery Museum, Terry Dietrich, Therese Ireland, and Hannah Nielson; at the Philadelphia Museum of Art, Kristina Haugland; at the Mary Pickford Foundation, Keith Lawrence; at Princeton University Library, Emily Belcher; at the Rhode Island Historical Society, Dana-Signe Munroe and Rick Statler; at the Rhode Island School of Design, Joy Emery; at the Rhode Island State Archives, R. Gwenn Stern; at the Rochester (New York) Museum and Science Center, Giancarlo Cervone and Vicki Schmidt; at the Rockingham Public Library (Vermont), Chris Burchstead and Raymond Massuco; at the Millicent Rogers Museum, William Ebie and Shelby Tisdale; and at the Helena Rubinstein Foundation, Pamela Johnson, Lori Shapley, and Elizabeth WatermanI want to thank Mike Coker at the South Carolina Historical Society; at the South Carolina State Department of Archives and History, Roy Tryon; at the Stewart Huston Charitable Trust, Scott Huston; at the Texas Fashion Collection, Myra Walker; at TimePix, Tom Gilbert; at the U.S. Coast Guard Historian's Office, Bob Browning; at the U.S. Coast Guard Museum, Cindy Herrick; at the University of Maryland, Julie Fife and Mark Leone; at the Valentine Museum, Colleen Callahan; at the Madam C. J. Walker Theater Center, Charles Blair; at the Maggie Walker National Historic Site, Hyman Schwartzberg; at the Wichita State University Archives Department of Special Collections, Michael Kelly and Mary Nelson; at Wichita-Sedgwick County Historical Museum, Jamie Frazer Tracy; at the Henry Francis DuPont Winterthur Museum, Leslie Bowman; at Women in Military Service for America, Britta Gramrud; at The Women's Museum: An Institute for the Future, Candace O'Keefe; and at YIVO Institute for Jewish Research, Erica Blankstein and Fruma Mohrer.

I am also grateful to the following individuals who have contributed in many different ways: Elaina Archer, A'Lelia Bundles, Cynthia Colin, John Josef Costandi, Jennifer Diener, Katherine Webster Dwight, Ellen Gordon, Ruth and Elliot Handler, Beth Holler, Marie Kargman, Victoria Kastner, Jeanne Farr McDonnell, Joan Meacham, Mary Lynn Oliver, Shirley Peppers, Dorothy Perry, Rosalind Webster Perry, Susan Peterson, Denise Pilato, Jane Plitt, Jo Anne Preston, Newbold Richardson, Coline Jenkins Sahlin, Pamela Townsend, and Joel Wyatt.

Jane S. Knowles
Project Manager